DALAI LAMA AND TIBET

ENCYCLOPAEDIA OF TIBET SERIES — 5

DALAI LAMA AND TIBET

Edited by
S.K. SHARMA & USHA SHARMA

ANMOL PUBLICATIONS PVT LTD
NEW DELHI-110 002 (INDIA)

ANMOL PUBLICATIONS PVT LTD
4374/4, Ansari Road Daryaganj,
New Delhi-110 002

Dalai Lama and Tibet
First Edition 1997

ISBN 81-7488-454-8

PRINTED IN INDIA

Published by J.L. Kumar for Anmol Publications Pvt. Ltd. New Delhi, Typeset by Akshar Graphics, Delhi and Printed at Mehra Offset Press, Delhi.

Dedicated

to

His Holiness Tenzin Gyatso the Fourteenth Dalai Lama

(For his distinguished writings on Buddhist philosophy, for the role he has played in fostering ecumenical relations between the great religions of the world and for his able leadership of the Tibetan people)

Preface

FOR CENTURIES, the unworldly world of Tibet has remained a mystery. Also known as—the Roof of the World, the Hidden Land, the Mystic Land, the Forbidden Land, or the Land of the Lamas—Tibet is situated on a high plateau surrounded by mountain passes. Covering an area in excess of 2.5 million square kilometers, it borders of India, Nepal, Bhutan and Burma to the south, Eastern Turkistan to the north and China on the east. Owing to its unique physical features, Tibet occupies not only the highest but also the most strategic position in Central Asia. In Tibet proper the mountain ranges, run from northwest to southeast with deep or shallow valleys forming innumerable furrows between them. The lofty Himalayan chain sprawls along the entire southern frontier and shuts off the warm monsoon from the Indian Ocean. Rich in minerals and with a variety of flora and fauna, Tibet is also the source of many great rivers — the Tsang-po (Brahmaputra), Senge Khabab (Indus), Drichu (Yangtse), Zachu (Mekong) etc.

Prjevalsky has described Tibet in the following words—"The grandeur of nature in Asia, revealing itself in endless forests and tundras of Siberia, or in the waterless deserts of an overwhelming grandeur in a wide flat upland which forms the southern half of the central part of this continent." Actually, everything that is said about Tibet, is full of significance, whether it be by Plano Carpini or Rubruquis or Marco Polo or Oodoric of Friuli or many other travellers. For them, Tibet has remained as something unusual and exotic.

Tibet is the homeland of a distinct and ancient nation. It is known as the ancient but yet a living home of Mahayana Buddhism. For centuries, Tibet remained a seat of Buddhist practices and learning. The impact of its smooth transmission was felt far and wide.

The Tibetan people have had a chequered history coupled with a unique cultural heritage. They are a distinct race with their own spoken and written language, own socio-cultural traditions, food and dress. Slowly but surely, it grew into a great military power and carved for itself a huge empire in Central Asia, and ultimately renounced the use of arms to practise the teachings of the Buddha. Unfortunately, on 17 March 1959, the Dalai Lama left Lhasa and escaped from pursuing Chinese to seek political asylum in India. He was followed by an unprecedented exodus of Tibetans into exile.

The study of Tibetan history, political developments, socio-cultural and religious traditions etc. is attracting the interaction of an increasing number of scholars all over the world. Viewing Tibet and the Tibetan people in a global perspective, the present theme—*Dalai Lama and Tibet* has been systematically and carefully conceived. It puts in detail the magnificent role of Dalai Lama in Tibetan history.

The editors of the present work made it a point to maximise the intellectual benefit of the wealth of literature embedded in the pages of various books, journals, newspapers, reports etc. Efforts have been taken to economise the precious time of scholars and the alike.

We feel much beholden to His Holiness, the Fourteenth Dalai Lama for many of his speeches/writings which we have incorporated in our humble attempt. We also express our deep gratitude to Dr. P. L. Mehra, Pema Rigzen and many others for their academic support. Finally, we gratefully acknowledge with thanks, the various institutions and a galaxy of authors whose contributions have become part and parcel of our present endeavour.

—Editors

Dedicated
to
His Holiness Tenzin Gyatso the Fourteenth Dalai Lama
(For his distinguished writings on Buddhist philosophy, for the role he has played in fostering ecumenical relations between the great religions of the world and for his able leadership of the Tibetan people)

Preface

FOR CENTURIES, the unworldly world of Tibet has remained a mystery. Also known as—the Roof of the World, the Hidden Land, the Mystic Land, the Forbidden Land, or the Land of the Lamas—Tibet is situated on a high plateau surrounded by mountain passes. Covering an area in excess of 2.5 million square kilometers, it borders of India, Nepal, Bhutan and Burma to the south, Eastern Turkistan to the north and China on the east. Owing to its unique physical features, Tibet occupies not only the highest but also the most strategic position in Central Asia. In Tibet proper the mountain ranges, run from northwest to southeast with deep or shallow valleys forming innumerable furrows between them. The lofty Himalayan chain sprawls along the entire southern frontier and shuts off the warm monsoon from the Indian Ocean. Rich in minerals and with a variety of flora and fauna, Tibet is also the source of many great rivers — the Tsang-po (Brahmaputra), Senge Khabab (Indus), Drichu (Yangtse), Zachu (Mekong) etc.

Prjevalsky has described Tibet in the following words—"The grandeur of nature in Asia, revealing itself in endless forests and tundras of Siberia, or in the waterless deserts of an overwhelming grandeur in a wide flat upland which forms the southern half of the central part of this continent." Actually, everything that is said about Tibet, is full of significance, whether it be by Plano Carpini or Rubruquis or Marco Polo or Oodoric of Friuli or many other travellers. For them, Tibet has remained as something unusual and exotic.

Tibet is the homeland of a distinct and ancient nation. It is known as the ancient but yet a living home of Mahayana Buddhism. For centuries, Tibet remained a seat of Buddhist practices and learning. The impact of its smooth transmission was felt far and wide.

The Tibetan people have had a chequered history coupled with a unique cultural heritage. They are a distinct race with their own spoken and written language, own socio-cultural traditions, food and dress. Slowly but surely, it grew into a great military power and carved for itself a huge empire in Central Asia, and ultimately renounced the use of arms to practise the teachings of the Buddha. Unfortunately, on 17 March 1959, the Dalai Lama left Lhasa and escaped from pursuing Chinese to seek political asylum in India. He was followed by an unprecedented exodus of Tibetans into exile.

The study of Tibetan history, political developments, socio-cultural and religious traditions etc. is attracting the interaction of an increasing number of scholars all over the world. Viewing Tibet and the Tibetan people in a global perspective, the present theme—*Encyclopaedia of Tibet*—has been systematically and carefully conceived, and finally categorized into the following volumes:

1. History and Geography of Tibet
2. Travel and Memoirs of Tibet
3. Society and Culture of Tibet
4. Religious Heritage of Tibet
5. Dalai Lama and Tibet
6. India and Tibet
7. Tibet and the World

The editors of the present work made it a point to maximise the intellectual benefit of the wealth of literature embedded in the pages of various books, journals, newspapers, reports etc. by way of compiling a multi-volume encyclopaedia. Efforts have been taken to economise the precious time of scholars and the alike.

We feel much beholden to His Holiness, the Fourteenth Dalai Lama for many of his speeches/writings which we have incorporated in our humble attempt. We also express our deep gratitude to Dr. P. L. Mehra, Pema Rigzen and many others for their academic support. Finally, we gratefully acknowledge the various institutions and a galaxy of authors whose contributions have become part and parcel of our present endeavour.

—Editors

Contents

Part C

INTERVIEWS / DIALOGUES

Part A

ARTICLES

1

The Hierarchy of the Dalâi Lama (1406-1745)

By

SARAT CHANDRA DAS

THE REFORMED Buddhist Church called Shawaser, the school of Yellow-cap Lamas, founded by Tson-khapa acquired such a celebrity within a few years of its birth that in the year 1406 Yunglo, the third Emperor of the Ta Ming dynasty sent an invitation to the great reformer to visit Peking. Finding, his time fully necessary for scriptural as well as monastic reformation, Tson-khapa was unable to comply with Yunglo's wish. He, however, sent his principal disciple to enlighten the devout monarch in the mysteries of Lamaism as developed in the reformed school, in the following year.

On his arrival at Peking, Sakya Yeses found the Emperor suffering from a serious illness. He performed several religious ceremonies, which was believed to have effected a speedy recovery. Under his direction a huge image of Maitreya, the coming Buddha, called Chamchen, was constructed and placed in the monastery of Yung-ho-kung founded by Yunglo himself. Sakya Yeses was appointed high priest of this monastery and given the title of Chamchen Choije. He founded the great monastery of Hwang-sze or Yellow Temple in one of the imperial gardens situated to the north of Peking. On his return journey to Tibet he took the circuitious Mongolian route and paid a visit to his tutor and chief Tson-khapa, making large presents to him. Shortly after his return to Lhasa, in the year 1418, he founded the great monastery of Sera Theg-chelin with the wealth which he had amassed during his residence in the capital of China. Sera, in time, rose to great distinction and was resorted to by Lamas as a seat of learning. It now contains 5,500 monks and is seconded only to Dapun in rank.

In 1408, shortly after establishing the grand annual congregational assembly called Monlam-chenpo at Lhasa, Tson-khapa founded the great monastery of Gahdan with 3,300 monks at a place some 20 miles to the East of Lhasa, and presided over it as the minister of the reformed Church till his death. He laid down the rule that his successors in the ministerial chair of Gahdan should be elected from among the most pious and learned of the brotherhood irrespective of their position in birth. Constitutionally therefore, the Gahdan Thipa become his successor in the ministry, the hierarch of the Yellow-cap Church.

From that time Gahdan became the chief seat of the reformed Church, the monks of which put on the yellow-cap to distinguish themselves from the followers of the older sects who generally wore the red-cap *(shwa-mar)* and were, therefore, called Shwa-ser Gelugpa, i.e., the order of which the religious badge was the yellow-cap. They were also called Gahdan-pa from the name of their monastery.

In 1415, one of Tson-khapa's disciples named Jam-yan Choije founded Dapun, now the premier monastery of Tibet, with 7,700 monks under the patronage of Namkha Zangpo, the then ruler of Tibet. In the year of the foundation of the monastery of Sera, the great reformer, whose real name was Lozan Tagpa but who is better known as Tson-khapa from the name of his birthplace Tson-kha (onion bank), in Amdo, passed away from mundane existence.

In 1446, Gadun-dub one of the later disciples of Tson-khapa founded the grand monastery of Tasi-lhunpo in Tsan. The establishment of these four great monasteries, — first Gahdan, then Dapun and Sera, and lastly, Tasi-lhunpo, — which have played such an important part in the political administration of the country, made the provinces of U and Tsan the headquarters of the Yellow Church. On account of his profound learning and holiness, though of humble and obscure parentage, Gadundub was regarded as a saint. He himself never pretended to have been a saintly origin, but people believed that he must have possessed in him the spirit of Bodhisattva Avalokitesvara— the guardian saint of Tibet. About three years after Gadundub's death the possibility of the reappearance of the spirits of deceased Lamas for the first time dawned in the minds of the members of the reformed Church. The monks of Dapun over which Gadundub had latterly presided thought that the spirit of one who had loved his country and all living beings so much could hardly have become freed from this longings, to work for them even when he had passed out of his mortal tenements. They, therefore, sent emissaries to the different places which the Lama had visited during his lifetime, to inquire if there was born seven weeks after his demise, any child in whom could be traced the signs of its indicating any incidents of Gadundub's life. They also consulted their tutelary deities for guidance in the right identification of Gadundub's spirit should it have re-appeared in any child.

At last, a child was discovered at Tanag born in the family of Sreg-ton Darma, who had settled in Tsan from Lower Kham. It revealed some signs of having been the re-embodiment of the Lama's spirit and successfully claimed as his own certain articles for which Gadundub used to evince much liking and which were kept mixed up with other people's properties. This fortunate child was removed to Tasi-lhunpo for religious and monastic education, His father, who was a lay Tantrik priest of the Nin-ma sect, instructed him in the Tantrik cult. When twelve years old he took the vows of an Upasaka (Lay devotee) from Panchen Lunrig Gya-tsho of Tasi-lhunpo; after which he was admitted into monkhood by the abbot of Ne-nin. When he passed all the examinations in the sacred scriptures, he was elevated to the highest rank in the order of monkhood, after being given the name of Gadun Gya-tsho and placed on the high priest's chair in 1511. He ably presided over the monastery of Tasi-lhunpo for a period of five years. He received instructions in the Buddhist scriptures and metaphysics from such eminent scholars as Ye-ses-zan, hierarch of Gahdan, Yontam Gya-tsho of Tsan and Panchen-ye-ses of Tasi-lhunpo. He founded the monastery of Choikhor Gyal in the plain of Metog-than in 1508. In the 43rd year of his age, in the year 1516, he was appointed to the abbotship of Dapun where he was better known by the title of Dapun Tulku or Avatara. In later times this Avatara, in his successive incarnations received the titles of Gyal-ba Rinpoche, Gyahvai Wanpo, Tale Lama, etc.

With him, in fact, originated the institution of incarnations in Tibet, which was but little known before and which since then has become general all over Tibet and Mongolia.

In the 52nd year of his age the Lamas of Sera elected him as their high priest, which office he held till his death in 1541. Since Kyisho, the district of which Lhasa is the chief town, had passed under the ruler of Tsan named Rinchen Pun-pa, for a period of nineteen years, the Lamas of Sanphu and Karma sects presided over the annual prayer assembly of Lhasa called the Monlam Chenpo. Under the auspices of Gadun Gya-tsho, the Lamas of Sera and Dapun regained their lost authority over the grand institution. Gadun wrote several works on the different branches of the sacred literature. At the age of 68, in the year called Water-Tiger, he departed from this life.

His spirit was discovered in a lad of four years born in the family of Ma Rinchen-chog at Toilun in the year 1546. When this boy was ten years old the Lamas of Dapun placed him on the chair of their high priest under the title of Sonam Gya-tsho. Formerly, when the Tartar Emperor Khublai Khan made rich presents to his spiritual tutor Lama Phag-pa, the latter had predicted that in time to come he would reappear on this earth as a Lama bearing the name—"Ocean," which in Mongolian was called Tale—Dalai, while the Emperor himself would reign as a king of the name Altan signifying gold in Mongolian.

Altan, the powerful Khan who ruled over Thumed Mongolia, being told by an astrologer that in a former life he was the great Khan of China, wished to know what became of the spirit of the Lama who had exercised so much influence over Emperor Khublai. Being informed that he too was reborn in the person of Sonam Gya-tsho, the incarnate Lama of Dapun, the monarch sent his general Tasi Rabdan to bring him to Mongolia.

In 1557, Sonam Gya-tsho became High Priest of Sera. Being in charge of both Sera and Dapun, he exercised great influence at Lhasa. In 1563, he took the final vows of monk-hood. In 1573, he founded the monastery of Namgyal Ta-tshan on Potala, but the Shwa-mar (red-cap) Lamas, whose power was again ascendant under the auspices of the ruler of Tsan, dispossessed him of this institution, converting it at the same time to a monastery of their own school. In 1574, the Tsan army under Rinchen Pun-pa invaded U and after subjugating it, withdrew to Tsan. About this time, the messenger of Altan Khan arrived and Sonam Gya-tsho was but too glad to accept the invitation for the purpose of converting the Mongolians to his creed. He set out on his journey to Mongolia in the company of the Khan's messenger, but owing to the numerous invitations he received on the way from the various chiefs and nobles of Tibet and who importuned him for his blessings, his journey was retarded. Tasi Rabdan, therefore, parted company with him at Raden and proceeded to Mongolia, in advance of the Lama. Being informed that the incarnate Phag-pa was coming, Altan Khan deputed three of his generals to welcome him. While passing through Arig-than, Nan-tsho and upper Mongolia, the Lama received the deputations which brought the tidings of the welcome that would be accorded him by the Khan. Altan himself advanced up to Tshab-cha, at the source of the Hoangho, a place situated to the South East of Lake Kokonor. At the first meeting the Khan addressed the Lama by the title—Tale Lama Vajradhara, Tale being the Mongolian equivalent of Gya-tsho which signifies "Ocean." But the Lama's real name was Sonam Gya-tsho which signified "The ocean of merit." Thus originated the name Dalai (from Tale) Lama by which the Buddhist hierarchs of the line of Gadundub came to be known in Mongolia, China and Tibet. From that time Gya-tsho became a necessary and inseparable part of the name of Gadundub's successors. The Mongolians readily embraced Buddhism and became devout followers of the Yellow-cap Church. With a view to commemorate his visit to Mongolia, Sonam Gya-tsho, under the auspices of the Khan, founded the monastery of Choi-khor-lin in the Mongol capital. About this time the monastery of Kumbum was founded at the birth place of Tson-khapa in Amdo.

On his return journey Sonam Gya-tsho visited Khukukhukto Lithang, Chamdo, Kham,

Apo, Chakyungtag, Ngan-tig Jomokhan, Chambabomling, etc., thus propagating the Buddhist faith in Mongolia, and the border lands of Tibet. Having been worshipped by all classes of people—from the Khans of Mongolia down to the barbarians of Ulterior Tibet—he returned to Tibet, full of glory. He died in 1587. The spirit of Sonam Gya-tsho was discovered in Mongolia, the favourite place of his sojourn, in the family of Sumi Thaiji, a direct descendant of Jenghis Khan, the great Tartar conqueror. The child was named Yontan Gya-tsho, the 'ocean of good quality.' This happy incident made the Mongolians firmly attached to the Yellow Church. They kept him in their country till the 15th years of his age. The authorities of Dapun, fearing lest the morals of their incarnate Lama might get stained by his continued residence in a country where chastity in the fair sex was unknown, brought him to Tibet at the budding of his youth. They gave him a good religious education before entrusting him with the duties of the high-priest of their monastery. About the time of Sonam Gya-tsho, the Kalmuk Tartars of Khalkha had set up a third hierarch of the Yellow-cap sect under the name of Je-tsun Dampa at Urga—the city of tents. A question arose as to the relative position, in spiritual rank of the high priest of the Mongolian monastery of Gahdan and the Khalka hierarch. The Tartars of the upper and lower Mongolia were about to go to war for its solution.

In 1605, the youg chief of the Celeuth Mongols effected reconciliation between the Kalmuks and his own tribe who had been quarrelling for sometime on the question of precedence between Gahdan and Urga. For this service the Emperor of China conferred on him the Buddhist title of Ta Kausri, from which circumstance he became known by the name of Gushi Khan.

In the year 1609, the armies of Tsan again invaded U, but encountering much opposition they were forced to withdraw from there. In 1611, Phun-tshog Namgyal who patronized the Shwa-mar (red-cap) Lamas, became the supreme ruler of Tibet. In the beginning of the 17th century the province of Tsan came to prominence on account of the power of its Teba or chief. He belonged to the Karmapa hierarchy known by the name of Shwa-mar which had its headquarters at Tshorpu and Ralun. With a view to put to shade Tasi-lhunpo they erected a large monastery in its immediate vicinity.

In the year 1615, Yontan Gya-tsho died, an event which was followed by the seige of the monasteries of Sera and Dapun by the armies of the Teba of Tsan in which several thousand Yellow-cap Lamas were killed. The news of this disaster to the Yellow Church enraged the Celeuth Mongols, whose general marched with a large army to Tibet and fought a fierce battle with the Tsan army at Kyan-than-gan, and killed several thousand Tibetans. In 1620, the Mongolians retired after restoring the lost territorial endowments of the Yellow Church to the monasteries of Sera, Dapun and Gahdan. About this time Sera and Dapun were presided over by the grand Lama of Tasi-lhunpo. In 1623, he was ordained and installed as the high priest of Dapun. About this time the Shwa-mar Lamas had regained their lost position and were vigorously presecuting the Yellow Church.

They had, in the meantime, influenced the Kalmuk Mongols whose chief had become a convert to their creed. In the year 1636, Gushi Khan espoused the cause of the Yellow Church and entered Kokonor with a large army. At the outset of this invasion he had to encounter with the Kalmuk Mongols who had taken up the side of the Shwa-mar Lamas. He completely defeated them after several engagements. From Kokonor, while proceeding towards Tibet, he heard that king Beri of Kham, who was a follower of the Bon religion, was preparing to invade Tibet. He, therefore, marched against him and reduced him to subjection. He again invaded Kham in 1639; this time, putting Beri to death, he annexed his territories to his Mongolian Kingdom.

In the year 1641, at the invitation and earnest entreaty of the Dalai Lama Nag-wan Lozan Gya-tsho, he entered Tibet with 30,000 Tartars and fought several battles with the Tsan army led by the powerful Teba of Tsan. After capturing Lhasa and other towns which had been in the occupation of the Teba, he put him to prison, annexed Upper Tsan of which Gyan-tse was the chief town, and proclaimed himself the supreme king of Tibet, assuming the Tibetan name of Tanzin Choi-gyal—the upholder of Religion or Dharma Raja.

He appointed Sonam Choiphel as Desrid (Governor) to rule over the country in his absence. Henceforth Tibet became a dependency of the Mongolian kingdom founded by Gushi Khan, the Celeuth chief, who owed but nominal allegiance to China. In 1643, six great nobles of China conspired against the last Ta Ming emperor Khrungtin (Tungtin), and their leader usurped the imperial authority for sometime. Shortly after, Shun-ti (also called Shunchi), a Mantchu chief, seized the throne and displaced the Ta Ming dynasty. So, owing to troubles in China and confusion during the period which preceded this dynastic change, no armed protest came from peking against Gushi Khan's military operations in Tibet and Kham. In 1644, Gushi Khan built a castle on the famous hill of Potala for the accommodation of his court.

As soon as Shun-ti found himself secure and firmly seated on the imperial throne, he took up the foreign affairs in hand. With a view to bring Tibet again under his direct control he sent an invitation to the Dalai Lama to visit Peking. In 1651, Nag-wan Lozan reached Peking where he was feted and loaded with honours. The Emperor, who with his whole family embraced the Lamaism of the Yellow Church in preference to that of the Red-cap school to which the Ta Mings were attached, decorated him with the exalted title of Ta Kausri. On this occasion, the Dalai Lama was greatly impressed with the power and splendour of the Emperor's court as well as the vastness of his dominions. With a view to make the position of his church secure in Tibet he prayed to the Emperor that China might take over the protectorate of Tibet in the manner it was done by Khublai Khan, the founder of the Ta Yen dynasty, when the Emperor himself had embraced the Lamaism of the Sakya-pa school. He also explained that the Ta Mings from the time they had displaced the Tartar dynasty proved themselves very staunch supporters of Lamaism and became pledged to the tenets of the Red-cap sect of the Karmapa hierarchy. Shun-ti very gladly acceded to the prayer. From that time the Mantchu dynasty became vouched, under solemn promises, to the protection of the authority of the Dali Lama in Tibet.

Shortly after this, Shun-ti proceeded to Mukden, his Mantchu capital, for offering prayers in the tombs of his ancestors, Lozan Gya-tsho accompanied him thither. At the end of the year 1652 the Lama returned to Tibet, visiting on the way the great monastery of Gon-lun in Amdo, then a flourising Yellow Church institution with 10,000 monks.

In 1653, Gushi Khan was succeeded by his son Da-yen Khan who appointed Lama Tin-leh Gya-tsho as Desrid of Tibet. The government having passed from the hands of a Tartar General to those of a Lama, the power of the Dalai Lama, who had lately returned from China, full of glory, greatly increased. Lozan Gya-tsho, besides being a scholar, well-read in the sacred literature, was a shrewd statesman of great ability. He made Tin-len unconsciously subservient to his wishes in the government of the country. In 1668, the Desrid died leaving the Government in the hands of a layman named Choipon Teba, and incident which afforded Lozan Gya-tsho a still better opportunity to exercise his influence more effectually in the affairs of the state.

In 1670, Da-yen Khan died leaving the throne to his son Ratna Talai Khan. On the retirement of Choipon Teba in 1674, Lama Lozan Jin-pa was appointed Desrid of Tibet. Since the conquest of Tibet by Gushi Khan, the internal administration of the country, which was vested in the Desrid, had been practically directed by Lozan Gya-tsho, who, since his return from China, was considered as the holiest man on the face of the earth on account of his having become the spiritual tutor of the Emperor of China. He was reverentially called Gonsa-napa-chenpo, the fifth supreme Lama—the four who preceded him being Gadundub the founder of the hierarchy, Gadun Gya-tsho, Sonam Gya-tsho and Yontan Gya-tsho.

Talai Khan having become powerless in Mongolia itself, his Desrid became a nonentity in Tibet. In the year 1678, Lozan Gya-tsho assumed the supreme control of the country and appointed Sanye Gya-tsho, a layman of great wisdom and learning, as Desird in the place of Lozan Jin-pa. Thus the sovereignty over Tibet and Kham practically passed from Talai Ratna Khan, the great-grandson of Gushi Khan, to the Tate Lama Nag-wan Lozan Gya-tsho, the supreme hierarch.

The ancient castle of Sron-tsan Gampo, the first Buddhist King of Tibet, which stood on the hill called Marpoi-ri (the red hill), was selected by Lozan Gya-tsho for his court. He transferred his residence and court called Choi-de Namgyal from Dapun to there, and laid the foundation of the famous palace of Phodan Marpo, now called Gahdan Phodan Choi-de Namgyal.

The name of the hill at the same time became changed into Potala, because the residence of Bodhisattva Avalokitesvara, the patron saint of Tibet, whose spirit was believed to have appeared both in King Sron-tsan Gampo and himself, was mentioned in the sacred books to have been on the top of a hill called Potola-giri (the harbour hill) somewhere in the south of India. Henceforth, from this circumstance, Potala became the chief place of pilgrimage of the Buddhists of the northern school who regarded the Dali Lama as the holiest of holies. His young Desrid, an adept in statecraft, than whom a greater statesman has not appeared in Tibet, in course of three years, firmly established the grand Lama's temporal authority all over the country, including Kham and Amdo. In 1681, Lozan Gya-tsho died, but the wily Tesrid managed to keep the occurrence secret from the public. He gave out that the Talai Lama, whose spirit was in communion with the gods, had entered into a *samadhi* (deep-meditation) under a solemn vow not to come out to public view for a period of twelve years. He now dressed himself in Lamaic robes, and assumed a holy character, for it was not desirable for a Tesrid not to be looked upon as a holy man. He was regarded as a wise minister and efficient ruler: in 1683 he wrote a valuable work on astronomy, astrology and chronology called *Vaidurya Karpo.* In 1693, he completed the nine-storeyed building called Vaidurya Marpo (the red-palace) on Potala, and entombed the remains of Gonsa-na-pa-chenpo, in the central hall, in a golden Chorten *(cuitya).* In the same year he installed, under the name of Tshon-yan Gyatsho, a child, three years old, as the incarnation of the deceased Dalai who had passed out of his body at the termination of his twelve years trance in profound *samadhi.* During this long period the Desrid had consolidated the Dalai Lama's authority, having governed the country with consummate skill. He being the central figure in the government and a layman, was called De-ba, and his government came to be known by the name of Shing. At the close of the year, with a view to commemorate the accession of his late master to the sovereignty of Tibet, he inaugurated the Tshog-choi the congregational service in connexion with the annual prayer meeting called Monlam Chenpo, of Lhasa, founded by Tson-khapa. In 1697, he wrote the work called *Vai-ser Choijun* the history of the rise of the Yellow Church. The boy Dalai Lama, as he grew up in age, shewed indifference to the performance of his religious duties. He failed in almost all the examinations that he was required to pass through before his ordination. He, however, displayed a tendency towards love-literature in which he acquired some proficiency. He selected from among the monks of Namgyal Ta-tshan young men for companions. He composed love songs and generally spent his time in the royal groves in the suburbs of Lhasa, where men and women of all classes and age came to receive his blessings. Here he got facilities for indulging in the pleasures of life, the enjoyment of which was strictly prohibited to monks. His attention to young ladies alarmed the Lamas. At first the courtiers interpreted this unholy tendency of the youthful Lama as a mark of his communion with the Khando (female angels) who, it was given out, paid him secret visits in the guise of young maidens for initiating him in the mysteries of Tantrik Buddhism; but later on, when the grand Lama ran to excesses, and sang love songs and behaved in utter disregard of the canonical rules, the public became undeceived. The Lamaic authorities of the monasteries of Sera, Dapun and Gahdan took steps for his removal from the hierarchial throne.

About this time the Chungar or the left branch of the Celeuth Mongols under the leadership of Tshe-wan Rab-dan had become very powerful, in consequence of which the influence of Gushi Khan's line over the Tartars greatly waned. The ambitious Tshe-wan Rabdan, who had made his power felt even in Russia in the north, was waiting for an opportunity to overrun Tibet.

The friends of the Desrid now courted his help against the enemies of the government who had reported the matter to the Emperor of China. In the year 1701, the abbots of the great monasteries with the help of the Desrid induced the prodigal youth to formally renounce the vows of celebacy and monkhood which he had taken from the grand Lama of Tasi-lhunpo. An incarnate Lama named Yeses Gya-tsho, who had come to Lhasa for that work, now took up the spiritual business appertaining to the Dalai Lama.

In 1702 Desrid Sangye Gya-tsho resigned his office and retired to private life. In 1705, the unfortunate Dalai Lama was removed from Tibet under a Chinese escort. He died on the way near lake Kokonur. When this news reached Peking, Emperor Kanghi ordered that a child in whom the spirit of Nag-wan Lozan may be discovered should be reported to him. In 1703, Lhabzan, son of Talai Ratna Khan, declared himself ruler of Tibet. He dismissed the militia and raised an army from among the Tartars. His first act was to surround the residence of the retired Desrid, his former chief, with a number of armed men and to kill him with four hundred of his devoted followers. In 1704 orders came from the Emperor to deport Tshan-yan Gya-tsho to China. The faction in the Yellow Church which was inimical to Lhabzan took immediate steps to elect a new Dalai Lama. They gave out that Nag-wan Lozan Gya-tsho who was reported to have entered *samadhi*, had actually died in the year 1681, and his spirit reappeared in one Pakar-dsin-pa Ye-ses Gya-tsho in 1685, whose claim to the hierarchial throne was set aside by the Desrid. Pakar-dsin-pa, who was an ordained monk of pure morals, was, however, holding the office of the high priest of Dapun. Accordingly, they set him up as the real Dalai Lama in 1706, but the public hesitated to accept the new pretender as their grand hierarch.

Lhabzan submitted to Chinese authority. The Lamas of the Yellow Church were now on their wit's end, being required to solve a problem of a novel nature. Emissaries were, therefore, sent to the different great monasteries of the Yellow Church in search of a new incarnation of the Dalai Lama. Applications came from the parents of different child-pretenders to the exalted office, which were carefully examined.

At last the real embodiment of the Dalai Lama was found at Kumbum—the birth-place of Tson-khapa, the founder of the Yellow Church. The council of Buddhist cardinals comprising of the abbots of Sera, Dapun and Gahdan, with the Tasi Lama as president, on whom devolved the responsibility of the right identification, resorted to all manner of religious rites and consultations with the gods for the purpose. All evidence having pointed towards and in favour of the discovery at Kumbum, in a child born in 1707, the matter was reported to the Emperor. Sanction having come, the princely child named Kalzan Gya-tsho was declared Dalai Lama, but, on account of his tender age, the child could not be brought in state to Tibet and installed on the throne of Potala. Kanghi, however, invested him with the insignia of an imperial order in 1709. But fresh dangers had in the meantime sprung forth which threatened Lhasa and also taxed the energies of the Emperor.

Tshewan Rabdan, the powerful chief of Chungar or the left branch of the Celeuth Mongols who had risen to eminence on the downfall of Gushi Khan's kingdom, had espoused the cause of the Tibetans. The friends of Desrid Sangye Gyatsho, with a view to avenge his death and to overthrow Lhabzan, had communicated to him all that had happened in Tibet. Accordingly, Tshewan Rabdan sent a large army to Tibet for punishing the enemies of the yellow Church. In 1716 the Chinese and Tibetan troops fought a great battle with the Chungar army but were defeated, Lhabzan being slain. In 1717, the victorious Chungars, at the instance of the Yellow Cap Lamas, sacked the monasteries of rival sects such as Tshurphu, Samdin, Nam-gyal-lin Dorje Tag, Mindollin and others, situated in the valley of the Tsangpo. In 1718 they returned to Mongolia.

About the time of the Chungar invasion the Tibetans had endeavoured to be independent, but Kanghi was determined to re-establish his authority over the whole of Mongolia and Tibet. In 1718, when order was restored in Tibet, the Chungar Mongolians being fully subjugated by the victorious Chinese, the young Dalai Lama was brought back to Lhasa from Kumbum by the command of the Emperor, who sent two high commissioners ostensibly to protect the Dalai Lama, but really to form an imperial residency at Lhasa which has since been controlling the political and military affairs of the country.

In 1722, the Chungar and the Celeuth Mongols of Kokonur fought with the imperial forces and were defeated. The Chinese killed upwards of seven hundred monks of all grades, including the abbot of Ser-khog-gon, called Chuzan Rinpoche, and destroyed many religious objects and burnt down many shrines and congregation halls. They demolished the great monastery of Shwa-khog. Many aged monks of Kumbum were also killed by them. In Amdo, in the following year, the Chinese generals Kung and Yo-u-then destroyed the temples and grand congregation halls of the Don-lun monastery. In 1725 and 1726 there arose internal dissensions in the Government at Lhasa, the Kahlons or ministers having risen against the Desrid-shan-khan Chenpo and killed him. About this time, general Phola Theji who had gone to Upper Tibet returned to Lhasa with troops from Ladak, Nahri and Tsan. He slew upwards of one thousand men who had been drawn from U and Konpo by the rebel ministers, and for a time restored order in the country. In 1727, Chinese troops came to his help and he was enabled to suppress the rebellion of U, killing the three ministers who had headed it. He removed the Dalai Lama to Kahdag, or Kathog monastery in Kham, thinking it would be unsafe to keep him in Lhasa at the time.

Note: This paper has been compiled from Tibetan histories such as *dPag-bsam-ljon-bzan*, *etc.*

[*Journal of the Asiatic Society of Bengal*, 1904.]

2

A Letter from Kien-lung, Emperor of China to Dalai Lama, the Sovereign Hierarch of Tibet, 1785 A.D.

PLACED by Heaven at the head of ten thousand kingdoms, my utmost endeavours are employed to govern them well. I nglect no means to procure peace and happiness to all that have life. I endeavour also to make learning and religion flourish. Lama, I am persuaded that you enter into my view, and that your intentions accord with mine. I am not ignorant that you do all, that depends on you, to omit nothing your religion prescribes, and to follow exactly all the laws. You are punctual at prayer, and you bestow the attention that praying well requires. It is principally by this that you become the most firm supporter of the religion of Fo (Buddha). I rejoice in it from my heart, and give you, with pleasure, the praises that are your due.

By the favour of Heaven I enjoy health. I wish, Lama, that you may enjoy the same blessing, and that you may long continue to offer up your fervent prayers.

The year before last the Panchen Irtinee (Pandit Ratna) set out from Tashi-lhunpo, in order to pray here, upon the occasion of my seventieth birth-day, to which I am drawing nigh. He performed his journey in good health. As soon as I was acquainted with his departure, and that he informed me he was to pass the winter at Kumbum, I sent the Lieutenant-General Ouau-fou, and another grandee, named Pao-tai, to meet him, and ordered them to convey to him a Soutchou (string) of pearls, that I had myself worn; a Saddle, and all the accoutrements of a riding horse; some utensils of silver, and other trifles. They found him at Kum bum treated him in my name with a feast of ceremony, and delivered these presents.

This last year, the Panchen Irtinee having left Kun-bum on his route to me, I sent to him a second time, the grandees of my presence, Our-tou-ksoon and Ta-fou, accompanied by Ra-koo, a Lama of the rank of Hou-touk-too. To these three deputies I committed one of my travelling chairs, one of my camp tents, the small flags, and other tokens of distinction proper to create respect with which he was to be complimented on my behalf.

They met him at the town of Houhou, and presented to him what they were commissioned with, after having given him as before a feast of ceremony.

When I learned tha the was no more than a few days journey from the frontiers, I despatched to meet him the sixth Ague, who is now the eldest of my sons, and caused him to be accompanied by the Houtouktou Chankya. They met him at the Miao, or temple of Taihan: There they saluted him on my behalf, gave him a feast of ceremony, and presented to him in my name of *Soutchou* of pearls, more valuable than those first sent: a cap enriched with pearls; a led horse, with saddle and accoutrements; some utensils of silver and other trifles.

After his departure from the Miao of Taihan, the Panchen Irtinee repaired to Tolonor (seven lakes), where he waited sometime in order to receive all I designed to send him. I deputed, for the purpose of saluting him, those princes of the blood, who have the title of Khawn (Khan), and guards of my person. They were accompanied by Fen-chen and Tehiloun, officers of rank, and by the Lamas of Avou-ang, Pa-tchou, and Ram-tehap. They presented to him in my name a cap of ceremony, oranamented with pearls, and many utensils of gold and silver.

On the 21st day of the seventh moon, the Panchen Irtinee arrived at Je-hole, where I then was, and gave me a feast of ceremony, to which the Lamas of his suite, from Tashi-lhunpo and Potala, were admitted. I gave in return a solemn entertainment, but apart, to all the Lamas of Je-hole, to the Lamas of Tchasaks, of the Eleuths, of the Kokonors, of the Tourgouths, and of the Turbeths.

During this festival the Mongoux (Mongolian) princes, the Begs, the Tai-dji, and other principal nobility of the different hordes, as well as the deputies, or ambassadors, from Coreans, the Mahomedans and others, who were assembled at Je-hole, did homage to him by performing the ceremonies of respect, used on such occasions.

Delighted with a reception so honourable and so uncommon, the Pan-chen Irtinee expressed marks of satisfaction that charmed all these strangers in their turn. He took this occasion to request that I would permit him to accompany me to Peking, to which I consented. The second day of the ninth moon was that, on which he made his entry, into this capital of my vast dominions. 'All the Lamas, many thousands in number, came forth to meet him, prostrated themselves in his presence, and fulfilled with respect to him the other duties which their customs prescribe. After all these ceremonies were finished, he was conducted to Yuen-ming-yuen, and I assigned for his habitation that part of my palace, which is named the golden apartment.

I gave directions that everything worthy of curiosity, in the environs, should be shewn to him: he accordingly went to Hiang-chau, to Ouan-cheou-chan, and other places deserving of notice.

He visited the Miao, or temples, of these different places, and was every where received with distinguished honours. He officiated in person, at the dedication of the Imperial Miao, which I had erected at Ouan-cheou-chan, and which was just then completed.

On the third day of the tenth moon I gave him a grand entertainment in the garden of Yuen-ming-yuen; "and, during the entertainment, I caused to be brought, in presence of all the court, the various articles I designed for him, and which I added to those already presented."

After the entertainment he repaired with the principal persons of his suite, to the Miao of the amplification of charity, and to that of concord. He offered up prayers in the one and in the other, for prosperity of my reign, and for the benefit and happiness of every living creature.

The Pan-Chen Irtinee, in undertaking a journey of twenty thousand *li*, to contribute to the celebrity of my Ouan-cheou did more than sufficient to entitle him to all the distinctions, that could evince my sense of his kindness; but the air of satisfaction and pleasure, which diffused itself on all around him, and which he himself manifested, whenever he was admitted to my presence, impressed on my mind on the most exquisite gratifications it ever felt. I remarked, with peculiar sentiment of affection, that he never once spoke to me on the subject of his return. He seemed disposed to fix his abode near my person. But, alas! how uncertain are the events of this life!

On the twentieth of the tenth moon, the Pan-chen Irtinee felt himself indisposed. I was informed of it, and instantly sent my psysicians to visit him. They reported to me that his complaints were serious, and even dangerous. I did not hesitate to go to him in person, in order to judge myself of his situation. He received me with the same tokens of pleasure that he had ever shewn when admitted to my presence; and from the words full of satisfaction with which he addressed me, I might have conceived that he was in the complete enjoyment of health. It was, however, far otherwise; and the venom of small pox had already spread itself through all parts of his body.

The second day of the eleventh moon, his disorder was pronounced to be incurable. The Pan-chen Irtinee suddenly changed his corporeal dwelling. The afflicting intelligence was immediately communicated to me.

The shock overcame me. With a heart full of the most poignant grief, and eyes bathed in tears, I repaired to Hwang-shi, the yellow chapel, where, with my own hands, I burned perfumes to him.

Although I am well aware that to come and to go are but the same thing to the Panchen Irtinee, yet when I reflect that he made a very long and painful journey, for the sole purpose of doing honour to the day of my Ouan-cheou; and that after having fulfilled that object, it was not his fate to return in tranquillity, as I had hoped, to the place of his usual abode; this reflection, I say, is distressing to me beyond all expression. To console me in some degree, or, at least to attempt so me alleviation of my griefs, I have resolved to render memorable, the day of his regeneration. I named for the guard of his body Chang-tchaopa, Soni-boun-gue and some other grandees, and gave them particular orders for the construction of a receptacle for it, worthy of such precious remains, which lie in the interior of the yellow temple. I gave directions also for making a shrine of gold, in which should be deposited the body of the Irtinee. This was executed by the twenty-first day of the twelfth moon. I then regulated the hundred days of prayer, counting from that day, on which he disappeared. It was only to alleviate, however little, the grief in which my heart was overwhelmed, that I acted so. I also caused several towers to be erected in different places, which I considered as so many palaces that he might have planned himself for varying his abode, or such as I might have assigned to him for his recreation. I bestowed bounties, on his behalf, to the most eminent of his disciples and to the principal Houtouktous. I gave them *Soutchous* of pearls, with permission to wear them; and I particularly distinguished the brother of Irtinee, by conferring on him the title of "prince of the efficient prayer." I did not neglect the Tchasak Lamas, in the distribution of my gifts. Several amongst them were decorated with honourable titles, and received from me, *Soutchous* of pearls, pieces of silk, and other things with which they appeared to be gratified.

My design in entering with you into this detail is to prove to you the estimation in which I hold whatever is connected with you, and the profound regard I have for your person. The number of one hundred days allotted to prayer was completed on the thirteenth of the second moon of the present year. I issued my orders for the departure; the body was conveyed with due pomp; and I joined the procession myself, in person, as far as it was proper. I should go. I depute the sixth Ague, now the eldest of my sonsr to accompany it to the distance of three days' journey from this capital; and I nominated Petchingue, mandarin in the tribunal of foreign affairs, and Iroultou, one of my guards, to accompany it all the way to Tashi-lhunpo. Although the Panchen Irtinee, has changed his abode, I have full confidence that, with the aid I have rendered to him, he will not long delay to be fixed in another habitation.

Lama, it is my desire that you show kindness to all the Lamas of Tashi-lhunpo, and respect them on my account; from the conduct they have observed, I judge them worthy of being your disciples. I recommend to you, especially those who accompany the body, and who will perform the number of prayers, that you shall regulate, for the completion of the funeral rites. I hope you will cheerfully execute what you know will be agreeable to me. It only remains for me to add, that I send you Petchingue and his suite, to salute you in my name, and inform themselves of the state of your health. They will deliver to you a *Soutchou* of coral to be used on grand festivals; a tea pot of gold, weighing thirty ounces; a bowl of the same metal, and the same weight; a tea pot and bowl of silver; thirty *soutchous* of various different coloured beads, and twenty purses great and small, of various colours.

The fourteenth of the second moon of the forty-sixth year of the reign of Kienlong.

A short account of Purnagir Gosain from Babu Gurudas Bysak's paper in the Journal, Asiatic Society of Bengal.

"The important features of the extraordinary character of Puran Gir, has been gleaned from the history of the mission to Tibet. He possessed remarkable intelligence and wisdom, a fund of inexhaustible energy, a mastery of many languages including Tibetan and Mongolian, a wide range of experience acquired by travel in and out of India, a practical insight into all the commercial relations of Asia of which Tibet formed the heart, and enjoyed and deserved a reputation for piety and integrity which made him the trusted agent of the Tashi-lhunpo authorities and the Bengal Government. Of the personal history of this remarkable and extraordinary Sanyasi; unfortunately there exists no record. Whatever was known of him, has, like that of most of our illustrious countrymen, passed into oblivion. It is a happy thing that so many particulars and incidents connected with his public life and such abundant testimony to his character, capacity and comprehensive knowledge of the important affairs of the time, have been preserved in the pages of Markham's Narrative of the Missions of George Bogle to Tibet"—a narrative the materials of which were traced by the author in the possession of private individuals and were not found in the public records of Government, and in the Reports of Captain Turner as well as of the Gosain himself. The statement of the Gosain was taken down by Turner and submitted to the acting Governor-General, Mr. Macpherson and this forms an annexure of the Report.

Among the papers…is a passport in Tibetan, which had been given to Puran Gir by the Tashi Lama for his pilgrimage to the celebrated Lake Manasarovara. This document shows what great regard and respect the Lama had for our Gosain, for whose comfort and convenience most minute injunctions were given in it. Some particulars about the Gosain have been gathered from the statements of the Mahatma of Bhot Bagan. According to him Puran was a Brahman by caste, though as a *Dandi* he had cast off his sacrificial thread. His title *Gir or Giri* shows that he was a follower of Sankaracharya's teachings and must have been initiated at the *Jyosi Moth* in Bedarikasram.

In the passport the Tashi Lama describes him as an Acharya. He was a young man when he went to Tibet as a pilgrim. He had fair features, and was tall, strong and sincere. His usual dress consisted of the Sanyas' *kaupina,* with a short red ochre-dyed piece of cloth wrapped round his lions, and a tiger skin thrown over his shoulder, but on certain public occasions he wore a kind of toga and covered his head with a *turban.*

[From *Indian Pandits in the Land of Snow,* by Sarat Chandra Das, 1893.]

3

The Dalai Lamas

By
CHARLES BELL

I SHALL perhaps be pardoned if I digress at this stage to describe from a more personal standpoint the lives of the priest-kings or god-kings, whose rule-period has formed the subject of the preceding chapter. The Dalai Lama is regarded by Tibetans as a Bodhisatwa, i.e. one who has attained the right to Nirvana, but consents to be reborn for the spiritual benefit of his fellow-creatures. In almost every Asiatic country which has had a spiritual ruler, the latter has been the object of veneration, but has not been allowed to exercise power and has been frequently kept more or less as a prisoner in his palace. The actual power has been wielded by a Minister, and has frequently been hereditary in the Minister's family. Even in Bhutan, a country adjoining Tibet and inhabited by men of Tibetan stock, the spiritual ruler, or Shab-tung Rim-po-che, known to Europeans and Indians as the Dharma Raja, did not govern. The duty of government was deputed to the Desi or Deb Raja, who was also a priest, and who in latter years had himself ceased to govern. The real power has lain for at least fifty or sixty years with the Penlop (Chief) of the Tongsa district, which covers the eastern half of Bhutan. The present Penlop has assumed the hereditary title of Regent of Bhutan and the Desi has retired. Thus in a country akin to Tibet in race, religion, and language, the actual power lay for many years not even with the second, but with the third man in the kingdom.

But Tibet has at times proved an exception to this almost universal rule. Since the time of the fifth Dalai Lama, i.e. from 1641, the Dalais, when they succeeded in attaining their majority, have at times ruled in fact as well as in name. A notable instance of this was the great fifth Dalai Lama, who himself conducted the administration for several years before placing it in the capable hands of his chief Minister, Sang-gye Gyatso. But the most striking example of all is the present God-king, who for the last twenty or thirty years, while introducing salutary reforms on the religious side, has also controlled the multifarious details of the secular government. How numerous and how varied the duties of Buddha's Vice-regent are, even I can in some measure realize after being in close contact with him for two years in India, and even more after eleven months' close personal intercourse in Lhasa.

When a Dalai Lama himself rules—and probably when a clever Minister rules in his name—his authority is unrivalled. Even though the Council and Parliament are united in opposition to his proposals, he can enforce them, and has not infrequently done so. Backed as he is by the veneration of a people who regard him as more than Pope, as in fact a Divinity ruling on earth, there can be no direct opposition to His Holiness's orders. The Nepalese have a characteristic proverb, which says:

There's no answer to an order;
There's no medicine for death.

Things are not indeed as strict as this in the Lama's domains, for the great wastes of Tibet cannot be controlled as easily as the fertile little lands of Nepal , and the Tibetan nomad wandering over his mountains is not so susceptible to discipline as the Nepalese peasant tied to his farm.

In practice also the Dalai's power is limited through his being kept in ignorance of events by monasteries, officials and others. His position precludes him from touring frequently and seeing things for himself. Governmental proposals and important events come to him from the Council, through the Lord Chamberlain or the Chief secretary, both of whom thus exercise great influence. But the Dalai has his private and semi-private employees, who bring him news and enable him to sift, in some degree, the official sources of information. In districts far from Lhasa, the natural independence—one might perhaps say the democratic tendency—of the Tibetan character asserts itself, and unpalatable orders are apt to be regarded but lightly.

A few of the earlier Dalai Lamas were born in aristocratic families. Among these was Yonten Gyatso, the fourth, the son of a Mongol, prince. But the 'Great Fifth' was apparently the son of a peasant at Chung-gye, two days' journey south-east of Lhasa. And in the later incarnations the Dalai Lama has almost invariably been chosen from a family of humble position. If he be selected from one of the leading families of the country, several of which are descended from the brothers of previous Dalai Lamas, that family is likely to become inconveniently powerful. Public appointments too are not usually given to members of his family during his lifetime. But these may hold, and usually do hold, private posts about his person, which carry great, though unacknowledged, influence.

Dalai Lamas do not drink wine or spirits, but they may and do eat meat, a necessary article of diet in Tibet, where the climate is cold and fruit and vegetables are scarce, often indeed unobtainable. As, however, the taking of life, even for food, is to Buddhists a sin, a religious ceremony is performed on behalf of the animals so killed, and this is held to insure their rebirth in a higher state of existence. Thus the loss of their lives means a gain to them. Dalai Lamas do not marry, but keep altogether apart from women.

The method of appointing a successor is unique. For the following description of it I am indebted to His Holiness the present Dalai Lama, to the late Prime Minister, and to other high Tibetan authorities.

Some Dalai Lamas are more believed in, some less. One of the former class, before he dies, ro—ar the Tibetans say—before he 'retires to the heavenly fields', will usually tell those round him where he will reincarnate. He may give particulars as to the house in which the small boy will be found, the stream, if any, near it, the shape of the mountains round it, etc. His entourage are themselves afraid to ask for these particulars, when they see their divinity ill, for they fear that they may thereby make him more eager to go.

Three or four years after the Dalai Lama has 'departed', the Tashi Lama, if of age, and fifteen or twenty other great lamas, e.g. the abbots of Sera, Drepung, and Ganden—the three huge monasteries near Lhasa—the State Oracle at Lhasa, known as the Nechung, and the Oracle at Sam-ye, one of the most famous monasteries in Tibet, decide as to the tract of country in which the new Dalai Lama will be found, the year of birth of his father, his mother, and himself, the kinds of trees growing near his house, and so forth.

Inquiries in the district indicated are then set on foot, and lead usually to the tracing of three or four boys whose birth has been heralded by heavenly manifestations. For instance, a rainbow has appeared over his house from a clear sky when he was born, and his parents have had heavenly visions concerning him. Particulars of these miraculous births are laid before the Oracles and lamas referred to above, and these decide which is the new Dalai Lama. The latter, a boy of three or four, has to recognize the sacred thunderbolt, the bell and other religious implements of his predecessor-or rather, as one should say, of himself in his previous life.

The young boy will be found to carry on his person some of the marks that distinguish the incarnation of the four-handed Chenrezi from ordinary mortals. Among such signs are:

(a) Marks as of a tiger-skin on his legs.
(b) Eyes and eyebrows that curve upwards on the outside and are rather long.
(c) Large ears.
(d) Two pieces of flesh near the shoulder-blades indicating the two other hands of Chenrezi.
(e) An imprint like a conch-shell on one of the palms of his hands.

The present Dalai Lama bears the last three signs. An unearthly light is believed to issue from his countenance when he blesses pilgrims, so that even his ministers and immediate attendants find it hard to look him in the face.

The names of the different candidates had, however, usually to be placed in the golden urn, presented in 1793 by the Chinese Emperor Chienlung. One was picked out with a pair of chopsticks, and opened by a Tibetan Grand Secretary. This contained the name of the new Dalai Lama. The Prime Minister asserted to me that this has always hitherto been the same as the name favoured by the Oracles. In the case of the present Pontiff the Tibetan Government represented to the Chinese Emperor that there was no doubt about the identity of the new Dalai Lama, and therefore no need for the Amban to perform the ceremony of picking out a name. The ceremony was accordingly remitted, an event which appears also to indicate that the Chinese suzerainty was then merely nominal.

By presenting the urn and arranging for the Amban to assist at the choice of each new Dalai Lama and other high Incarnations, the Chinese Government no doubt hoped to gain some hold over the personage who influences not only Tibet but Mongolia, and is revered by many millions in Asia, and even by some in European Russia. For the Lama, owing his accession in some measure to their representative. might naturally feel bound to repay his debt by subservience to their requests. According to Chinese accounts they had good grounds for their innovation, for at the time the choice of a high Incarnation was often made corruptly. A ruler of Ladakh had many relatives who were chosen among the highest of the Incarnations. A Tashi Lama chose a Dalai Lama from a prominent family in the Tsang province; the latter in turn made his first cousin Tashi Lama when the former Tashi Lama died. But the climax was reached when the Ne-chung Oracle of Lhasa declared that the reincarnation of the Grand Lama of Urga would be the child that the wife of the reigning prince of the Tushot Mongols was expected to bring forth. For the child was born, but proved to be a girl.

Lonchen Shatra, the later Prime Minister—whose early death was a very heavy loss to his country—told me the story of the finding of the present Dalai Lama, then a boy or two or three years old, in words somewhat as follows:

'The Ne-chung Oracle gave certain particulars, showing the names of the father and mother, the approximate whereabouts of his house, the kind of country round it, and so on. The Oracle of Sam-ye also gave some particulars; e.g. that a mountain by the house was "shaped like an elephant."

After this, a leading lama, with a number of doctors of divinity in attendance, was instructed to go to a lake named "Mu-li-ting" in Sanskrit-Tibetan and "Cho-kor Gyal-ki Nam-tso" in popular Tibetan. Here he was to see an image of the Dalai Lama's house and surrounding country. The lama went accordingly, but found the lake frozen and under snow, so wondered how he could see as directed. But soon afterwards a strong wind got up and blew off the snow, making the ice clear to the lama, who was looking at it from a neighbouring hill. Then, so the story goes, the lake rose up on end and the lama looked into it as into a glass. And in it he saw the image as foretold.

'Later on in a dream the lama saw the baby Dalai in his mother's arms. When he arrived at the house, he found the baby in the arms of his mother, and the face of the boy corresponded with the face in the dream.

'A deputation of priests and officials waited on the boy, who picked out property of the late Dalai Lama from among a large number of articles. And in spite of his tender years he was able to indicate occurrences that had happened in the lifetimes of previous Dalai Lamas. Among other cases he indicated that of a Chief of Li-tang, to whom a former Dalai Lama had given an image of Buddha. For fear of losing this, the Chief had encased it in a golden urn, and hidden it in a beam in his house, unknown to anybody. The young Dalai Lama told people that the Chief or Li-tang had done this.

'Dalai Lamas cease identifying property and telling of such occurrences, when they grow older.

'If there is no doubt as to the true Dalai Lama, the names are not put into the golden urn. The names of the 9th Dalai Lama, Lung-tok Gyatso, and of the present one were not put into it.

The Prime Minister, who narrated this account to me, was a man of exceptional intelligence and strong common sense. As Tibetan Plenipotentiary at the diplomatic Conference in 1913-14, he proved himself to be more than a match for his Chinese colleague. But in matters of religion Tibetan faith is strong and deep.

The father of a Dalai receives the rank of Kung, the highest rank held by a layman in Tibet. He receives also the insignia of the Ruby Button and the Double-Eyed Peacock Feather. There are very few Kungs; they are descended from the fathers of recent Dalai and Tashi Lamas.

The abandonment by China of the use of the golden urn in the choice of the present Pontiff is a measure of the growing impatience felt by Tibet towards the Chinese suzerainty, and of the steady decline of the latter. This decline is further evidenced by the attainment to his majority of the present Dalai. The four immediately preceding him all died before they could take up the reins of government. Thus for nearly a hundred years Tibet was administered by Regents. This enabled the Chinese to enjoy greater power in Tibet than would have been likely under the administration of the Dalai Lamas themselves.

When seven years old, or even earlier, the Dalai is brought to Lhasa, and takes up his residence in his palace, known as the Potala. At the age of eighteen be is entitled to receive his full powers. The present Dalai Lama was taken from his mother when about three years old and brought to Lhasa. His father and mother thereafter saw him only at occasional visits. 'The Master of the Bed Chamber', so the Lord Chamberlain informed me, 'took his mother's place, fondling him in his arms, and looking after him in every way. He also gave him his early education, and it is largely owing to him that the Dalai Lama has become so learned and wise.'

The title Dalai Lama (or more properly Ta-le Lama), being of Mongolian origin, is used mainly by Chinese and Mongols. The TIbetans know him rather as *Kyam-gon Rimpo-che,* 'The Precious Protector'; *Gye-wa Rim-po-che,* 'The Precious Sovereign': *Buk,* 'The Inmost One'; *Kyam-gon Buk,* The Inmost Protector'; *Lama Pon-po,* 'The Priest Officer'; sometimes also as'The Presence', *Kun-dun.*

The Dalai Lama informed me that he had five chief seals of office. 'The Golden Seal of the Rainbow and of the Earth' bears on it the name of the Emperor of China, who ruled at the time of the fifth Dalai Lama. It is a red seal, about one inch square. It is supposed to be kept in the personal custody of the Lama himself, and is one of the chief symbols of his authority. It is not stamped on documents nowadays, but is found on some of the more ancient title-deeds of the old families of Tibet. Another seal of primary importance, known as 'The Inmost Seal', bears on it the words 'Gan-den Po-trang', 'The Blissful Palace', and 'Dalai Lama'. It is red, square, and a little larger than the first seal. It is applied to title-deeds of large properties, and to other documents issued by the Lama himself. A large photograph of His Holiness, Which I took for him, and which he presented to me, shows him seated on his throne, and arrayed in the robes in which he blesses the pilgrims and others in his Palace at Lhasa. This he signed himself and sealed with the Inmost Seal. The signature runs, 'In accordance with the Precepts of the Lord Buddha the Great Dalai Lama, Unchangeable, Holder of the Thunderbolt, the Thirteenth in the line of Victory and Power.'

In foreign affairs the Dalai Lama is expected to act in conjunction with the two Councils, the Greater and the Lesser, and with the National Assembly. Until the expulsion in 1912 of the Chinese Amban and his troops from Lhasa, it was the custom, when the matter was one of great importance, that their decision should be communicated to the Amban, who in his turn submitted it to the Chinese Government. The TIbetan report was known as 'The Request for Power', and the Amban's communication as 'The Golden Ears'. After sending their report, the Tibetan authorities considered themselves at liberty to act according to their decision, without awaiting the Emperor's reply, which was not received in less than three months, even in urgent cases. By this practical method they gained their own way, while satisfying the dictates of Oriental courtesy.

It is indeed clear that, for many years prior to 1904, China had very little control over Tibetan foreign policy. Nor indeed was Tibet in the habit of acknowledging her authority, except when desirous of avoiding foreign pressure. In such cases, the Tibetan Government was able to plead the Chinese relationship, and the consequent impossibility of taking action until a report had been submitted to the Emperor and a reply obtained from him, a plea by which several months' delay could always be assured. Among other instances in which the Tibetans availed themselves of the Chinese relationship may be mentioned the Dalai Lama's refusal to reply to the two letters that the Viceroy of India wrote to him in 1900 and 1901. As regards the first letter he wrote, 'The Ambans, when they first came here, made an arrangemetn forbidding us to correspond direct with your Government'. Lord Curzon's second letter to the Dalai Lama was returned unopened.

Per contra Their disavowal of the Chinese suzerainty is evidenced by their refusal to acknowledge the Anglo-Chinese Convention of 1890 as binding on Tibet, when Colonel Younghusband in 1903 pressed for its observance. Similarly by their refusal to permit the Amban to go the meet the Expedition of 1904. And once again, by their refusal to acknowledge the deposition of the Dalai Lama by the Chinese Emperor after this Expedition. The Emperor's proclamation was mutilated and bespattered with filth, and the Tibetan Government continued to submit matters for the orders of the Lama, though His Holiness was absent in Mongolia.

In the internal administration also a Dalai Lama is supreme. An appeal lies to him against the decision of the Council in cases of exceptional importance. If, for instance, the dispute is between persons of high rank, or if a large landed property is involved, the party aggrieved by the decision of the Council may apply for the intervention of the 'Precious Sovereign'. Such appeals are known as 'The Placing of the Names of the King and Ministers'; and are so-called from the fact that the petition is addressed in the names of the Dalai Lama and Council. In every murder case also the decision of the Court used to be submitted to the Dalai Lama for confirmation. But the present Dalai Lama gives his Prime Minister full control in criminal cases, for it is held to be unfitting for His Holiness to touch things of this kind.

Although in Tibet, as elsewhere, rank and position are shown by the height of the seat above the floor of the room, yet a Dalai Lama, the Supreme Head of Tibet, will frequently sit on a lower seat than a learned Lama, when taking lessons in religion from the latter. This happens especially when the Dalai Lama is a youth. But even when His Holiness was 36 years old, at the time of his flight to India, there were in Tibet two learned Lamas, who were privileged to sit equal with the Dalai Lama himself. Such is the respect paid to learning by the Buddhists of Tibet, where it is regarded as the highest of all moral attainments. To the Christian, Love is the greatest virtue; to the Tibetan Buddhist, Learning. In India the man or woman who desires to please, will address you as 'Protector of the Poor' or 'Incarnation of Justice', but in Tibet as 'Learned Sir'.

[From *Tibet—Past and Present,* 1924.]

The two leading officers in the Dalai Lama's household are the Lord Chamberlain and the Chief Secretary. The former is the head of all the ecclesiastical officials in Tibet. The recent incumbent was a clever doctor, and, as such, always attended His Holiness in addition to his ordinary duties, which include, among - other charges, the control of the parks round Lhasa.

The Chief Secretary is the main medium of communication between His Holiness and the outside world. As such, he has many enemies, but his power is very great. For, when the Dalai Lama, dissatisfied by the Council's handling of some important issue, takes the direct control in his own hands—as happened once during my year in Lhasa—the Chief Secretary for the time supersedes the Prime Minister and the Council.

The Chief Secretary has ten assistants who combine the duties of secretaries and aide-de-camps. One of these was attached to my Mission in Lhasa; his alertness, political acumen, and knowledge of his own national concerns, would have made him a man of mark in any cuntry.

The Master of the Bedchamber, the Court Chaplain, and the Chief Butler wield considerable power indirectly, because they have access to His Holiness, and can put in a word on this side or that. The four orderlies are men of great stature: when we were in Lhasa, all were well over six feet and one was just seven feet in height. They and the soldiers of the Bodyguard are patient with crowds, but are not to be lightly disregarded.

4

The Dalai Lamas

THE TITLE "Dalai Lama' (Ocean of Wisdom) is Mongolian and was offered to the third incarnation, Sonam Gyatso (1543-1588), by the Mongolian ruler Altan Khan in 1578 A.D.

The Dalai Lama is the spiritual and temporal leader of the Tibetans. We believe there is but one Dalai Lama who chooses to take rebirth to serve all sentient beings. Buddhists all over the world revere the Dalai Lama as the manifestation of *Chenresig*, the Buddha of Compassion.

Other titles by which the Dalai Lama is known to Tibetans and Buddhists in the Himalayan region are: *'Yeshin Norbu'* (The wish-fulfilling Jewel), *'Kundun'* (The Presence), *'Gyalwa Rinpoche* (The Precious Victor), *'Gongsa Chog'* (The Highest One).

The Present Dalai Lama

The present Dalai Lama, his Holiness Tenzin Gyatso, (Ocean of the holder of the Faith), is the fourteenth incarnation. The first Dalai Lama, Gedun Drup, was born in 1391. From the time of the fifth incarnation, Ngawang Losag Gyatso (1617-1682), the Dalai Lamas assumed spiritual and temporal leadership of the Tibetans.

His Holiness Tenzin Gyatso was born on July 6, 1935, in a small village called Tagtser, in Dhome province (north-east Tibet). His father. Chokyong Tsering, and mother, Sonam Tsomo (Whose name was changed into Diki Tsering later), were simple farmers. His Holiness was first named Lhamo Thondup which has changed upon his being formally recognised the reincarnation of the XIII Dalai Lama at the age of four and a half. The story of his recognition is told vividly in his autobiography, *'My Land and My people.* His Holiness now has three brothers and one sister.

His full title is, *Jetsun Ngawang Losang Yeshi Tenzin Gyatso Sisum Wangyur Tsumgpa Nepai Dhe Palsangpo,'* a rough literal translation of which is, 'Venerable, having authority over his speech, kindhearted wisdom, Ocean of the holder of the Faith, ruler of the three worlds, the peerless One.'

His Holiness moved from his home to Lhasa, the Capital of Tibet, in October, 1939. His enthronement ceremony took place on February 22, 1940.

His Education

His Holiness Tenzin Gyatso underwent traditionally system of education-from the age of six, in the Potala and Norbu Lingka, his winter and summer residences respectively. His Holiness had two official preceptors: Yongzin Ling Rinpoche (1903-1983) and Yongzin Trichang Rinpoche (1901-1982). At 25 His Holiness took his preliminary examinations in the three big monastic universities of Sera (established in 1419), Drepung (1416) and Gaden (1409). His final examinations were held at the Jokhang (641, the Central Cathedral and the first temple of Tibet) in Lhasa during the annual *Monlam*, (great prayer festival) in 1959. In the morning of the examination day he was examined in turn by 30 scholars in the field of *Tsenma* (logic). In the afternoon, His Holiness debated with 11 scholars on the subject of *Uma* (Middle path) while in the evening 35 scholars tested his knowledge of Dhulwa (the canon of monastic discipline) and the study of *Pharchin* (Metaphysics). His Holiness passed all these oral examinations and received the Geshe Lharampa title (equivalent to a doctorate in Buddhist Philosophy) in the same year.

Responsibilities of State

Though all his predecessors assumed full charge of office at the age of 18 only, His Holiness Tenzin Gyatso was called upon to assume the responsibility at the tender age of 16. By late 1949 Communist China had entered Tibet by force. Influenced for centuries by the Buddhist principle of non -violence, Tibet was virtually unprepared for this brazen show of force. In the wake of this invasion, the people of Tibet supplicated to His Holiness to lead them against this. After assuming complete power (on November 17, 1950), His Holiness tried for peaceful coexistence with the Chinese for nine years. He also took steps to promote the well-being of his people. One of his first steps was to appoint a reforms committee which proposed various measures to ease the burden of the Tibetan people. However, due to Chinese intervention the committee's recommendations could not be carried out.

In 1954, His Holiness visited China at the invitation of the Chinese Government. While there he met with Mao Tse-tung, Chou-en-Lai, Deng Xiaoping and others. His Holiness also met Jawaharlal Nehru, Indira Gandhi, N. Krushchev and Bulganin who were at that time a Peking.

Two years later (in 1956), His Holiness visited India to participate in the 2500th Buddha *Jayanti.* While there he met with Nehru and informed him about the situation in Tibet created by the arrival of the Chinese. His Holiness extended an invitation to Nehru to visit Tibet to see the actual situation. Nehru accepted the invitation but was later forced to canel it due to Chinese intervention. In India His Holiness also met Chou-en-Lai who was there then.

It was during this visit that His Holiness went to Rajghat to pay homage to the memory of Gandhiji.

His feelings on reaching the *Samadhi* is succintly written in his autobiography, *My Land and My People:*

I felt I was in the Presence of a noble soul—the soul of the man who in his life was perhaps the greatest of our age, the man who had contended till death itself to preserve the spirit of India and mankind—a true disciple of Lord Buddha and a true believer in peace and harmony among all men. As I stood there, I wondered what wise counsel the Mahatma would have given me if he had been alive. I felt sure he would have thrown all his strength of will and character into a peaceful campaign for the freedom of the people of Tibet.

I wished most fervently that I had the privilege of meeting him in this world. But standing there, I felt I had come in close touch with him, and I felt his advice would always be that I should follow the path of peace. I had and still have unshaken faith in the doctrine of non-violence which he preached and practised. Now, I made up my mind more firmly to follow his lead whatever difficulties might confront me. I am determined more strongly than ever that I could never associate myself with acts of violence.

Flight to India

Despite his best efforts His Holiness could not kept the Chinese at bay. The Chinese were gradually annexing entire Tibet and were also attempting to harm the person of the Dalai Lama. This was evident when His Holiness received an 'invitation' from the Chinese for a theatrical show at their military headquarters on March 10, 1959. They wanted His Holiness to come unaccompanied by his usual personal securitymen. This alarmed the Tibetan people and they rose up in a spontaneous uprising on March 10. The Tibetan people, now fearing for His Holiness' safety, requested him to seek refuge in India. So on March 17, His Holiness along with a small group of attendants left Norbu Lingka, in the guise of an ordinary layman. After enduring all hardships on the way, His Holiness crossed over into India on March 31 and was given a warm welcome by the Government and the people of India.

Since then, His Holiness has been living in India, first in Mussoorie and presently in Dharamsala, a hill station in the Indian state of Himachal Pradesh, where a Tibetan Government in Exile has been set up.

Even in exile His Holiness has been continuously taking up the cause of Tibet. It was at his request and on the sponsorship of some justice loving countries that the United Nations took up the Tibetan issue. Three resolutions were passed in 1959, 1961 and 1965 condemning the Chinese invasion of Tibet.

His Holiness has also been looking to the needs of Tibetan refugees. With gracious assistance from the Government of India and philanthropic organisations and individuals, he has been able to resettle his people, and to provide educational facilities to the young Tibetans. In 1963. His Holiness promulgated a draft constitution for future Tibet which assured a democratic form of government.

In 1979, dialogue with China was initiated. In the same year, the first fact-finding delegation visited Tibet. This was followed by three others in 1980 and 1985. In 1982 and 1984, two exploratory-delegations held talks with the Chinese in Peking.

On September 21st, 1987, His Holiness presented a Five Point Peace Plan on Tibet to the Congressional Human Rights Caucus in the United States. The Five basic components are:

1. Transformation of the whole of Tibet into a zone of Peace;
2. Abandonment of China's population transfer policy which threatens the very existence of the Tibetans as a people;
3. Respect for the Tibetan people's fundamental human rights and democratic freedom;
4. Restoration and protection of Tibet's natural environment and abandonment of China's use of Tibet for the production of nuclear weapons and dumping of nuclear wastes:
5. Commencement of earnest negotiations on the future status of Tibet and of relations between the Tibetan and Chinese peoples.

This peace proposal was widely welcomed all over the world. The United States Congress, the West German Bundestag (parliament), the European Parliament, the Dutch Parliament and the Swedish Parliament unanimously supported the plan.

On June, 15, 1988, His Holiness further elaborated the fifth point of the Peace Plan, while addressing the European Parliament at Strasbourg.

Contact with East and West

His Holiness Tenzin Gyatso has the distinction of being the first Dalai Lama to travel beyond India, China and Mongolia.

Starting from 1945 when he made his first trip to China, His Holiness has visited 30 countries to date. During these tours he has met with a number of religious and political leaders, philosophers, scientists and political thinkers.

His Holiness met the late Pope Paul VI in 1973 and frequently meets the present Pope John Paul II. In all his tours, His Holiness has taken the message of love and spoken on the need for peace in the world and for better understanding among different faiths.

International Recognition

Ever since the emergence of the institution, the Dalai Lamas have attracted the attention of foreigners, beginning with the Mongolians and the Chinese. Today, His Holiness the Dalai Lama attracts worldwide attention for his simplicity and devotion to universal brotherhood. In recent years, a number of universities and institutions have conferred peace awards and honorary doctorate degrees upon His Holiness, for his distinguished writing on Buddhist philosophy, for the role he has played in fostering ecumenical relations between the great religions of the world and for his able leadership of the Tibetan people. Among them are the following:

— Doctor of Philosophy, Benares Hindu University, 1959;
— Ramon Magsaysay, national award for community leadership, Philippines, 1959;
— Palketta Award, Norway, 1973;
— Peace Medal, for services to humanity for Peace, Asian Buddhist Council for Peace, Mongolia, 1979;
— Doctor of Divinity, Carroll College, Waukesha, Wisconsin, U.S.A. 1979;
— Lincoln Award, for distinguished leadership in the service of freedom, Research Institute of America, 1979;
— Doctor of Buddhist Philosophy, University of Oriental Studies, California, U.S.A., 1979;
— Doctor of Humanities, Seattle University, Washington, U.S.A., 1979;
— Honorary Doctorate, University of Paris, Nanterre, France, 1984;
— Albert Schweitzer Humanitarian Award, Human Behavioural Foundation, U.S.A., 1987;
— Dr. Leopold Lucas Prize, University of Tubingen, West Germany, 1988;
— Foundation for Freedom and Human Rights Award, Switzerland, 1988.

Besides, His Holiness has been conferred with honorary degrees by many universities and made honorary citizen of some USA States. Those who have had the privilege of meeting His Holiness and talking with him have been astounded by his simplicity, blending the traditional with modern.

The Dalai Lama's Message

During all his travels abroad, His Holiness has spoken out strongly for better understanding and respect among the different peoples and faiths of the world. He has given many public talks where he has imparted the message of universal responsibility, love compassion and kindness. In his famous talk in 1973 on 'Universal Responsibility and the Good Heart,' he said:

The need for simple human to human relationship is becoming increasingly urgent .... Today the world is getting smaller and more interdependent. One nation's problems cannot be solved by itself completely. Thus without a sense of universal responsibility, our very survival is threatened. Basically, universal responsibility is feeling for other people's sufferings just as we feel our own. It is the realization that even our enemy is entirely motivated by the quest for happiness. We must recognise that all beings want the same thing that we want. This is the way to achieve a true understanding unfettered by artificial consideration.

His Holiness bears no ill-will even towards the Chinese. Only compassion and gratitude pours forth, for 'The kind of love we advocate is love you can have even for someone who has done you harm.'

His Holiness always places great emphasis on the individual's contribution towards creating peace in the world, and the vital role of mental peace:

My personal Philosophy is something like this: not to care too much about the past, the past has disappeared into space. The important thing now is the future. The future depends on the present, on today. Therefore, in our own actions and behaviour lies the real answer for the future. That too depends largely on our motivation, which is why we must have a pure honest and warm-hearted motivation, and on top of that, determination, optimism, hope and the ability not to be discouraged. The whole of humanity depends on this motivation......

To begin with, of course, we must control the anger and hatred in ourselves, and as we learn to remain in peace, then we can demonstrate society in a way that makes real statements for world peace. If we ourselves remain always angry and then sing about world peace, it has little meaning.

I feel that the present crisis is a very real one, not a question of one or two nations, but a crisis for the whole of humanity. It is the question of the survival of civilisation itself. Making, more weapons and creating more competition, and then more fighting, it is quite clear, cannot achieve what we want. So there is no alternative but through peace of mind.

Wherever he has gone, His Holiness' visits have had a tremendous impact on the general public. The underlying theme of all his public talks, and indeed his very presence, will resound for a long time in the memories of all who have heard and met him.

His whole outlook is characterised by his one statement:

'My religion is very simple—my religion is kindness.'

5

Dalai Lamas: Past and Present

I.	dGe-'dun-grub	1391 - 1475
II.	dGe-'dun-rgya-mts'o	1475 - 1542
III.	bSod-nams-rgya-mts'o	1543 - 1588
IV.	Yon-tan-rgya-mts'o	1589 - 1617
V.	Nag-dban-blo-bzan-rgya-mts'o	1617 - 1682
VI.	Ts'ans-dbyans-rgya-mts'o	1683 - 1706
VII.	Blo-bzan-bskal-bzan-rgya-mts'o	1708 - 1757
VIII.	'Jam-dpal-rgya-mts'o	1758 - 1804
IX.	Lun-rtogs-rgya-mts'o	1806 - 1815
X.	Ts'ul-k'rims-rgya-mts'o	1816 - 1837
XI.	mK'as-grub-rgya-mts'o	1838 - 1856
XII.	'P'rin-las-rgya-mts'o	1856 - 1875
XIII.	T'ub-bstan-rgya-mts'o	1876 - 1933
XIV.	bsTan-'dzin-rgya-mts'o	1935 -

6

Decision of the Dalai Lama

By
JAWAHARLAL NEHRU

THREE DAYS ago when speaking about the recent happenings in Tibet, I said that I would keep the House informed of every fresh development. In the last two days we have been receiving a number of messages. They were often delayed because they had to come through a rather devious route.

Yesterday I was thinking of informing the House of a certain development, but I hesitated to do so, because I wanted it to be fully confirmed. I was waiting for some details which we received last evening. We could have issued this news to the Press last evening, but I thought I should inform the House first.

The facts are that on April 1, that is, the day before yesterday morning, we received a message *via* Shillong dated March 31 evening that an emissary with a message from the Dalai Lama had arrived at our border check-post at Chutangmu in the North-East Frontier Agency. The emissary had arrived there on March 29 Stating that the Dalai Lama requested us for political asylum and that he expected to reach the border on March 30, that is, soon after he himself had come. We received the message on April 1. The same evening a message was received by us again *via* Shillong dated April 1 which informed us that the Dalai Lama with a small party of eight had crossed into our territory on the evening of March 31.

Expecting that some such development might occur, we had instructed the various check-posts there what to do. So, when the Dalai Lama crossed over into our territory, he was received by our Assistant Political Officer of the Tawang Sub-Division, which is a part of the Kameng Frontier Division of the North-East Frontier Agency. A little later, the rest of his party, the entourage, came in. The total number who have come with him or after him is 80. From the evening of yesterday, we learn that this party in two groups is moving towards Tawang, which is the headquarters of that subdivision, and that he is expected to reach Tawang the day after tomorrow, Sunday, April 5, in the evening.

A Member: I want a clarification. There is a report in the Press that the New China News Agency had published the very same news yesterday. How is it that the Government of India here did not get confirmation even till last evening? May I know whether we are going to give political asylum to the Dalai Lama?

Another Member: The Dalai Lama is the temporal and spiritual head of Tibet. Does the asylum confer the same right on him and will he be functioning in the same capacity on Indian soil?

The Prime Minister: So far as spiritual rights, etc., are concerned, I cannot answer the question. It is a complicated matter which will have to be considered. But there is no doubt that he will receive respectful treatment.

A Member: I would like to ask whether it is a fact that the Dalai Lama was injured.

The Prime Minister: No, Sir; he is quite healthy. As for the other question, I myself stated that we knew the day before yesterday evening about his having crossed the frontier, but we wanted certain confirmation about details—whether the whole party had crossed over, where they were and so on, before I mentioned it to this House. Yesterday morning I was not in a position to do so although I had known that he had crossed the border. In the evening I was, but I wanted to wait for the meeting of the Lok Sabha today.

[*Statement in the Lok Sabha,* 3 April, 1959.]

7

Tutor to the Dalai Lama

By
HEINRICH HARRER

AFTER FILMING the scenes in the Norbulingka I was riding slowly home when, a little way out of Lhasa, I was overhauled by an excited soldier of the bodyguard, who told me that they had been looking for me everywhere and that I must at once ride back to the Summer Garden. My first thought was that the cinema apparatus was out of order, as I could hardly imagine that the young ruler, still a minor, would override all conventions and summon me directly to see him. I immediately turned round and was soon back at the Norbulingka, where everything was now peaceful and still. At the door of the yellow gate a couple of monks were waiting. As soon as they saw me they signalled to me to hurry up and when I reached them they ushered me into the Inner Garden. There Lobsang Samten awaited me. He whispered something to me and put a white scarf in my hand. There was no doubt about it. His brother was going to receive me.

I at once went towards the cinema, but before I could enter the door opened from the inside and I was standing before the Living Buddha. Conquering my surprise I bowed deeply and handed him the scarf. He took it in his left hand and with an impulsive gesture blessed me with his right. It seemed less like the ceremonial laying-on of hands than an impetuous expression of feeling on the part of a boy who had at last got his way. In the theatre three abbots were waiting with bowed heads—the guardians of His Holiness. I knew them all well and did not fail to observe how coldly they returned my greeting. They certainly did not approve of this intrusion into their domain, but they had not dared openly to oppose the will of the Dalai Lama.

The young ruler was all the more cordial. He beamed all over his face and poured out a flood of questions. He seemed to me like a person who had for years brooded in solitude over different problems, and now that he had at last someone to talk to, wanted to know all the answers at once. He gave me no time to think over my answers, but pressed me to go to the projector and put on a film which he had long been wanting to see. It was a documentary film of the capitulation of Japan. He came with me to the apparatus and sent the abbots into the theatre to act as spectators.

I must have seemed slow and clumsy in handling the projector as he impatiently pushed me on one side and, taking hold of the film, showed me that he was a much more practised operator than I was. He told me that he had been busy the whole winter learning how to work the apparatus and that he had even taken a projector to pieces and put it together again. I observed then, for the first time, that he liked to get to the bottom of things instead of taking them for granted. And so, later on, like many a good father who wishes to earn the respect of his son, I often spent the evening reviving my knowledge of half-forgotten things or studying new ones. I took the utmost trouble to treat every question seriously and scientifically, as it was clear to me that my answers would form the basis of his knowledge of the Western world.

His obvious talent for technical things astonished me at our first meeting. It was a masterly performance for a boy of fourteen years to take a projector to pieces and then to reassemble it without any help, for he could not read the English prospectus. Now that the film was running well, he was delighted with the arrangements and could not praise my work too highly. We sat together in the projecting-room and looked at the picture through the peep-holes in the wall and he took the greatest pleasure in what he saw and heard, often clasping my hands excitedly with the vivacity of youth. Although it was the first time in his life that he had been alone with a white man he was in no way embarrassed or shy. While he was putting the next film on the reel, he pressed the microphone into my hands and insisted on my speaking into it. At the same time he looked through the peep-holes into the electrically lit theatre in which his tutors sat on carpets. I could see how keen he was to observe the wondering faces of the worthy abbots when a voice should suddenly come out of the loudspeaker. I did not want to disappoint him so I invited the non-existent public to remain in their seats as the next film would present sensational scenes from Tibet. He laughed enthusiastically at the surprised and shocked faces of the monks when they heard my cheerful, disrespectful tones. Such light, unceremonious language had never been used in the presence of the Divine Ruler, whose gleaming eyes showed how he enjoyed the situation.

He made me turn the film which I had made in Lhasa while he looked after the switches. I was as curious as he was to see the results, as this was my first full-length picture. An expert could have picked out faults in it, but it seemed quite satisfactory to us. It contained my shots of the "little" New Year Festival. Even the formal abbots forgot their dignity when they recognised themselves on the flickering screen. There was a burst of laughter when a full-length picture appeared of a Minister who had gone to sleep during the ceremonies. There was a burst of laughter when a full-length picture appeared of a Minister who had gone to sleep during the ceremonies. There was no malice in their laughter, for each of the abbots had sometimes to struggle to keep awake during these endless festivities. All the same the upper classes must have got to know that the Dalai Lama had witnessed his Minister's weakness, for afterwards whenever I appeared with my camera, everyone sat up and posed.

The Dalai Lama himself took more pleasure than anyone in the pictures. His usually slow movements became youthful and lively and he commented enthusiastically on every picture. After a while I asked him to turn a film which he had made himself. He very modestly said that he would not dare to show his 'prentice efforts after the pictures we had already seen. But I was anxious to see what subjects he had chosen for filming and persuaded him to put his roll on to the screen. He had not, of course, had a large choice of subjects. He had done a big sweeping landscape of the valley of Lhasa, which he turned much too fast. Then came a few under-lighted long-distance pictures of mounted noblemen and caravans passing through Sho. A close-up of his cook showed that he would have liked to take film portraits. The film he had shown me was absolutely his first attempt and had been made without instructions or help. When it was over he got me to announce through the microphone that the performance was over. He then opened the door leading into the theatre, told the abbots that he did not need them any more and dismissed them with a wave of the hand. It was again clear to me that here was no animated puppet, but a clear-cut individual will capable of imposing itself on others.

When we were alone we cleared away the films and put the yellow covers on the machines. Then we sat down on a magnificent carpet in the theatre with the sun streaming through the open windows. It was fortunate that I had long acquired the habit of sitting cross-legged, as chairs and cushions are not included in the Dalai Lama's household furniture. At the start I had wished to decline his invitation to sit down, knowing that even Ministers were not supposed to sit in his presence, but he just took me by the sleeve and pulled me down, which put an end to my misgiving.

He told me that he had long been planning this meeting as he had not been able to think of any other way of becoming acquainted with the outside world. He expected the Regent to raise objections but he was determined to have his own way and had already thought up a rejoinder in case of opposition. He was resolved to extend his knowledge beyond purely religious subjects, and it seemed to him that I was the only person who could help him to do so. He had no idea that I was a qualified teacher, and had he known this it would probably not have influenced him. He asked my age and was surprised to learn that I was only thirty-seven. Like many Tibetans he thought that my "yellow" hair was a sign of age. He studied my features with childish curiosity and teased me about my long nose, which, though of normal size as we reckon noses, had often attracted the attention of the snub-nosed Mongolians. At last he noticed that I had hair growing on the back of my hands and said with a broad grin: "Henrig, you are as hairy as a monkey." I had an answer ready, as I was familiar with the legend that the Tibetans derive their descent from the union of their god Chenrezi with a female demon. Before coupling with his demon-lover Chenrezi had assumed the shape of a monkey, and since the Dalai Lama is one of the Incarnations of this god, I found that in comparing me with an ape he had really flattered me.

With remarks such as this our conversation soon became unconstrained and we both lost our shyness. I now felt the attraction of his personality, which at our earlier fleeting contracts I had only guessed at. His complexion was much lighter than that of the average Tibetan. His eyes, hardly narrower than those of most Europeans, were full of expression, charm and vivacity. His cheeks glowed with excitement, and as he sat he kept sliding from side to side. His ears stood out a little from his heads. This was a characteristic of the Buddha and, as I learned later, was one of the signs by which as a child he had been recognised as an Incarnation. His hair was longer than is customary. He probably wore it so as a protection against the cold of the Potala. He was tall for his age and looked like reaching the stature of his parents, both of whom had striking figures. Unfortunately, as a result of much study in a seated posture with his body bent forward, he held himself badly. He had beautiful aristocratic hands with long fingers which were generally folded in an attitude of peace. I noticed that he often looked at my hands with astonishment when I emphasised what I was saying with a gesture. Gesticulation is entirely foreign to the Tibetans, who in their reposeful attitudes express the calm of Asia. He always wore the red robe of a monk, once prescribed by Buddha, and his costume differed in no way from that of the monastic officials.

Time passed swiftly. It seemed as if a dam had burst, so urgent and continuous was the flood of questions which he put to me. I was astounded to see how much disconnected knowledge he had acquired out of books and newspapers. He possessed an English work on the second world war in seven volumes, which he had had translated into Tibetan. He knew how to distinguish between different types of aeroplanes, automobiles and tanks. The names of personages like Churchill, Eisenhower and

Molotov were familiar to him, but as he had nobody to put questions to, he often did not know how persons and events were connected with each other. Now he was happy, because he had found someone to whom he could bring all the questions about which he had been puzzling for years.

It must have been about three o'clock when Sopon Khenpo came in to say that it was time to eat. This was the abbot whose duty it was to look after the physical welfare of the Dalai Lama. When he gave his message, I immediately rose to my feet meaning to take my leave, but the God-King drew me down again and told the abbot to come again later. He then, very modestly, took out an exercise book with all sorts of drawings on the cover and asked me to look at his work. To my surprise I saw that he had been transcribing the capital letters of the Latin alphabet. What versatility and what initiative! Strenuous religious studies, tinkering with complicated mechanical appliances, and now modern languages! He insisted that I should immediately begin to teach him English, transcribing the pronunciation in telegant Tibetan characters. Another hour must have passed, when Sopon Khenpo came in again and this time insisted that his master should take his dinner. He had a dish of cakes, white bread and sheep's cheese in his hands which he pressed on me. As I wanted to refuse it, he rolled the food up in a white cloth for me to take home with me.

But the Dalai Lama still did not want to end our conversation. In wheedling tones he begged his cup-bearer to wait a little longer. With a loving look at his charge the abbot agreed and left us. I had the feeling that he was as fond of the boy and as devoted as if he had been his father. This white-haired ancient had served the thirteenth Dalai Lama in the same capacity and had remained in the service. This was a great tribute to his trustworthiness and loyalty, for in Tibet when there is a change of masters, there is a change of servants. The Dalai Lama proposed that I should visit his family who lived in the Norbulingka during the summer. He told me to wait in their house till he should send for me. When I left him he shook my hand warmly—a new gesture for him.

As I walked through the empty garden and pushed back the gate bolts, I could hardly realise that I had just spent five hours with the God-King of Tibet. A gardener shut the gate behind me and the guard, which had been changed more than once since I came in, presented arms in some surprise. I rode slowly back to Lhasa and, but for the bundle of cakes which I was carrying, I would have thought it was all a dream. Which of my friends would have believed me if I had told him that I had just spent several hours alone in conversation with the Dalai Lama?

Needless to say I was very happy in the new duties that had fallen to my lot. To instruct this clever lad—the ruler of a land as big as France, Spain and Germany put together—in the knowledge and science of the Western world, seemed a worthwhile task, to say the least.

On the same evening I looked up some reviews which contained details of the construction of jet planes about which my young pupil had that day asked me questions to which I did not know the answers. I had promised to give him full explanations at our next meeting. As time went on I always prepared the materials for our lessons, as I wanted to introduce some system into the instruction of this zealous student.

I had many set-backs on account of his insatiable curiosity, which drove him to ask me questions that opened up whole new regions. Many of these questions I could answer only to the best of my lights. In order, for example, to be able to discuss the atom bomb, I had to tell him about the elements. That led to a disquisition on metals, for which there is no generic word in Tibetan, so I had to go into details about the different sorts of metals—a subject which, of course, brought down an avalanche of questions.

My life in Lhasa had now begun a new phase. My existence had an aim. I no longer felt unsatisfied or incomplete. I did not abandon my former duties. I still collected news for the Ministry: I still drew maps. But now the days were all too short and I often worked till late into the night. I had little time for pleasures and hobbies, for when the Dalai Lama called me, I had to be free. Instead of going to parties in the morning, as others did, I came late in the afternoon. But that was no sacrifice. I was happy in the consciousness that my life had a goal. The hours I spent with my pupil were as instructive for me as they were for him. He taught me a great deal about the history of Tibet and the teachings of Buddha. He was a real authority on these subjects. We often used to argue for hours on religious subjects and he was convinced that he would succeed in converting me to Buddhism. He told me that he was making a study of books containing knowledge of the ancient mysteries by which the body and the soul could be separated. The history of Tibet is full of stories about saints whose spirits used to perform actions hundreds of miles away from their physical bodies. The Dalai Lama was convinced that by virtue of his faith and by performing the prescribed rites he would be able to make things happen in far-distant places like Samye. When he had made sufficient progress, he said he would send me there and direct me from Lhasa. I remember saying to him with a laugh "All right, Kundun, when you can do that, I will become a Buddhist too."

Unfortunately we never got as far as making this experiment. The beginning of our friendship was darkened by political clouds. The tone of the Peking radio became more and more arrogant and Chiang Kai-shek had already withdrawn with his Government to Formosa. The National Assembly in Lhasa held one sitting after another; new troops were raised; parades and military exercises were carried out in Sho, and the Dalai Lama himself consecrated the army's new colours.

Fox, the English radio expert, had much to do, as every military unit had to have at least one transmitting set.

The Tibetan National Assembly, by whom all important political decisions are taken, is composed of fifty secular and monastic officials. The Assembly is presided over by four abbots from Drebung, Sera and Ganden, each of whom has a monk and a finance secretary attached to him. The other members of the National Assembly, whether secular or religious, belong to the different government offices but none of the four Cabinet Ministers is a member. Custom provides that the Cabinet should meet in an adjoining chamber and should see all the decisions of the Assembly, without possessing the right of veto. The final decision in all questions belongs to the Dalai Lama or, if he is still a minor, to the Regent in his stead. Of course no one would dare even to discuss a proposal coming from such a high authority.

Until a few year ago the so-called Great National Assembly was convoked every year. This body was composed of officials together with representatives of the guilds of craftsmen—tailors, masons, carpenters and so on. These annual meetings of about five hundred persons were quietly discontinued. They had really no value except to satisfy the letter of the law. In effect the power of the Regent was supreme.

In these difficult times the State Oracle was frequently consulted. His prophecies were dark and did not help to raise the morale of the people. He used to say "A powerful foe threatens our sacred land from the north and the east." Or "Our religion is in danger." All the consultations were held in secret but the oracular utterances seeped through to the people and were spread abroad by whisperers. As is usual in times of war and crisis, the whole town buzzed with rumours like a beehive, and the strength of the enemy was swelled to fabulous dimensions. The fortune-tellers had a good time, for not only was the fate of the country in the balance but everyone was interested in his own personal welfare. More than ever men sought counsel of the gods, consulted the omens and gave to every happening a good or bad meaning. Far-sighted people already began to send away their treasures to be stored in the south or in remote estates. But the people as a whole believed that the gods would help them and that a miracle would save the country from war.

The National Assembly had soberer views. It had at last become clear to them that isolationsim spelt a grave danger for the country. It was high time to establish diplomatic relations with foreign states and to tell the whole world that Tibet wished to be independent. Hitherto China's claim that Tibet was one of her provinces had remained without contradiction. Newspapers and broadcasters could say what they liked about the country: there was never an answer from Tibet. In conformity with their policy of the complete neutrality the Government had refused to explain themselves to the world. Now the danger of this attitude was recognised and people began to grasp the importance of propaganda. Every day Radio Lhasa broadcasted its views in Tibetan, Chinese and English. Missions were appointed by the Government to visit Peking, Delhi, Washington and London. Their members were monastic officials and young noblemen who had learnt English in India. But they never got farther than India, thanks to the irresolution of their own Government and the obstruction by the great powers.

The young Dalai Lama realised the gravity of the situation but he did not cease to hope for a peaceful outcome. During my visits I observed what a lively interest the future ruler took in political events. We always met alone in the little cinema-theatre, and I was able to understand often from trifling indications how much he looked forward to my coming. Sometimes he came running across the garden to greet me, beaming with happiness and holding out his hand. In spite of my warm feelings towards him and the fact that he called me his friend, I always took care to show him the respect due to the future king of Tibet. He had charged me to give him lessons in English, geography and arithmetic. In addition I had to look after his cinema and keep him conversant with world events. He had my pay raised on his own initiative, for though he was not yet constitutionally entitled to give orders, he had only to express a wish for it to be executed.

He continually astonished me by his powers of comprehension, his pertinacity and his industry. When I gave him for homework ten sentences to translate, he usually showed up with twenty. He was very quick at learning languages, as are most Tibetans. It is quite common for people of the upper class and business men to speak Mongolian, Chinese, Nepalese and Hindi. My pupil's greatest difficulty was to pronounce the letter "F", which does not occur in Tibetan. As my English was far from being perfect, we used to listen to the English news on a portable radio and took advantage of the passages spoken at dictation speed.

I had been told that in one of the government offices there were a number of English school books stored in sealed cases. A hint was given to the Ministry and on the same day the books were sent up to the Norbulingka. We made a little library for them in the theatre. My pupil was delighted at this discovery, which was something quite out of the ordinary for Lhasa. When I observed his zeal and thirst for knowledge I felt quite ashamed at the thought of my own boyhood.

There were also numerous English books and maps from the estate of the thirteenth Dalai Lama but I noticed that they looked very new and had obviously not been read. The late ruler had learnt much during his long journeys in India and China, and it was to his friendship with Sir Charles Bell that he owed his knowledge of the Western world. I was already familiar with the name of this Englishman and had read his books during my internment. He was a great champion of Tibetan independence. As political liaison officer for Sikkim, Tibet and Bhutan, he had got to know the Dalai Lama on his flight to India. This was the beginning of a close friendship between the two men which lasted for many years. Sir Charles Bell was, doubtless, the first white man to come into contact with a Dalai Lama.

My young pupil was not yet in a position to travel, but that did not diminish his interest in world geography, which was soon his favourite subject. I drew for him great maps of the world and others of Asia and Tibet. We had a globe, with the help of which I was able to explain to him why Radio New York was eleven hours behind Lhasa. He soon felt at home in all countries and was as familiar with the Caucasus as with the Himalayas. He was particularly proud of the fact that the highest summit in the world was on his frontier, and like many Tibetans was astonished to learn that few countries exceeded his kingdom in area.

our peaceful lessons were disturbed this summer by an untoward event. On August 15th a violent earthquake caused a panic in the Holy City. Another evil omen! The people had hardly got over their fright caused by the comet, which in the previous year had been visible by day and night like a gleaming horsetail in the heavens. Old people remembered that the last comet had been precursor of a war with China.

The earthquake came as a complete surprise, without premonitory tremors. The houses of Lhasa began suddenly to shake and one heard in the distance some forty dull detonations, caused no doubt by a crack in the crust of the earth. In the cloudless sky a huge glow was visible to the east. The after shocks lasted for days. The Indian radio reported great landslides in the province of Assam, which borders Tibet. Mountains and valleys were displaced and the Brahmaputra, which had been blocked by a fallen mountain, had caused immense devastation. It was not till a few weeks later that news came to Lhasa of the extent of the catastrophe in Tibet itself. The epicentre of the earthquake must have been in South Tibet. Hundreds of monks and nuns were buried in their rock-monasteries and often there were no survivors to carry the news to the nearest District Officer. Towers were split down the middle, leaving ruined walls pointing to the sky, and human beings, as if snatched by a demon's hand, disappeared into the suddenly gaping earth.

The evil omens multiplied. Monsters were born. One morning the capital of the stone column at the foot of the Potala was found lying on the ground in fragments. In vain did the Government send monks to the centres of ill-omen to banish the evil spirits with their prayers, and when one day in blazing summer weather water began to flow from a gargoyle on the cathedral, the people of Lhasa were beside themselves with terror. No doubt natural explanations could have been found for all these happenings, but if the Tibetans lost their superstitiousness they would at the same time lose an asset. One has to remember that if evil portents can demoralise them with fear, good omens inspire them with strength and confidence.

The Dalai Lama was kept informed of all these sinister events. Though naturally as superstitious as his people, he was always curious to hear my views on these things. We never lacked matter for conversation and our lesson time was all too short. He actually spent his leisure hours with me, and few people realised that he was using his free time for further study. He kept punctually to his programme, and if he awaited my coming with pleasure, that did not prevent him from breaking off as soon as the clock told him that our conversation time was over, and that a teacher of religion was waiting for him in one of the pavilions.

I once learned by chance what store he set by our lessons. One day, on which many ceremonies were to take place, I did not expect to be called to the Norbulingka and so went with friends for a walk on a hill near the town. Before I started, I told my servant to flash me a signal with a mirror if the Dalai Lama sent for me. At the usual hour the signal came and I ran at top speed back into the town. My servant was waiting with a horse at the ferry but, fast as I rode, I was ten minutes late. The Dalai Lama ran to meet me and excitedly grasped both my hands, calling "Where have you been all this time? I have been waiting so long for you, Henrig." I begged him to pardon me for having distressed him. It was only then that I realised how much these hours meant to him.

On the same day his mother and youngest brother were present, and I showed them one of the eighty films which the Dalai Lama possessed. It was very interesting for me to see the mother and son together. I knew that from the moment of the official recognition of the boy as the Incarnate Buddha the family had no more claim on him as a son or brother. For that reason his mother's visit was a sort of official event, to which she came in all her finery and jewels. When she left, she bowed before him and he laid his hand on her head in blessing. This gesture well expressed the relation of these two persons to one another. The mother did not even receive the two-handed blessing, which was accorded only to monks and high officials.

It very seldom happened that we were disturbed when we were together. Once a monk of the bodyguard brought him an important letter. The huge fellow threw himself three times to the ground, drew in his breath with a panting sound as the etiquette demands, and delivered the letter. He then withdrew from the room, walking backwards, and closed the door silently behind him. In such moments, I was very conscious how greatly I myself offended against the protocol.

The letter I have mentioned came from the eldest brother of the Dalai Lama, the abbot of Kumbum in the Chinese province of Chinghai. The Reds were already in power there and they were now hoping to influence the Dalai Lama in their favour through his brother Tagtsel Rimpoche. The letter announced that Tagtsel was on the way to Lhasa.

On the same day I visited the Dalai Lama's family. His mother scolded me when I arrived. Her mother's love had not failed to notice how much he depended on me and how often he had looked at the clock as he waited for my coming. I explained why I had not come in time and was able to convince her that my unpunctuality had not been due to casualness. When I left her she begged me never to forget how few chances of enjoying himself in his own way her son had. It was perhaps a good thing that she had seen herself how much our lesson hours meant to the Dalai Lama. After a few months everyone in Lhasa knew where I was riding about noon. As was to be expected, the monks criticised my regular visits, but his mother stood up for her son's wishes.

The next time I came through the yellow gate into the Inner Garden I thought I noticed the Dalai Lama looking out for me from his little window, and it seemed as if he was wearing glasses. This surprised me as I had never seen him with spectacles on. In answer to my question he told me that he had for some time been having difficulty with his eyes and had therefore taken to wearing glasses for study. His brother had procured him a pair through the Indian

Legation. He had probably damaged his eyes when he was a child, when his only pleasure was to look for hours together through his telescope at Lhasa. Moreover continuous reading and study in the twilight of the Potala were not exactly calculated to improve his sight. On this occasion he was wearing a red jacket over his monastic robe. He had designed it himself and was very proud of it, but he allowed himself to wear it only in his leisure moments. The chief novelty about this garment was the fact that it had pockets. Tibetan clothes do not have any, but the designer had noticed the existence of pockets in the illustrated papers and in my jackets and had realised how useful they might be. Now, like every other boy of his age, he was able to carry about with him a knife, a screw-driver, sweets, etc. He also now kept his coloured pencils and fountain pens in his pockets and was, doubtless, the first Dalai Lama to take pleasure in such things. He was also much interested in his collection of watches and clocks, some of which he had inherited from the thirteenth Dalai Lama. His favourite piece was an Omega calendar-clock which he had bought with his own money. During his minority he could only dispose of the money which was left as an offering at the foot of his throne. Later on the treasure vaults of the Potala and the Garden of Jewels would be open to him and, as ruler of Tibet, he would become one of the world's richest men.

[From *Seven Years in Tibet*.]

8

Asylum for the Dalai Lama

By

JAWAHARLAL NEHRU

MR. BHUPESH Gupta asked rather rhetorically, "Do we stand by Panchsheel?" So far as India is concerned, we have earnestly striven to stand by these principles and I do not think we have offended any principle. If these principles are right, we should hold by them and we hold by them. Some people, taking advantage of the occurrences in Tibet, have raised the cry that India should now consider how far she can adhere to the policy of non-alignment. That shows a strange misunderstanding of our ways. Non-alignment, despite the negative form of the term is a positive concept, and we do not propose to have a military alliance with any country, come what may. The moment we give up the idea of non-alignment, we lose every anchor that we hold on to and we simply drift.

The present difficulties that we have to face in relation to the happenings in Tibet will, I hope, gradually pass. But it is a tragedy that something that we have laboured for all these years, something which may be said to be enshrined in Panchsheel or in Bandung, has suffered considerably in people's minds. I may I shall hold on to it, but the fact is that in people's minds there is a crack, there is suffering, there is uneasiness. Words like Bandung and Panchsheel have begun to lose their shine and to be hurled about without meaning, even as the word "peace" has become almost a thunderbolt.

We have received the Dalai Lama and party and, subsequently, some thousands of refugees. We have given them asylum. As a sovereign country we have every right to do so, and nobody else can be a judge of that except ourselves. If it is suggested by some people outside India that we should have refused to give asylum to the Dalai Lama when he asked for it, well, I can tell them that the hundreds of millions of Indians would have become angry t any such decision. It would have been utterly wrong for us to do otherwise.

Now it is said that the commanding centre of the rebellion in Tibet has shifted to Mussoorie. And why? Because the Dalai Lama is there and because the brother of the Dalai Lama, who normally lives in Darjeeling, went to see him, and, after seeing him, went back to Darjeeling of Kalimpong. These are very serious charges against a country's leaders being made irresponsibly in this way by the leaders of a people whom we have not only honoured and respected but whom we have considered particularly advanced in culture and politeness and the gentler art of civilization. It has been a shock to me beyond measure.

An extraordinary thing has appeared in the newspapers in Peking. They refer to some memoranda that we had sent in 1950 when Chinese armies were entering Tibet. They were polite memoranda but the answers were not very polite. The point is that now they say that we wrote them after consultation with the British Government, and that though we called ourselves independent we really acted as stooges or tools of the British Government.

Of course, it is completely untruthful. There was no question of our consulting the British Government. Our view on Tibet was different from that of the British Government.

Some foreign newspapermen said, about two days after the Dalai Lama had come to Mussoorie, that we were keeping him behind barbed wire. That sounds horrible. The fact was that the Mussoorie police, to lighten their burden, because of all kinds of curious people trying to go into the compound of the house, had put a little barbed wire on the compound before he came, for his security and general protection. It was not to keep him in, and I believe he goes about in Mussoorie.

It is no use my repeating what I have said earlier that the Dalai Lama is not kept under duress here, that he did not enter India under any duress, excepting the duress of circumstances. And having met him and talked to him, I can certainly say that he is staying there of his own free will.

Hon. Members might have seen some newspaper headlines to the effect that I said I would be happy if the Dalai Lama went back to Tibet. When somebody asked a question I said, "Naturally I would be happy if he went with dignity." That does not at all mean that I am going to push the Dalai Lama out. It is entirely for him to decide what to do and when to do it.

I may refer one more matter to the Press. I do not fancy the constant sensational way of referring to the Dalai Lama as the God-king, and I do not think he likes it either. This is not the Indian way; it is a foreign way of doing things. I hope that world will not be used. It is good enough to refer to him as the Dalai Lama.

[From *Reply to Debate on Tibet in Rajya Sabha*, 4 May, 1959.]

9

The Tibetan Uprising and the Flight of the Dalai Lama

IN ORDER to obtain a correct prespective of the events leading up to the flight of the Dalai Lama from Tibet and his arrival in India on March 31st, 1959, it will be necessary to go into the back-ground and examine in greater detail some of the important facts and events which took place in Tibet between 1951 and 1959.

Although there is nothing in the Seventeen-Point Agreement to suggest that Tibet was to be carved up, Tibet was in fact divided into three parts, one of which was put under the control of Chamdo Liberation Committee headed by General Wang Chi Mei, a Chinese general, the second under the Panchen Lama's Bureau and the third, which came to be described as the Local Government, was nominally under the jurisdiction of the Dalai Lama and his Government.

The Dalai Lama in his Tezpur statement has mentioned that the "Tibetan Government did not enjoy any measure of autonomy even in internal matters and the Chinese Government exercised full powers in Tibetan affairs." In his press statement of June 20th, 1959, he said:

> "Although they had solemnly undertaken to maintain my status and power as the Dalai Lama, they did not lose any opportunity to undermine my authority and sow dissensions among my people. In fact, they compelled me, situated as I was, to dismiss my Prime Ministers under threat of their execution without trial, because they had in all honesty and sincerity resisted the justified unsurpations of power by representatives of the Chinese Government in Tibet.
>
> "Far from carrying out the agreement they began deliberately to pursue a course of policy which was diametrically opposed to the terms and conditions which they had themselves laid down. Thus commenced a reign of terror which finds few parallels in the history of Tibet. Forced labour and compulsory exactions, a systematic persecution of the people, plunder and confiscation of property belonging to individuals and monasteries and execution of certain leading men in Tibet, these are the glorious achievements of the Chinese rule in Tibet."

In addition to this, large-scale immigration and colonization by the Chinese had started in eastern and northeastern regions. In the press conference held a Mussoorie the Dalai Lama stated:

> "The ultimate Chinese aim with regard to Tibet, as far as I can make out, seems to attempt the extermination of religion and culture and even the absorption of the Tibetan race. Besides the civilian and military personnel already in Tibet 5 million Chinese settlers have arrived in eastern and northeastern Tso, in addition to which 4 million Chinese settlers are planned to be sent to U and Sung provinces of Central

Tibet. Many Tibetans have been deported to China, thereby resulting in the complete aborsption of these Tibetans as a race, which is being undertaken by the Chinese."

About the end of 1955 uprisings took place in the northeastern and eastern region of Tibet which were under the Chamdo Liberation Committee and the Panchen Lama's Bureau. Soon these uprisings spread westwards. In 1956 the Dalai Lama visited India and remained in India till April 1957. Little was known at the time of the serious situation in Tibet and the extremely difficult position in which the Dalai Lama found himself. The Dalai Lama in his press statement of June 20th 1959 has stated "as I was unable to do anything for the benefit of my people I had practically made up my mind when I came to India not to return to Tibet until there was a manifest change in the attitude of the Chinese authorities. I therefore sought the advice of the Prime Minister of India who has always shown me unfailing kindness and consideration. After his talk with the Chinese Prime Minister and on the strength of the assurance given by him on behalf of China, Mr. Nehru advised me to change my decision." Mr. Nehru in his speech in the Indian Parliament of April 27th, 1959 has confirmed that he did give such advice to the Dalai Lama on the assurance he had received from Mr. Chou En Lai, who had been on a visit to India in December 1956.

In 1957 the situation had worsened and evidently, in an attempt to placate the outraged Tibetan sentiments, Mao Tsetung, in his well-known 'Hundred Flowers Speech' said that reforms would not be introduced in Tibet during the period of 1958-62 and that thereafter the introduction of reforms would depend on the wishes of the Tibetan people.

The risings took place in Lithang, Ba, Chantin, Gyal-thang, Lingharzy-pa, Dhan-go, Golak, Sertha, Lha-dhe, Gu-rak, Amcheck, Chebc-she, Choney, Dzo-goy, Tso and Nyapa in Amdo; and the three regions of Golak as well as what are known as the eighteen kingdoms of Gyerong.

Flight of the Dalai Lama

Coming now to the recent incidents in Lhasa, which ulitmately led to the flight of the Dalai Lama, a little background to the immediate flare-up may be useful. A number of incidents had happened in the last two years, when high personages, believed not to be sympathetic to the Chinese, were invited to parties by the Military Commanders. These were either killed or imprisoned. This was widely known in Tibet. The names of the Lamas and the regions where they came from are:

1. Head Lama Amdo—Sharkelden Gyalto (killed)
2. Head Lama Amdo—Kunchok Lhundup (killed)
3. A very famous Lama Kham—Pandit Shi Chen (killed)
4. Another famous Lama Kham—Kathok Situ (imprisoned)

The Dalai Lama had received an invitation from the military commander to attend a cultural programme on March 10th, 1959 at the military headquarters; he was asked to come unaccompanied by any of his ministers or his body-guard, a most unusual request. In view of the stories mentioned above, as soon as the news of the invitation became known, a large number of people surrounded the Norbulinga Palace, where the Dalai Lama was in residence. This happened on the 10th. All the ministers except one gathered in the palace. The exception was a minister who was considered to be pro-Chinese who was prevented by the people from entering the palace.

The Dalai Lama asked the people to be calm and announced that he would not go to the show. In spite of this the people continued to stay round the Palace throughout the night of the 10th.

On the 11th of March 1959 a meeting of all Government officials was called at the Palace, a few pro-Chinese officials did not attend and a proclamation was issued in the name of the Cabinet that Tibet was independent. Among the Cabinet Ministers present at the meeting were:

Surkhang, Neushar, Gastang, Shasur.

These gentlemen are at present in India with the Dalai Lama.

On this day about 5,000 women also gathered. A deputation of some of them went into the Palace asking the Dalai Lama to proclaim independence.

On March 12th, 1959, a large meeting was held at Shol—below the Potala Palace. Almost the whole population of Lhasa seem to have been present. At this meeting it was decided to prepare documents regarding the claim of independence. A letter was sent to Mr. Shakabpa, which never reached him, mentioning these facts and he was asked to announce to the world the facts about the Chinese oppression and the decision of the Tibetan people regarding independence. This meeting was almost in continuous session between 12th and the 17th of March and the people gathered were entirely unarmed. After nightfall, two shells were fired on the Palace but fell in an artificial lake in front of the Place. Machine-gun firing was heard. At 10.30 p.m. and thereafter the Dalai Lama and some of his party, which arrived in India, left the Palace one by one.

The shells were evidently fired by the Chinese as a warning in the hope of getting the Dalai Lama to surrender, but nothing happened on the 18th. On the early morning of the 19th at 1 a.m. a serious bombardment of the Palace began. The Chinese were evidently not aware that the Dalai Lama had left 24 hours earlier. This bombardment greatly damaged the Norbulinga Palace and the city was also greatly damaged. The accounts of refugees point to a large loss of life. There were sufficient Chinese troops in Lhasa at the time who could have taken perhaps milder action, but the continuous bombardment was intended to strike terror among the people.

Since, in spite of the bombardment, the Dalai Lama did not come out and surrender, the Chinese suspected that the Dalai Lama had left and as a result numerous aerial search parties were sent. These planes flew low and machine-gunned groups of people on sight. This was done indiscriminately in many places on the possible escape routes of the Dalai Lama in the hope that the group might consist of the Dalai Lama's party.

Every valid order of the Kashak (Cabinet) must ordinarily be sealed with the seals of the three monasteries Drepung, Sera, and Gaden, which are all in Lhasa. The first and the second mentioned monasteries were also shelled and very badly damaged.

The struggle is still continuing and judging from Tibetan sources the Chinese claim that the revolt has been put down does not seem to be justified, excepting insofar as the area in and around Lhasa is concerned. In an interview given by the Dalai Lama to Mr. Mahesh Chandra, special correspondent of the *Statesman* (India) on June 6th, 1959, the Dalai Lama stated that the news from Tibet he had lately been receiving was sad to the extreme. There was much trouble for his people. Every day he heard of fresh atrocities. He appealed to the editor of this newspaper to help in bringing the terrible happenings in Tibet to public notice. He used the words "Please help us."

He further said that both the Tibetans who had remained behind and those who had come away were suffering equally, the first physically and the second mentally. "But we both feel the same pain. Those who are left behind are being subjected to unbearable tortures day and night." He ended by saying "Despite all these difficulties, and come what may, our spirit will never die. Tibet will live. One day our beloved country will arrived at journey's end, when truth shall triumph."

Nature of the Uprising

As to the nature of the uprising the Chinese have claimed that it has all been engineered or organized by the upper class reactionaries.

By the end of May 1959, there were about 15,000 refugees in India. There are some in Sikkim, Nepal and Bhutan. Enquiries show that the refugees are not what has been described by Communist China as as "reactionaries;" the overwhelming majority are the common and the poor people.

The leaders of the rebellion have banded themselves in an organization called "Ten-Soung-Ma-Ghar," viz. the National Voluntary Defence Army of Tibet. A reference of the National Voluntary Defence Army has been made by the Dalai Lama in his press conference. A recent statement by the leaders of this army discloses that on January 1, 1959 a declaration made by them set out radical changes in social and political organization of the country which they advocate. The proposals include acquisition of large landed estates on payment of compensation, the introduction of the elective system on the basis of adult suffrage and the principles of individual liberty according to modern constitutional concept. They have stated, "We pledge ourselves for the improvement of the condition of our people and their standard of living. We engage ourselves to introduce all necessary reforms in the country in accordance with the natural conditions, customs and genius of our people. In the field of economic development we pledge ourselves to improve the life of our nomadic people, of the tillers of the land, of the artisans and the handicrafts men to the best of our ability and to effect changes in all spheres of our national life. It is our avowed policy to bring about these changes by peaceful means."

They claim that this declaration was backed by the masses of the people and they refute the allegation of the Chinese authorities that the rising was the handiwork of a few reactionaries instigated by "imperialist powers." They claim that the widespread revolt is a national upsurge of people who are fighting for their existence and their identity.

It may be of interest to note that Mr. Nehru, Prime Minister of India, in his speech to Parliament on April 27th, 1959, says:

"To says that a number of 'upper class reactionaries' in Tibet were responsible for this appears to be an extraordinary simplification of a complicated situation. Even according to the accounts received through Chinese sources, The revolt in the Tibet was of considerable magnitude and the basis of it must have been a strong feeling of nationalism which affects not only upper class people but others also. No doubt, vested interests joined it and sought to profit by it. The attempt to explain a situation by the use of rather worn-out words, phrases and slogans, is seldom helpful."

[From *Truth About Tibet*.]

10

An Abridged Report on the Second Delegation of the Dalai Lama to Tibet

[Based on the talk given by Tenzin N. Tethong, the leader of the Second delegation of the Dalai Lama to Tibet at the Asia Society, New York City on October 2, 1980.]

Status of Religion

Before our arrival in Peking, we studied the constitution of the People's Republic of China, and paid particular attention to Article 46 which pertains to religious freedom. Article 46 guarantees the right to believe in religion, the right not to believe in religion and the right also to propagate atheism.

In spite of the introduction of "lenient policy" two years ago, it is apparent that the political climate is more favourable to the non-practice of religion and that the propagation of atheism then it is to the freedom to practise religion. Although a few existing temples are opened to the public, people are free to recite only the Tibetan Mantras and turn prayer wheels in the privacy of their homes. However, since, any propagation or explanation of the meaning or benefits of the Mantras or Buddhism would invite trouble, it appears that Article 46 is more an attempt to improve China's world image of religious tolerance rather than actual implementation of the freedom to worship.

From our extensive travels, we can safely say that more than 99 per cent of Tibet's monasteries and temples have been destroyed. They stand in ruins or have been ploughed into wheat fields. Remaining portions of some monasteries are used for gain storage. Tibet. Dotted with more than 3,700 monasteries and temples before the Chinese military occupation, today has only a few temples in Gyangtse, Shigatse, Lhasa and some parts of Amdo where the central temples exist. In Gyangtse, we visited the main cathedral, Jokhang, and the well-known Pagoe Chorten (Stupa). All the smaller chapels, hostel for monks and classrooms surrounding the central temple are destroyed. In Shigatse Tashi Lhunpo, the fourth largest monastery in Tibet, is in ruins except for its central temple. In Lhasa, we visited the Potala and Jokhang, the central cathedral. We learned that Jokhang had been occupied by Chinese troops as a garrison for many years and the main temple had been used as a pigsty before its recent renovation.

After considerable renovation and refurbishment, it is "presentable" to foreign visitors. During our visit to Norbulingka, one Tibetan daringly gestured to a palace not on our official itinerary. Peering inside, we saw vast mounds of broken Buddha statues a sight as forlorn as a car junk yard in the United States.

In Kham, eastern Tibet, the famous monasteries of Ba, Karze, Chamdo, Dragyab and Lithang are in ruins. The Chinese officials told us that they were destroyed during the Cultural Revolution, but we learned that initially there had been extensive destruction in 1956 during Chinese attacks on the monasteries. In

1959, and during the Cultural Revolution in the mid-1960s the destruction was completed.

The nature of plundering and devastation of these monasteries can best be illustrated by the systematic destruction of Ganden Monastery which was the third largest monastery in Tibet. Ganden Monastery was founded in 1409 by Tsongkhapa, the founder of the Gelugpa school of Tibetan Buddhism. From 1959 through the mid-1960s, Ganden was occupied as a garrison by Chinese troops and used also for grain storage.

At the outset of the Cultural Revolution, Chinese Officials from the Mineral Department in Lhasa removed all the precious stones studded on the thousands of statues, images and ritual objects that were housed in the Ganden Monastery. Pillaged stones included diamonds, emeralds, rubies, coral, turquoise and pearls. Later, Chinese carried away all religious objects and images made of gold and silver and other metals. The third act of vandalism was the removal of all other goods, including furniture, art works, painting and everything else of value. Finally, a few of the largest buildings at Ganden were dynamited and reduced to rubble.

At this stage, the last remnants of wood from the pillars and ceilings were carried away by nearby members of the communes to be used for firewood and building materials.

On July 27, 1980, we went to see the ruins of Ganden. There we were met by about 3,000 Tibetans who saluted us, wept and shouted their devotion to the Dalai Lama. These Tibetans came from Lhasa and near by villages and towns in 83 Chinese trucks. The trucks were driven by Tibetans. It was very moving to know the sacrifices these people had made to be there. They well knew that they would be arrested and jailed for an indefinite period for their activities. Even as the demonstration was going on, Chinese official photographers were busy taking their pictures.

During our last meeting with Minister Yang Jiren of the Minority Nationalities in Peking, we learned that an investigation committee has been set up to document the actual destruction of Ganden.

Aware of the impact that the devastation of Ganden might have and presumably expecting possible demonstration, the foreign correspondents who were in Lhasa at the time were not allowed to come with us to Ganden. The Chinese authorities cannily told the journalists that the road to Ganden was damaged. Therefore, there was no foreign press reportage of the tremendous, spontaneous outbursts of expressions of Buddhist faith and support for the Dalai Lama on that day.

Over the past 21 years, the Chinese have attempted to eradicate the Tibetan people's faith in Buddhism. They have desecrated all the holy places, Buddhist scriptures, images and everything that is sacred to the Tibetans. They have humiliated and ridiculed the high lamas and have demanded them to perform miracles. Lamas, monks and nuns have been tortured and killed in mass numbers. People have been imprisoned for reciting Tibetan mantras, turning prayer wheels and having in their possession a photograph of the Dalai Lama. Nevertheless, the Tibetan people's faith in Buddhism retains its vital strength, bravely upheld by numerous groups of monks who secretly gather for prayers.

The strong faith of the lay people is clearly manifest in their behaviour towards the representative of the Dalai Lama. Last year, when the first delegation visited Tibet, they were mobbed by crowds day and night who eagerly snatched bits of hair and clothing as talismans. The Dalai Lama's elder brother Mr. Lobsang Samden often returned to his lodgings stripped of his upper garment and with other pieces in tatters. Again, during our visit thousands of people came to see us and asked to be touched and given blessings. In some cases, they collected locks of our hair. Even young children would hold our hands and would tell us about their prayers and their wishes for the Dalai Lama.

Since the introduction of the lenient policy, pilgrims are streaming towards the holy city, Lhasa, from all over Tibet. A large number come from the Amdo and Kham areas. These people walk to Lhasa and are occasionally given free rides by Tibetan truck drivers. (They usually have no bedding, food or money with them). We met many of them on several occasions during our sojourn from the eastern to the central Tibet. Even groups of youngsters in their early teens walk to Lhasa from Kham, a pilgrimage that will probably take them months.

Actually, these people are not officially allowed to make these pilgrimages. As a punitive action against them, their work-points are cut down and their wages consequently diminished.

Desecration of religious objects and images is evident everywhere. In many places we saw that the holy Mantra-Stones (stones on which holy scriptures are engraved) were used for doorsteps, foot paths, construction of public lavatories and also for the drainage of human waste. Furthermore, the Tibetan term for religious faith is no longer in use; now it is called "blind faith" or "faith of ignorance." We challenged these contentions wherever we went, stating that such official attitude towards religion counteracts the religious freedom established in the Chinese constitution. We also pointed out that Buddhism is an integral part of the Tibetan culture, and hence it should be respected at least for its cultural value.

In Tibet today, Buddhism has been replaced by Communism. Every office, every hall, every house is adorned with the portraits of Communist "God" : Marx, Stalin, Mao and Hua.

The Present Status of Culture

Buddhism has traditionally been woven into the fabric of Tibetan daily life. Today, since Communist ideology takes precedence, daily habits and customs are changing. Everyone must listen to Chinese propaganda broadcast at least three times a day. This constant barrage of speeches interspersed with music permits little time for people to relax or to think quietly.

In terms of dress, most Tibetan men wear the Chinese Mao jackets and caps and many women wear pants. Even among the women who wear the Tibetan *Chuba*, the national dress, the style is modified: the length is shorter and worn with pants clearly showing beneath the hemline.

In every town which we visited, there was a cultural performance. Most of these performances are not different from what one could see in Peking. Although the actors are Tibetan, there is virtually no true representation of Tibetan culture in these shows. Only rarely does one hear of traditional Tibetan tune and if so the lyrics are new, sung in Chinese style, glorifying Mao and the Communist Party.

One encouraging cultural aspect is the revival of the *Lhamo* (Tibetan Opera). We were told that there are several such troops in Lhasa, and the best group is in Shol, at the foot of the Potala. We saw performances of "Dowa Sangmo" in Lithang and an extract of "Achi Nangsa" in Gyangtse. We noted, however, that the performance in Gyangtse subtly portrays the "evils" of the old society.

The use of Chinese language is predominant in Tibet. All road signs and signboards are in Chinese. The first public sign in Tibetan that we saw was for a Men's toilet in the Ngapa area of Eastern Tibet. All official ranks and administrative units in Tibet are in Chinese language even though it may be written in the

Tibetan script. The Tibetan word "Dzong" for district headquarters, which literally means fortress or government house, is replaced by the Chinese word "Shen;" the Tibetan word for leader "Utre," is replaced by the Chinese word "Turin." Likewise, the Tibetan word "gyalrab" for history is banished from the Tibetan vocabulary when referring to Tibetan history. Instead, the word "Logyu" is used which means story. However, when a reference is made to Chinese history, the word "gyalrab" is used. Tibetan kings are termed "Lonpo" which means minister. Tibet's 33rd king who lived in the early seventh century is so called Lonpo Songtsen Gampo.

It is not suprising to learn that the Tibetan cadres are now given Chinese names to be used for their official matters. The giving of names to Tibetan children is a cultural and religious custom that dates back to centuries. It was customarily done by Tibetan lamas. However, today, the Chinese have given strange, statistical names to Tibetan children that simply accord with their weight at the time of their birth or the day or month of their birth, i.e., names like "Six-Thirteen" referring to the month and date of their birth or "Seven and Half" referring to their birth-weight. We were often asked by parents to rename their children. We took the liberty of conferring the first name of His Holiness the Dalai Lama, Tenzen, and a suitable second Tibetan name to these children.

The Present Status of Education

Owing to China's claim in the past years of the establishment of numerous schools and higher educational institutions in Tibet, our expectations were high. But we were shocked to learn the dismal reality of standards of education in the country. In the eastern parts of Tibet, no Tibetan language it taught in the so-called regular school. Aside from some mathematics and general science, the most important subject is Marxist ideology and Chinese is the medium of instruction.

In the Ngapa area of Amdo province, some Tibetan is taught at a Tibetan Medical School and a Tibetan Teacher's Training School. The teacher's training course is for three years, and some of these prospective teachers come to the school with no knowledge of the Tibetan language. After three years, they graduate as "qualified" teachers!

During our stay in Tibet and China, we told the Chinese official that we would like to meet with Tibetans who had completed university education. To our disappointment, we did not meet a single Tibetan who has received university education.

When the Chinese talk about higher education for Tibetans, they are referring to the Nationalities Institutes in Peking and Chengtu; plus a few other schools which the Chinese label higher institutes such as the "medical" schools in Chamdo, Thartsedo and Nyitre. We visited all these schools.

Students at these schools have prior schooling of five years, often less, and they graduate after three or four years. The curriculum included: Chinese language and Marxist ideology. The medical schools are similar to the other so-called higher institutions. Students at medical schools have had only two or three years of primary education and graduate after three years as qualified "doctors."

In most cases, these "doctors" do more harm than good. Once our interpreter, appointed by Peking, was ill. The medicine given to him did not cure him; instead, produced a rush all over his body. Then he was given an injection which worsened his condition. Finally, he was taken to a hospital where he recovered after three days.

There are only four or five "big" hospitals in Tibet all of which are located in towns. Therefore, the 99 per cent of the Tibetans who live in the countryside are at the mercy of "doctors" whose training is dangerously inadequate, according to other sources.

The Present Status of Communication

During the last 30 years, the Chinese have built roads in Tibet. The obvious question: are these roads of benefit to the Tibetan people whose contribution is sweat and blood is far greater than that of the Chinese engineers and technicians? During our travel throughout Tibet, we were convinced that the roads are used principally for Chinese military purposes. Each day we travelled, sometimes for eight or more hours, we met only convoys of army trucks. During the three-month period, we ran into only about 10 public buses. There are no paved roads in Tibet except the road between Yangpachen and Lhasa which is about 40 kilometers.

There are airfields in Karzi, Chamdo, Damshung, Gongkar and Shigatse, but only Gongkar is used for civilian purposes. All the rest for military use.

There are telephone lines in most parts of Tibet, but no one has a telephone at home for private use. There are telephones in offices used for official purposes only. These telephone services are primitive. We had to wait for hours before we were able to get a line on which to make a call.

The Military Presence

The presence of the People's Liberation Army (PLA) is highly visible and extensive. Almost every town and village has a PLA unit. In each of the 137 districts in Tibet, we were told that there are 500 to 1,000 troops with a total of about 140,000. According to other sources, the figure is considerably higher between 300,000 to 400,000 troops.

We also learned that a large number of Tibetans were sent to fight the Vietnamese during the Sino-Vietnamese War in early 1979. We met many families whose sons died in Vietnam.

Government

The present system of government in Tibet is neither democratic nor a people's government. Rather, it is authoritarian in nature, dominated by the Chinese Communist Party officials.

Until two years ago, almost all positions above a district head were held by Chinese. Today, although most district heads are Tibetans, all decisions are made by Chinese officials.

One of the strongest features of government in Tibet is the Political Consultative Committee. The Committee consists of former aristocrats, lamas and local leaders. The members include: Phakpa Gelek Namgyal, a high lama from Chamdo; Samding Dorjee Phakmo, a female incarnate; Thupten Lhautara and other ranking aristocrats from the former government.

These people are from the so-called upper class and some of them were criticized and publicly humiliated and imprisoned in the early 1960s and during the Cultural Revolution. Today, they are well-paid, well-treated spokesmen for foreign journalists, highly regarded in protocol and highly visible without having actual portfolios or real power. Supposedly they are consulted on "important policy matters."

The State of Economy

In terms of statistics, the Tibetan economy has improved during the past two decades. The Chinese readily boast about the recent production figures and compare them with figures of pre-1959. However, they fail to take into account the increase in the Tibetan population or the large number of Chinese immigrants and PLA units. In many towns, especially in the warmer areas that we visited, the Chinese population outnumbers the Tibetan.

In general, there is a clear distinction between the Tibetan Autonomous Region and the Autonomous Prefectures which are under Chinese provincial governments. And also owing to the presence of large Chinese population in towns and cities, the urban areas are usually much better off than the rural areas.

The local Chinese officials have always provided inflated figures for production and living standards. In Dragyab Kham, the Chinese officials told us that the local Tibetans receive about 550 pounds of grain per year per person. But when we visited the town and spoke to the people, we found the figures quite different. Many families of two or three persons received each only about 350 pounds of grain a year. The per capita cash income a Tibetan peasant family may be less than $68 a year.

The Chinese agricultural policy in Tibet is a case of Communist Party mismanagement. Disregarding and ignoring the local Tibetans' expertise in farming, the Chinese policy for a number of years was to introduce winter wheat crops and to cultivate all available land, including grasslands which were used for grazing by nomadic herds. In the first year, the crop yields were dramatically increased, then gradually they began to drop. Winter wheat sucked the soil dry of nutrients and the soil was soon exhausted and useless. Traditionally in Tibet, sections of farm land were left to lie fallow for at least a year before the next crop was planted.

Misguided and dictatorial agriculture policies pushed by the Chinese dominated regional government contributed to year of disastrous harvests. Large tracts of grasslands were destroyed and, as a consequence, the herds began to die of starvation. Near famine gripped many areas of Tibet. In Dragyab and Karze, celebrated in the past for their abundant output of grain, people were reduced to beggars and were forced to abandon their towns in search of food.

Other factors have contributed to the poor state of economy in Tibet. Last year bad weather and bad policies compounded with a plague of insects produced a crop failure unprecedented in modern times. In spite of these conditions, it was mandatory that each Tibetan provide at least 1,000 pounds of grain as an annual tax. In consequence, Tibetans were compelled to live on semi-starvation rations. It is rare that a family will have meat, butter or cheese in their larder.

Poor living conditions are further exacerbated by the housing shortage. In many towns or cities like Chamdo, Shigatse and Lhasa, the Chinese have built many new houses which outnumber the old. Occupancy of 90 per cent of these houses is by Chinese and a few Tibetan cadres. Tibetans live in government-owned old, ram-shackle houses. Collection of rent is prompt. Renovation is seldom effected.

The Present Status of Industry

One of the most visible signs of industrialization are the ubiquitous electricity plants. Lights, however, are automatically switched on at 7 p.m. and switched off at 11 p.m. The only power stations capable of producing considerable electricity seems to be the ones near Chamdo and in Tharsedo in eastern Tibet.

Chamdo also has a cement plant if properly used, could be of considerable benefit to the Tibetans. The many leather factories and dairy plants that we visited are mainly geared for Chinese needs and their products sent to China. Another sad aspect of these operations is that only a few Tibetans have been taught industrial skills or technical knowledge.

At the same time, Tibet's traditional handicrafts have been ignored for the past 20 years and under attack as capitalist enterprises. In the last year, some effort has been made to revive them. The carpet weaving centre in Gyangtse in regarded as one of the best centres in Tibet. The wool used here is better quality than those used in the exiled's carpet centres in India and Nepal. Nevertheless, the quality of weaving is inferior to those produced by the exiles. We also visited the woollen mills in Tharsedo and Kongpo Nyitre. Here the wool is used for making blankets and materials. In the Tharsedo woollen mill, there are some 600 workers, of which only 33 are Tibetans. The ration of Tibetan and Chinese worker is similar in many plants and factories in Tibet.

One industry which amazed us was the lumber industry in eastern Tibet. In the Ngapa, Karze and Dechen areas, an extensive lumber industry is in operation. Some mountains and hills have been completely denuded. All of this timber has been transported to China by road and by river. Tibetans do not receive any compensation or payment for this lumber. Despite their poor living conditions, Tibetans are forced to purchase everything from a cap to a shoelace from Chinese shops which only sell goods manufactured in China.

People's Feeling

The feeling of the Tibetan people were clearly demonstrated to the visiting delegations sent by the Dalai Lama. So far, three delegations visited Tibet, each travelling extensively in the country. The visit of fourth delegation planned for last August has been postponed for an indefinite period.

More than 99 per cent of the Tibetans in Tibet want their country to be an independent and sovereign state. They acknowledge the leadership of the Dalai Lama and his exiled government as the legitimate government of Tibet. Under the present circumstances, the Tibetans strongly urge the Dalai Lama not to return to Tibet. Older Tibetans wish to see the Dalai Lama before they died. Both young and old send messages of their fellow Tibetans in exile to serve the Dalai Lama for the cause of Tibet. If this was not possible, they urged the exiles, never to go against the wishes of the Dalai Lama.

In 21 years of Chinese occupation, Tibet has met the cultural, religious and economic devastation. Virtually all Tibetans have been degraded to second class citizens, they have no voice in their governing. Almost all Tibetans have been reduced to the status of beggars. Instead of benefiting from the modern technology promised by the Chinese, the Tibetans, for the first time in their history, have been forced to live on starvation rations on which thousands have died. Their traditional way of life has degenerated into nothingness.

[From *"Liberation to Liberalisation: Views on Liberalised Tibet." Information Office of His Holiness the Dalai Lama,* 1982.]

11

The Ocean of Wisdom: H.H. the Dalai Lama

By
SARDAR BUTA SINGH

THE "Ocean of Wisdom," the Bodhisattva of Mercy, Avalokitshwara, His Holiness The Dalai Lama is, indeed, compassion-incarnate. Spreading the gospel of peace and non-violence in the strife-torn world, His Holiness has given the message of hope to humanity. He has asserted that the salvation of the human race lies in Ahimsa from which flows compassion for all and genuine peace. He also reminded the world that mere absence of war is not peace. It is much more than that. Genuine peace prevails when man is free from fear and want, when individual freedom is universally respected, when no one undergoes avoidable suffering, when the fate of people in any country is the legitimate concern of the entire human family, when every human being has the right to pursue happiness and live in peace and freedom.

During the struggle for our freedom from colonial rule, Mahatma Gandhi put the infallible weapons of Truth, Non-Violence, Non-Cooperation and Sacrifice in the hands of our people and ultimately Truth prevailed and India emerged as a free nation. Today, His Holiness The Dalai Lama is not only inspiring his own people with the same ideals, but is tirelessly going around the world with the message of Truth, Non-violence, Compassion, Sacrifice, Peace, Love and Tolerance giving new hope to the suffering humanity the world over.

The people of India and Tibet always had unique cultural and spiritual relationship. His Holiness has always cherished this relationship. The people of India have always revered His Holiness and his great predecessors as the great spiritual Gurus and standard bearers of the message of Universal Love and Ahimsa preached by Lord Buddha.

Born in the Amdo Province of Tibet in 1935, the spiritual and religious leadership of Tibet was conferred on him in 1939 at the tender age of four and he became the 14th Dalai Lama. When the Chinese army violated Tibetan sovereignty and besieged Dalai Lama's residence in Lhasa in 1959, His Holiness had to leave Tibet along with lakhs of his followers. He came to India and made Dharamsala (Himachal Pradesh) the Headquarters of his Government-in-Exile.

Ever since, he has been raising the question of Tibet's independence in international organizations. Though he has been leading the struggle for the rights of the people of Tibet, yet as a true saint he has not shown any rancour against the Chinese Government and the Chinese people. He has not even used harsh language against the Chinese. He simply asserted that the people of Tibet have the right to decide and shape their own destiny without any outside interference. He has drawn the attention of the world community to the systematic efforts of the Chinese authorities to settle large number of people of Chinese origin in Tibet, with a view to reducing the people of Tibet into minority in their own homeland.

To resolve the problem of Tibet in a peaceful manner His Holiness has established direct contact with the Chinese Government. To protect the mutuality of interests and to develop mutual confidence, His Holiness has proposed a Five Point Plan to the Chinese Government to peacefully and equitably resolve that question of Tibet's independence. He has also made an offer to the Chinese authorities to discuss the matter without pre-conditions. In the true Buddhist tradition, he has suggested the adoption of the Middle Path which can lead both sides to the goal of mutual trust and confidence.

The members of the Vishwa Manav Ekta Kendra feel deeply honoured by honouring His Holiness The Dalai Lama and join in prayer with millions the world over for the success of his mission to secure justice for his people and the suffering humanity a large with the confidence that ultimately the truth prevails and love triumphs.

[*10 August 1993, New Delhi*.]

12

Buddhism at a Glance

By
THE DALAI LAMA

JUST AS a particular disease in the world can be treated by various methods in medicine, so there are different religions that bring happiness to human beings and others. Different doctrines have been expounded by different exponents at different periods and in different ways. But I believe they all fundamentally aim at achieving the same noble goal, in teaching moral precepts to mould the functions of mind, body and speech. They all teach us not to tell lies, or bear false witness, or steal, or take the lives of others, so on. Therefore, it would be better if disunity among the followers of different religions could come to end. Unity among religions is not an impossible idea. It is possible, and in the present state of the world it is especially important. Mutual respect would be helpful to all believers; and unity between them would also benefit to unbelievers, for the unanimous flood of light would show them the way out of their ignorance. I strongly emphasise the urgent need for flawless unity among all religions. To this end, the followers of each religion should know something of the religion of others, and that is why I am presenting a brief introduction to the Buddhism of Tibet.

I must begin, however, by saying that it is very difficult to find exact English equivalents for the philosophical terms of Buddhism expressed in Tibetan. It is hardly possible (at present) to find a scholar who has both a perfect knowledge of English and a perfect knowledge of Tibetan Buddhist philosophy and religion. Also, there are not many authentic translations for reference. Books written or translated in the past have certainly done a great service to Buddhism, but some of them are rather rough translations, providing only a superficial interpretation. I hope scholars in the future will solve this problem so that the more profound aspects of our religion can be communicated in English. In this article a very free translation is being used so that the English is as simple as possible. At present, I can only write on these matters with confidence in Tibetan, and for an English translation I have to rely on others. I can only hope that the translation is a precise rendering.

I have already explained in My Land and My People that we Buddhists believe that all being are reborn, and strive, through a series of lives, towards the perfection of Buddhahood. We do not take it for granted that this perfection will be attained in a single lifetime, although it can be possible.

Of the mind and body of a man, we consider the mind superior; both speech and body are subject to it. Sins do not affect the intrinsic nature of mind. The essential mind is naturally pure. Sins are the defects of the peripheral or secondary minds. In the quest for enlightenment, these defects are removed one by one from the peripheral minds, and when all defects are removed from them true perfection, or Buddhahood, is attained.

We believe that during the present Kalpa (aeon) the incarnations of a thousand supreme Buddhas will take place in this world. Like ourselves, these Buddhas were living being before they attained perfection. These Buddhas have the power to project re-incarnations of their mind, body, and speech into millions of forms within a moment of time. And they do this for the benefit of all living beings of worlds like ours. Each of these supreme incarnations will preach his own doctrine, and will work eternally for the salvation of all living beings.

We regard Lord Buddha, or Gautama Buddha, as he is also called, one of these one thousand Buddhas. He was born in a royal family in India over 2,500 years ago. In the early part of his life, he lived as a prince; but he noted instances of suffering which made him realise that human existence was precarious. He renounced his princely life and became an ascetic. From the point of view of ordinary beings, which is limited, his life was marked by twelve main events; his descent called Tushita, his conception, birth, schooling, marriage, renunciation, penance, meditation under the Bodhi tree (the tree of enlightenment), conquest of Mara (the tempter), attainment of Buddhahood, preaching, and departure from Samsara (the round of existence).

His teaching differs from that of other Buddhas; while most of them preached only on Tantras (instructions on spiritual method).

After he attained Enlightenment, the Perfection of Buddhahood, at Buddha Gaya, he preached three different sermons, each at a different place in the part of India known as Bihar. The first, at Varanasi (Banaras), was on the Four Noble Truths, about which I shall have more to say. I was mainly addressed to the Sravakas (hearers) who were people gifted spiritually but of limited outlook. The second sermon, at Girdhakuta, was on Sunyata (Voidness), the non-existence of an ultimate self-nature. I shall refer to this again. This was addressed to Mahayanists, or followers of the Great Way, who were men of very high intellect. The third sermon, at Vesali, was intended primarily for Mahayanists of a lesser calibre.

Thus, he not only preached on Sutras for Mahayanists and Hinayanists (followers of the Greater and Lesser Ways, the two main schools of Buddhism), but after attaining the status of Vajra Dhara, that is to say, on his initiation into the most profound methods, he also preached many Tantras for Mahayanists. The great scriptures (translated in Tibet under the title of Kangyur) are all Lord Buddha's teachings.

The Kangyur has a Sutra and a Tantra section. The Sutra section is further divided into three subjects. Vinaya, which concerns the principles of morality; Sutantra concerning meditation; and Abdidharma concerning philosophical work related to transcendental wisdom. These three sub-divisions are called Tripitakas, and their fundamental principles are known in Sanskrit as Shila, Samadhi and Prajnya. The Tantric part of Kangyur has four subdivisions. In Tibet these sub-divisions of Tantra are sometimes included in the Sutanta division of the Sutra of Tripitaka.

The Four Noble Truths

Lord Buddha said: "This is true suffering; this is true cause; this true is cessation; this is the true path." He also said "Know the sufferings; give up their causes; attain the cessation of suffering; follow the true paths." Again, he said: "Know the sufferings although there is nothing to know; relinquish the causes of misery of although there is nothing to relinquish; be earnest in cessation although there is nothing to cease; practise the means of cessational though there is nothing to practise." These are three views of intrinsic nature, action and ultimate result of the Four Noble Truths.

According to the Madhyamika theory (originally taught by Nagarjuna, a scholar of third century of Christian era), a theory which remains supreme among all the theories of different Buddhist schools, the explanation of these Truths is this; True suffering means Samsara (the entire round of existence, of birth and rebirth), arising from Karma (this is, action and re-action) and from delusion. True cause means Karma and delusion, which are the causes of true suffering. True cessation means the complete disappearance by degrees of the preceding two truths. The true path is the method by which we arrive at true cessation.

Thus the true cause of suffering leads to true suffering, but in following the true path, we arrive at the goal of true cessation. Although this is the natural sequence, Lord Buddha preached the Fourth Truths by placing the effects first and the causes after. The reasons for this is that if the nature of suffering is determined, the cause of it may be deduced; and when this desire to eliminate the cause (of suffering) is strong, means will be found to abandon it.

Samsara and Beings

Samsara is the whole round of existence. Samsara, with its miseries, is the true cause of suffering. To Samsara belongs everything which does not contain its own sufficient cause, everything which proceeds from a chain of other causes and which is thus involved in Karma and delusion. Its essential nature is misery; its function is to provide a basis for the spread of misery and by nature to attract miseries for the future.

Spatially, Samsara is divided into three worlds—the world of the Senses, the world of Form and the world of the Formless. The beings in the first of these worlds enjoy external sensual pleasure. The second, the world of Form, consists of two parts. In the lower part beings cannot enjoy external sensual pleasures but enjoy the undisturbed pleasure of internal contemplation. In the world of the Formless, the objects of the five senses do not exist nor the five sensual organs with which we enjoy them. There is only a bare mind, devoid of distractions. This exists and dwells entirely in a state of equanimity.

Samasara may also be divided according to the nature of the beings it contains; and by this system there are six divisions:

Gods: These include beings in the world of celestial forms and of formless spirits, and the six categories of gods found in the sensual world.

Demi Gods, or Titans

These are mischievous beings who are like gods in every respect.

Human beings—Yi Dag or Pretas

Living spirits who are afflicted constantly with the miseries of hunger and thirst.

Animals

Hells: There are different regions of hell, and the living beings in each of them also vary in nature, according to their past Karma.

The causes of the miseries of Samsara

The true causes of suffering are Karma and delusion. Karma has been defined as "concordant action and reaction." According to the higher schools of Buddhism, Karma has two aspects, known in Tibetan as Sempai Le and Sampai Le. Sempai Le is the latent stage of Karma in which physical action is yet to take shape; the stage where the impulse to act is sub-conscious. Sampai Le is the manifest stage in which physical and oral actions occur. With regard to its results, there are three kinds of Karma. Meritorious Karma cause beings to take rebirth in the realms of gods, demi-gods, and men. Demeritorious Karma causes rebirth in the lower religions of animals, pretas and hells. Finally, Achala Karma, Invariable Karma, cause beings to take rebirth in the upper worlds, Rupa and Arupa Dhatu, the worlds of the Form and the Formless. The effects of Karma may be experienced in this present life, or in the next life, or in subsequent lives.

Delusion is not a part of the essential or central mind, which, as I have said, is intrinsically pure; it is a defect of one of the peripheral or secondary minds. When this secondary mind is stimulated, delusion becomes influential; it dominates the central mind and causes sin.

There are very many kinds of delusion; passion, anger, pride, hatred, hostility and so on. Passion and hostility are the main delusions; by passion we mean a passionate attachment to men or things. Passion may express itself as self-attachment or egoism and from it one may develop pride through a sense of superiority; or, on encountering hostility towards oneself, one may develop a counter-hatred. Again, through ignorance and lack of understanding, one may be led to oppose the truth. This strong "I consciousness' has been fostered in all beings in Samsara since time immemorial, and they are so habituated to it that they experience it even in their dreams.

In fact, all cognizable things are empty by their very nature, but through delusion they appear as self-originating and as self-sufficing entities. Conversely, this distorted concept is at the root of all delusion.

The essence of Nirvana

Samsara, in another sense, implies a bondage, Nirvana implies a liberation from this bondage: the true cessation, the third of the Noble Truths. I said that the causes of Samsara are Karma and delusion. If the roots of delusion are thoroughly extracted, if creation of new Karma to cause rebirth in the cycle of Samsara is brought to an end, if there are no more delusions to fertilize the Karma persisting from the past, then the continual rebirth of the suffering being will cease. Such a being, however, will not cause to exist. It has always existed in a body with a mortal residue, a body born because of previous Karma and delusion. But after the cessation of rebirth, after the liberation from Samsara and the achievement of Nirvana, it will continue to have consciousness and a spiritual body free of delusion. This is the meaning of the true cessation of suffering. Nirvana can indicate a lower stage, in which there is simply no suffering, and also it can mean the highest stage, called Buddhahood. This is the stage of supreme Englightenment, total and unqualified, free from all moral and mental defilement, and from the defilement caused by the power of discriminative thought.

Hinayana

A prescribed path must be followed to attain either of the states of Nirvana described above; the true path, the fourth of the Noble truths. Hinayana and Mahayana represent two schools of thought by which we discern this path. Hinayanists, the followers of the Lesser Way, basically seek to attain Nirvana for the individual's own sake. According to this school, the mind should be trained to exercise a strong will in order to renounce Samsara; it should pursue religious ethics (Shila), and simultaneously practise concentration (Samadhi) and meditation (Vipassana: Tibetan-Lhagthong), so that delusion and the seeds of delusion may be purged, and may not grow again. Thus Nirvana is attained. The paths to be followed include the Paths of Preparation, Application, Seeing, Practice and Fulfilment.

Mahayana

Mahayanists aim at attaining the highest stage of Nirvana, Buddhahood, for the sake not only of individual but of all other sentient beings. Motivated by the thought of Englightenment (Bodhi-chitta) and by compassion, they follow almost the same paths as those of Hinayana. But in addition to those paths, they practise other methods (Upayas) such as the six Paramitas (transcendent virtues). By this practice, Mahayanists seek not only to rid themselves of delusion but also of the defilement of sin, thereby working to attain Buddhahood. The five Mahayanic paths are likewise known as the Paths of Preparation, Application, Seeing, Practice and Fulfilment. But although the name of the paths are the same as those of Hinayana, there is a qualitative difference between them. And since Mahayanists have a different fundamental motive and in general follow different paths and practise different methods, the final goal which they achieve is different.

The question is sometimes asked whether Hinayanists, having achieved Nirvana, will be confined to the stage they have attained, or whether they will subsequently follow the Mahayana. The answer is that they will certainly not regard their own stage of Nirvana as the final goal but will certainly adopt ways to attain Buddhahood.

Tantrayana

The paths I have mentioned are doctrinal paths, and they must be followed to provide a sound foundation before Tantrayana (the way of Yogic Method) is practised. In Tibet the greatest care was taken before any Tantric doctrine was introduced. Spiritual teachers always investigated whether the doctrine was among those preached by Lord Buddha, and submitted it to logical analysis by competent Pandits, and also tested its effects in the light of experience, before they confirmed its authenticity and adopted it. This was necessary as there were many non-Buddhist Tantric doctrines which are apt to be confused with those of Buddhism because of superficial resemblances.

The Tantrayana falls into four classes, and it has vast number of treatises which cannot be enumerated here. In the simplest terms, this is its system: as already explained, bad Karma are held responsible for the various kinds of miseries we suffer. The bad Karma are created through delusion. Delusion is essentially due to an indisciplined mind. The mind should therefore be disciplined and controlled by exercises that stop the flow of evil thoughts. This flow may be stopped, and the wandering or projecting mind brought to rest, by concentration on the physical make-up of one's body and the psychological make-up of one's mind.

The mind may also be focussed on external objects of contemplation. For this, strong contemplative powers are needed, and the figures of deities provide—it has been found—the most suitable objects. For this reason, there are many images of deities in Tantrayana. These are arbitrary creations. Images, as objects of contemplation to purify the body, mind and senses have to be created in wrathful as well as peaceful aspects, sometimes with multiple heads and hands, so that they suit the physical, mental and sensuous aptitudes of different individuals striving for the final goal. Progress towards this goal is achieved in some cases mainly through strong faith and devotion, but in general it is achieved by the power of reason. And if the transcendental path is systematically followed, reason itself will provide during the pursuit many causes for heartfelt belief.

The Three Refuges

It is imperative that men understand the Refuge (sharangaman) and the universal law of Karma and its fruits—moral or psychological cause and effect—for the mind to be wedded to the path of religion.

The Refuges

There are three Refuges—Buddha, Dharma (the Law or Doctrine) and Sangha (the Order).

Buddha

He who has cleansed his mind of all impurities and has removed the motives and inclinations that lead to them—freeing himself thereby from the defilements of sin—becomes omniscient and is known as the Buddha. Such a person has perfect knowledge of phenomena occuring in space and time, and such a person is Buddha, the Refuge, a guide to health like a physician.

Dharma

The Dharma is the true Refuge: and one arrives at the goal of Dharma—the noble paths (arya marg) of deliverance by practising properly the method of overcoming evil and of removing its taints. In this sense Dharma can be compared to the practice of medicine.

Sangha

The order of Sangha comprise all beings who have attained Darshan Marg (the Path of Seeing). Darshan Marg or the Seeing is the stage of perfection in which one perceives the reality of all objects; Bhavana Marg or the Path of Practice is a stage in the way to Buddhahood realized—through meditation; Ashaikshita or the Path of fulfilment is the stage in which one no longer needs guidance. These are the Three Noble Paths. The Order is the friend who helps us to realize the Refuge. The Order may be compared to the nurse who administers the medicine.

Karma

Good or bad every result must necessarily have a cause. The Three Gems constitute the cause, and the realization of the Three Gems comprise the Effect. The Cause and the Effect of the Three Gems—Buddha, Dharma, and Sangha (the Teacher, the Teaching, and the Taught)—are related to Two Refuges.

The Cause Refuge is the Three Gems realized through the personality of another being. The Effect Refuge is the Three Gems realized by oneself in the future. In the former case the Three gems are to be considered external entities while one is perfecting oneself, i.e. while one takes refuge objectively. In the latter case when one has attained perfection the three Gems are to be considered internal entities i.e. one takes refuge subjectively. As a stronger man must provide refuge or protection to the weaker, the more powerful of the two refuges, Cause Refuge protects and harbours the seeker. When the weak becomes strong through the help of the protector and teacher, and his status is powerful, he attains the Three Gems of the Effect Refuge.

Efforts to actually realize the characteristic conditions of the Three Gems should be made during this life. And for this one must practise the Three Moral Precepts (the Trishiksha). The Three Moral Precepts are :

1. Adishila-shiksha (the Training in Higher Conduct).
2. Adisamadhi-shikha (the Training in Higher Meditation).
3. Adiprajnya-shiksha (the Training in Higher Wisdom).

In terms of analogy Adishila-shikha is the strength of a person; adisamadhi, his sure hand, and adiprajnya, his sharp axe. Using his sure hand and backed by his virile strength he chops the wood (symbolizing the notion of a permanent self and the defilements of sin) into pieces.

Training in Higher Conduct

The First Moral precept: Adishila-shiksha, which can be termed as the foundation of the Three Moral Precepts, has many aspects. All these aspects are based on the precept that one must abandon the Ten Immoralities. Of the ten Immoralities three pertain to bodily action, four to activity of speech, and three to the function of mind. The three immoralities pertaining to the body are:

1. The taking of the life of any living being-ranging from men to the smallest insect, whether directly or indirectly.
2. Stealing or taking away without consent another's property, directly or indirectly, whatever be its value.

3. Committing adultery and indulging in perverted forms of sexual intercourse.

The four immoralities pertaining to speech are:

1. Being guilty of falsehood by leading others through false or wrong advice or information, and through all forms of physical indications.
2. Being guilty of calumny by causing disunity where unity exists, and by aggravating disunity where disunity already exists.
3. The use of harsh and abusive language.
4. Indulgence in gossip mongering out of sheer lust and passion.

The three immoralities pertaining to the functions of the mind are:

1. Covetousness or the desire to possess the thing that belongs to other.
2. The desire to harm others.
3. Heresy related to disbelief in re-birth, the Law of Causation and Effect and Three Refuges.

The anti-thesis of the ten Immoralities are the Ten Virtues. When one practises the Ten Virtues one is actually practising Adishila-shiksha or Higher Conduct.

Training In Higher Meditation

The Second Moral Precept: During meditation the mind must be fixed on a single object so that it develops a "One-pointedness of mind." Mental concentration consists in withdrawing the mind gradually from the sense objects and conceptual notions so that the focus of the mind will be unwavering and fixed on an object until it is steadied and calm, permitting both body and mind to experience a rapturous ecstasy.

When "mental quiescence" is attained, besides the resultant experience mental and physical ecstasy, the mind also is under complete control. Such a mind can be employed to concentrate on any object of merit with effortless ease. And at the same the vehicle of concentration becomes possessed with super-natural psychic powers and can perform miracles and other supramundane feats.

The chief merit of Samath Bhavana (mental quiescence achieved through concentration) is that, if by the acquirement of Samath Bhavana, Vipassana or penetrative insight (which realizes Sunyata) is attained the phenomenon of Samsara can be demolished altogether. Besides, it bears many other good results. For instance, almost all the knowledge of Tri-Yana (I) Sravaka Yana (2) Pratekya Yana and (3) Mahayana are derived from Samath Bhavana. If the concentration is practised with the motive of attaining the Buddhist Refuges it becomes Buddhist concentration. If the concentration is practised with the motive of Bodhichitta, it becomes Mahayanic Buddhist concentration. For Samath Bhavana to be successful the following conditions must be fulfilled :

1. The place of meditation should be secluded, quiet and climatically congenial. Noise distracts meditation.
2. The person who is meditating must be well-contented and have few wants. He should have severed himself from every impurity in the world and he should be determined not to indulge in any immorality of action or speech.
3. He must grasp comprehensively the instructions and the methods of deep meditation. He should be fully aware that craving has its retribution and that the phenomenal world is ephemeral.

Samatha is achieved according to Arya Bodhisatva Mitreya by relinquishing the Five Shortcomings and by adopting the Eight Introverting Mental Faculties.

The Five Shortcomings to be relinquished

are:

1. Laxity resulting from a lethargic attitude towards meditation.
2. Forgetfulness concerning the object of meditation.
3. Interruptions that make the mind either sluggish or intensely agitated (because of lust).
4. The inability to prevent these interruptions.
5. Imaginary interruptions and the adoption of false counter-measures.

The Five shortcomings can be avoided by adopting the Eight Introverting Mental Faculties. They are:

1. Belief in the virtues of meditation and the ability to discern them.
2. The earnest desire to meditate and the ability to do so.
3. Perseverance and a happy frame of mind.
4. Experience of mental and physical ecstasy.
5. Conscientious effort at concentrating on the object of meditation.
6. A conscientious watch on any inclination towards sluggishness or intense agitation. (Assuming that the mind is divided into five parts one part must restrain the mind as a whole from becoming sluggish or intensely agitated when the other four parts are collectively engaged in deep concentration on the object of meditation).
7. Immediate readiness to counteract the danger of distraction the moment it is perceived.
8. Relaxation of counter-measures if and when the counter-measure achieves the desired purpose.

The practice and exercise of the Eight Introverting Mental Faculties eliminate the Five Shortcomings, resulting in the gradual increase in the power of concentration. This process has to proceed through nine stages of mental concentration.

The Nine Stages of Concentration

The first stage consists of fixing the mind on the object of concentration. The second stage consists of endeavouring to prolong the concentration on the object of meditation at each successive phase of the process. The third stage consists of perceiving immediately any diversion of the mind and to bring it back to the object of concentration. The fourth stage consists of maintaining a clear conception of even the minutest detail of the object of concentration. The fifth stage consists of strengthening the efforts of concentration by making the mind realize the virtues of the meditation. This helps to strengthen the effort of concentration. The sixth stage consists of dispelling any averse feeling towards meditation, such as indolence, so that the mind becomes pacified. The seventh stage consists of perserverance in maintaining the equanimity of the mind by dispelling even the slightest disturbance. The eighth stage consists of taking the mode of concentration to the furthest limit so that, free of all distraction, it achieves the perfect "one-pointedness of mind' in meditation. The ninth stage is a stage the person meditating reaches when he does not require any assistance, such as the effort of memory or of consciousness.

The above nine stages of Meditation can be accomplished by the help of the six faculties. These are :

1. The Faculty of Hearing.
2. The Faculty of Reflection.
3. The Faculty of Memory.
4. The Faculty of Consciousness.
5. The Faculty of Mental Energy.
6. The Faculty of Perfection.

The first stage of Meditation is attained through the Faculty of Hearing—for instance, listening to instruction on meditation given by a great teacher.

The second stage is attained through the Faculty of Reflection.

The third and the fourth stages of Meditation are attained through the Faculty of Memory.

The fifth and the sixth stages of Meditation are attained through the Faculty of Consciousness.

The seventh and the eighth stages of Meditation are attained through the Faculty of Mental Energy. The ninth stage of Meditation is attained through the Faculty of Perfection.

The Four Comprehensions

There are four steps in the realization of a full comprehension of the Nine Stages of Meditation. They are :

1. *The first step:* The first step in the realization of the first and second stages of meditation demand the most strenuous absorption of the mind on the object of concentration.

2. *The Second Step:* The second step is concerned with the realization of the next five stages (3,4,5,6 and 7) of meditation. Here concentration on the object of meditation is not extended over long periods but is desultory i.e. the process of concentration goes on intermittently.

3. *The Third Step*: The third step is concerned with the realization of the eighth stage of meditation. At this point the mind is capable of concentrating on the object of meditation without any interruption whatsoever.

4. *The Fourth Step* : The fourth step is concerned with the realization of the ninth stage of meditation when concentration on the object of meditation is possible with the minimum of conscious effort.

When one has wholly comprehended the nature, the order of the stages in meditation, and the distinction between the different steps in concentration, and when one practises meditation in conformity with the knowledge thus gained, it will be possible to accomplish perfect meditation in about a year's time. This type of meditation through concentration is of a general nature. However, if the object of concentration is in one's own mind the means of deep meditation are different.

An understanding of the nature of the mind is necessary before commencing any meditation by way of inner mental concentration. Mind is not visible. It has no shape, size, or colour. It is as empty as the Void. And yet it generates such characteristic functions as thought, imagination, etc. and it can identify anything that can be felt or that arises in the thought process. The method of inner mental concentration of meditating on an internal object—is the same as the methods used for general meditation. We must observe the avoidance of the Five Shortcomings, and adopt the Eight Introverting Mental Faculties in the Nine Stages of Meditation. When this semi-ultimate phase of meditation through inner and spontaneous concentration is attained there is the gradual realization of mental and physical ecstasy. When mental and physical ecstasy are realized the unwavering "One pointedness" of meditation is the result. This achievement (in meditation) can be classified as preparatory in the stages of bodily meditation which is one of the four forms of meditation.

Thus the mind will be completely brought under control through the accomplishment of mental quiescence effected by concentration (Samath Bhavana). Such a mind is all-powerful in comprehending the meaning of any subject.

The foregoing section on Training in Higher Meditation is a very brief synopsis of the instruction on meditation given by Arya Bodhisattva Maitreya and Acharya Asanga.

Training in Higher Wisdom

Training in higher wisdom is the third

moral precept (Adiprajnya-shiksha). It is concerned with two kinds of wisdom:

1. Wisdom which comprehends the relative nature of things, i.e. empirical knowledge.
2. Wisdom which comprehends the absolute nature of things, i.e. transcendental knowledge.

Wisdom which destroys all moral and mental defilements, and defilements caused by the power of discriminative thought, i.e. wisdom which comprehends Sunyata is described here.

Sunyata

Sunyata is the knowledge of the ultimate reality of all objects, material and phenomena. Sunyata exists but its existence has not been effected by the miracle-performing powers of the Buddhas nor is it dependent on the karmic fruits of sentient beings. Sunyata exists and the nature of Sunyata pervades all elements. Whatever creations the new objects be, and whatever be their designation, the ultimate nature of all elements, all objects is Sunyata. By their very nature all Dharmas have the mark of emptiness. To quote from a Sutra: "Whether the Buddhas appear into this world or not, Sunyata, the ultimate nature of all objects, is absolute and eternal." Sunyata is a principle that negates all contradictions in "self" existence. Sunyata only negates but does not affirm. To quote Acharya Chandrakirti, the Madhyamika philosopher: "The word `self' denotes any self-existing essence or substance in anything whatever that is not dependent on others. Negation of the self is Sunyata." The method for comprehending Sunyata is the study and application of the Middle Path (Madhyamika) logic.

Generally speaking, the knowledge of the ultimate nature of all Dharmas is actually a contradiction of what we think we know. The truth is that the ultimate nature of all elements of all objects is Sunyata.

And so it naturally follows that all objects which bear the ultimate mark of Sunyata are non-self existent.

But because we are accustomed to regard illusion (what we think we know) as the reality—a habit acquired from the very beginning of the originless samsaric existence—men have gone on believing that the distorted conception of the Dharmas of all objects is the true reality, and as such regard it as a self-originating and self-sufficing entity. Thus all phenomenal and unsubstantial conceptions that are taken as true by the mind run counter to the knowledge of the immanent nature of the Dharmas of all worldly objects. As a result the mind gets confused and is not able to distinguish between appearance and the deduced reality. The notion of deduced reality is mistaken for the notion of self-entity. This gives rise to maljudgment, i.e. false perception and thinking. When the biassed mind, which has been unpholding mistakenly the notion of mere conception for the reality, realizes that no such object of reality actually exists, it becomes aware of the Non-Absolute, Non-Self-Existent Nature. At that point the Non-Self-Existence of all elements and objects (Sunyata) becomes vividly clear.

A proper understanding of the manner in which our mind works forms a significant basis for the understanding of Sunyata. To understand this complex we must analyse the self or the "I consciousness." If we accept the conception that the self is no other than the "I", i.e. that "I-consciousness" is self-immanent, then by implication it will be devoid of any cause dependence. As this "I" is not dependent either on the body, or the mind, or the aggregates of skandhas, the "I" therefore must be an entity separate and different from all of them. In other words, the one is not dependent on the others. As such when my body suffers pain, it will not mean that the "I" suffers pain. When my hunger is satisfied. But this cannot be so. For when my body suffers pain, it follows the "I" is suffering pain. Similarly when my mind is sad it will mean the "I" is feeling sad. So, the logical conclusion would be that no entity can have a separate independent existence on its own.

In case that the "I" is the same as the aggregate of skandhas, then the latter must be one single unit. But the aggregates of skandhas consist of five different parts. If this is so, there should be five different "I." But again to take the instance of the "I" and the body. In case the body is the same as "I", when the present body disintegrates, the "I" should also disintegrate. But this is not so. Therefore, the logical conclusion is that the "I" and the body are not the same. Similarly the "I" and the continuity of skandhas, the "I" and the mind, are not the same.

It is also not correct to say that the "I" is neither identical nor different from the aggregates. When there is an "I" which appears to manifest itself as self-existent, either it must be identical to or different from the aggregates. It cannot be argued in any other way. Therefore, the "I", which to the mind seems to be the one and the only reality, is neither identical nor independent of the aggregates. So, we are led to the conclusion that there must not be an "I." Now, we have arrived at the premise that such an "I" does not exist. But, at the same time we cannot dogmatically deny the non-existence of such an "I." The formation of the notion of the denomination "I" is dependent on the aggregates—a mere designation, or a mere appellation. This designation "I" enables the formation of a concept in which the "I" enjoys eating, drinking etc. is born again and again in Samsara: practises religion and attains enlightenment. This "I" is distinct from the four-fold categories of Self-Existence, Non-Existence, both Self-Existence and Non-Existence, neither Self-Existent nor Non-Existent. To quote Nagarjuna :

"All Dharmas are neither self-existent, nor non-existent, neither both self-existent and non-existent nor different from both." Again, "when one is definite about the meaning conveyed by this "I" as being a mere designation separate from the logic of fourfold categories, then one has grasped the real significance of the non-existence of "I."

Similarly, by taking the instances of one's eyes, ears, etc. form, sound, smell, taste, etc. and even Sunyata itself, this logic of four-fold categories can be used to prove the relativity and non-existence of all elements and objects. To consider Sunyata itself as self-existent is to take fatalist view of things.

For a correct comprehension of the significance of non-self-existence of objects of the world, a deep, penetrating study of the Doctrine has to be made. Hearing instruction from learned masters and teachers, and such other sources, results in the realization of "theoretical wisdom." Thinking again and again on the real meaning of what one has learnt results in the acquirement of "Practical Wisdom."

Vipassana

If one were to make concentrated meditation on the fathomed meaning of Sunyata obtained from the process of such wisdom, one will be able to comtemplate with one pointed concentration on Sunyata by virtue of the great power obtained from the accomplishment of mental quiescence (Samath Bhavana). This wisdom which accomplishes Samath Bhavana is the "Meditative Wisdom." Samath Bhavana is the steppingstone to Vipassana Bhavana. Unlike in Samath Bhavana, if concentration during meditation is aided by the power of reasoning, the experience that results is an unique mental and physical ecstasy. This unique experience of mental and physical ecstasy is the realization Vipassana. When Vipassana Bhavana is successful it is known as the fusion of mental quiescence (Samath Bhavana) and direct intuitive insight (Vipassana) with any object selected for the purpose of concentration.

The knowledge of the Path of Application is the stage reached when one acquires Vipassana with Sunyata as the object of concentration. When the true meaning of Sunyata is fully realized, further efforts are to be made. (1) One must remove the things that are to be discarded in the step-by-step stages of the Paths of Seeing, Practice and Fulfilment. (2) When this leads to the destruction of all moral and mental defilements, and the defilements caused by the power of discriminative thought.

I have given here only a condensed account of Adiprajnyashiksha.

Of the three moral precepts, the third is generally assumed to be superior to the preceding ones. in considering the development of the moral mind, the first one forms the basis of the second, and the second, the basis of the third. Hence the very first one, i.e. training in higher conduct is most important of all.

Pursuing religious ethics and simultaneously practising concentration and meditations (penetrative insight) on the basis of taking refuge in the Three Gems, and making one's thought and action conform to the Law of Karma and its fruits, one can liberate oneself from the Wheel of Existence. Going a step further, if one faithfully pursues the Three Moral Precepts, having been motivated by the thought of the precious Bodhichitta of love and compassion, one will attain the "superior release" of omniscient Buddhahood.

Bodhi Citta

All religions, in teaching moral precepts to mould the functions of mind, body and speech, have primarily the same noble goal. They all teach us not to lie or bear false witness, not to steal or take other's lives, and so on. That there are so many different religions to bring happiness to mankind is analogous to the treatment of a particular disease by different methods. For, in the most general terms, all religions aim to help each living being to avoid misery and acquire happiness. Thus, although we can find causes for preferring individual interpretations of religious truth, there is much greater cause for unity stemming from the heart. In the present state of the world, the need to evolve a great measure of unity among the followers of the different religions has become especially important. Moreover, such unity is not an impossible ideal.

Bodhi-citta forms the central theme of Mahayana Buddhism in Tibet. We believe that the concept of the Bodhi-citta will go a long way in helping to achieve basic unity and a spirit of cooperation among the followers of different creeds. We believe that striving in itself will effect great results. The Blessed. One acquired Bodhi-citta after making innumerable sacrifices and powerfully concentrated efforts. For three immeasurable acons, he practised the deeds of a Bodhisattva, making unstinting sacrifices and undergoing great hardships, thus gradually acquiring the dual accumulations of merit and wisdom. Finally, at Buddha Gaya, he attained to the supreme Enlightenment which is called Buddhahood. Emancipated from the misery that follows clinging to the extremes of the mundane and the sublime, he reached that perfect equanimity that flows from the ultimate, ineffable peace called Nirvana, free of every fault, his intellect perfected beyond the minutest error or illusion, he proceeded to evolve the many forms of the Holy Dharma, turning the Three Stage Wheel of the Dharma, in accordance with the system of the Four Noble Truths and of Interdependent Origination, all in revelation of dual Truth (relative and absolute).

The inspiration to achieve this ineffable Bodhi-mind can be expressed in this way: "I must attain the supreme state of omniscient Buddhahood, so that I can liberate all sentient beings from this ocean of misery, Samsara, and establish them in the ultimate happiness of Nirvana." This inspiration creates a longing to devote one's energy to both the profound and extensive stages of the path of Mahayana. it is the root of the practice for accomplishing the Bodhisattavacarya, which connotes charity, morality, patience, perserverance, meditation and wisdom. To be more precise, from the first three, charity, morality and patience, stems the accumulation of virtue. From the last two, meditation and wisdom, stems the accumulation of sublime wisdom. And the fourth one, perseverance, leads both accumulations. In short, the key to the practice of Mahyana Buddhism in Tibet is dual co-ordination at every level, the coordination of virtue and wisdom, method and knowledge, Tantra and Sutra, relative and absolute. Simultaneously, careful attention must be paid to the inherent moral implications of all of the Buddha's teachings, i.e. desisting from harming others and cultivating the spirit of loving-kindness. Viewed from the perspective of the Bodhi mind, the goal is to maintain undiscriminating compassion towards all living beings, without making any distinction of race, nationality, class or tenous status of friend or enemy. In time, the great nations of the world, inspired by the Bodhi-mind may cease to manipulate everything, both sacred and profane, in a vain pursuit of power, and instead try to create a peaceful world by regulating the mind's activities to accord with Dharma, the inexhaustible panacea.

Compassion

In our approach to life, be it pragmatic or otherwise, a basic fact that confronts us squarely and unmistakably is the desire for peace, security and happiness. Different forms of life at different levels of existence make up the teeming denizens of this earth of ours. And, no matter whether they belong to the higher groups such as human beings or to the lower groups such as animals, all being primarily seek peace, comfort and security. Life is as dear to a mute creature as it is to a man. Even the lowliest insect strives for protection against dangers that threaten its life. Just as each one of us wants happiness and fears pain, just as each one of us wants to live and not to die, so do all other creatures.

The faculty of reasoning, the ability to think and the power of expression distinguish man as a being superior to his mute friends. In the quest for peace, comfort and security, the methods applied by man are diverse and, sometimes, radically opposed to one another. All too frequently, the means adopted are cruel and revolting. Behaving in a way that is utterly unbecoming to his human status, man indulges in inhuman cruelties, torturing his fellow men as well as members of the animal kingdom just for the sake of selfish gain; such behaviour has almost become the order of the day. Such unskilled actions bring suffering to oneself as well as to others. Having been born as human beings, it is vitally important for us to practice benevolence and to perform meritorious deeds for ourselves and others in this life and in lives to come. To be born a human being is a rare experience, and it is meet to use this golden opportunity as wisely and skillfully as possible.

Buddhism, with its emphasis on universal love and compassion impregnated with ideas that are wholly non-violent and peaceful, offers a means, at once unique and eternal, for the successful attainment of that state of security and happiness wherefrom man and beast can derive common benefaction. It can rightly be asserted that loving-kindness and compassion are the two corner stones on which the whole edifice of Buddhism stands. Destruction or injury to life is strictly forbidden. Harming or destroying any being from the highest to the lowest, from a human to the tiniest insect, must at all cost be avoided. The Blessed One says: "Do not harm others. Just as you feel affection on seeing a dearly beloved person, so should you extend loving-kindness to all creatures. "Those who follow the Mahayanist way are admonished not only to abstain from doing injury but also to cultivate a great spirit of compassion involving an eager longing to save all sentiment beings from pain and misery.

The arising of Maha Karuna in the mind will prepare the ground for the perfect fruition of the precious Bodhi-citta, which is a necessary condition for attaining the supreme status of Bodhisattva. One is called a Bodhisattva when his mind is filled with the pure compassion and equanimity which proceed from Bodhi-citta. As whatever we do in our every day life results from the functioning of our minds, ultimate peace and Buddha hood are the result of Bodhi-citta and compassion. The Lord Buddha has said: "Bodhi-citta is the seed of all Dharmas." Acharya Nagarjuna says: "If you wish to acquire the supreme status of Bodhisattva, you must cultivate the quality of Bodhi-citta which should be as firm as a rocky mountain." Another Buddhist scholar, Acharya Chandra Kirti, says: "In the beginning Maha Karuna (boundless compassion) is like a seed; it becomes as water and manner in the middle, and as the ripe fruit at the end." All these sayings emphasize the matchless efficacy of Bohhi-citta. The intention to do good to others; the persistent thought in ones heart of the welfare of others will spontaneously create happiness among the people around us. To return good for evil, benevolence for injury, love for hate, and compassion for harm, are some of the characteristics of the quality of Bodhi-citta. Deeds of benevolence and loving-kindness not withstanding ill-will from other side will delight the hearts of all. Indulgence in resentment and vengeance will only further increase misęrses to oneself and others in this life and in lives to come.

Whatever method is adopted for the cultivation of the quality of Bodhi-citta, the fact remains that the birth-cycles of all sentient beings are beginingless, and that numberless times in their previous lives they have each fulfilled the role of a mother. The feeling of a mother for her child is a classic example of love. For the safety, protection and welfare of her children, a mother is ready to sacrifice her very life. Recognising this, children should be grateful to their mother and express their gratitude by performing virtuous deeds. In the same way, a person motivated by the thought of Bodhi-citta strives with all his might for the welware of every sentient being whether it be a human or a beast or fowl of land or sea. At the same time, he will treat all the beings as he treats his cultivation of compassion and loving-kindness for all sentient beings will bring peace and happiness to oneself and others. Ill-will, malice and malevolent acts will only be a source of suffering to all.

The noble aspiration to attain Buddhahood, to cultivate Bodhi-citta in the mind and to practise charity, forbearance, morality, kindness and so on are all for the sake of living beings. It is for them that these ennobling and uplifting qualities are sought. The creatures that inhabit this earth-be they human beings or animals—are here to contribute, each in its own peculiar way, to the beauty and prosperity of the world. Many creatures have toiled singly or jointly to make our life comfortable. The food we eat, the clothes we wear have not just dropped from the sky. Many creatures. Have laboured to produce them. That is why we should be grateful to all our fellow creatures. Compassion and loving kindness are the hall marks of achievement and happiness. Let us practise them for the welfare of all.

Dual Truth

Buddhism has flourished in Tibet for over a thousand years. During these centuries, it has been carefully pre-served and has become the basis of our culture. Nevertheless, although our culture has been nourished by many things of worth from neighbouring countries, we have on the whole been very much on our own.

In Tibet we practise Buddhism in its entirety. In garb and conduct, the monks practise according to he rules of Vinaya Sutras; in the training of mind, we follow the Mahayana philosophy; and we also practise Tantric Buddhism. That why I have used the phrase "in its entirety."

The world today is engulfed in conflicts and sufferings to such an extent that everyone longs for peace and happiness; that longing has unfortunately led them to be carried away by the pursuit of ephemeral pleasure. But there are a few learned people who dissatisfied by what is ordinarily seen or experienced, think more deeply and search for true happiness. I believe that the search will continue. As we make greater material progress and are able to satisfy our daily needs more fully, man will continue to search for Truth, not being satisfied with material progress. Indeed, I am convinced that the search for Truth will still grow keener.

In past centuries, there have been many learned Teachers, who have laid down various paths to the realization of Truth. Among them, Lord Buddha is one, and my study of Buddhism has led me to form the opinion that, despite the differences in the names and forms used by the various religions, the ultimate Truth to which they point is the same.

In Buddhism we have Relative Truth and Absolute Truth,. From the view point of Absolute Truth, what we feel and experience in our ordinary daily life is all delusion. Of the various delusions, the sense of discrimination between oneself and others is the worst from, as it creates nothing but unpleasantness for both sides. If we can realise and meditate on ultimate Truth, it will cleanse our impurities of mind and thus eradicate the sense of discrimination. This will help to create true love for one another. The search for Ultimate Truth is, therefore vitally important.

In the search for Ultimate Truth, if it fails to dawn on us it is we who have not found it. Ultimate Truth exists. If we think deeply and reflect carefully, we shall realize that we ourselves have our existence in Ultimate Truth. For example, I am talking to you and you are listening to me. We are generally under the impression that there is the sound of words being spoken: but, in Ultimate Truth, if I search for myself I will not find it, and if you search for yourselves you will not find them. Neither speaker nor audience, neither words nor sound, can be found. They are all void like empty space. Yet they are not completely non-existent. They must exist, for we are able to feel them. What I am saying is being heard by you, and you in turn thinking on the subject. My speech is producing some effect, yet if we search for them we cannot find them. This mystery relates to the dual nature of Truth.

Anything whose existence directly perceivable by us can be classified as pertaining to Relative Truth. But, in ultimate Truth, neither the searcher nor the object being searched for exists. Ultimate Truth is void like empty space, beyond every form of obstruction and complication. Once we understand this, we can achieve true mental peace. It is my hope that, as the world becomes smaller and smaller owing to material progress and better communications, we shall, as a result, all be able to understand more about Ultimate Truth. When this happens, I have great hope that we shall achieve true world peace.

The Source of Suffering

The faculty of reasoning distinguishes man from animals and other living creatures. Human being are capable of investigating and understanding many things which animals cannot. Because they are able to discover and perceive things lying beyond the direct perceptions of their sense-organs, most men, whether they are Buddhists, Hindus, Christians or belonging to any other denomination, offer up prayers or devotional recitations of one kind or another. Are such prayers and recitations due merely to custom, are they mere rituals to embellish daily life? The answer is definitely negative, because controlling and disciplining the mind is or should be the primary purpose of all prayers and religious recitations.

Though there are various methods of disciplining mind, to think primarily for the benefit of other is immensely important. Benevolent thought for others will bring happiness both to them and oneself, whereas if one thinks only of one's own selfish comfort and happiness, nothing but suffering can result. As the great Indian Pandit Shanta Deva has said: "All suffering in this world is due to egoistic desire for selfish comfort and happiness of others."

Happiness, whether it is transient or ultimate, is a direct or indirect result of a sincere desire for the welfare of others. The main cause of suffering is egoistic desire for one's own comfort and happiness or its in direct effects. In this strife-torn world of ours, this is always true, no matter whether the sufferings in question are on a large scale such as those resulting from disagreement between different nations or the perpetration of a wicked act which brings about the loss of many lives, or on a smaller scale such as the bickering between insects. In all such cases, egoism is the root cause.

When mutual co-operation between neighbours and nations in motivated by benevolent thought for each other, such motivation is of the highest value. It is fitting that we should attach greater importance to unselfish desire for the comfort and happiness of others than to egoistic desire for self-beatitude and happiness. Generally speaking, all beings possessing mind feel discomforted when they come across something unpleasant which they cannot withstand, however trivial it may be. Knowing the others, too suffer when they encounter things that discomfort them, one should make every effort to avoid doing anything that might be the cause of discomfort or suffering to another being. This principle can be the foundation of peace and of all means of bringing about or consolidating world peace, such as disarmament. When all thoughts likely to cause suffering, such as a desire to resort to war, are erased from the mind, when speech and action, which stem from thought, will be devoid of evil intent. Similarly, the success of disarmament and other peace movements stems from a determination to achieve peace which first takes form in the mind, and is subsequently translated into speech and action. Speech and action unsupported by firm intention in the mind will achieve nothing, howsoever one may try. Basically, the inability to control and discipline the mind is at the bottom of all the troubles and problems of the world. Therefore, in this life or ours, whether we believe in rebirth or not, if we generate and send our benevolent thoughts towards all beings from men down to the tiniest insects, the world will inevitably be a happier place to live in. Happiness is gained for oneself and others by concentrating chiefly on other by concentrating chiefly on others. What the world needs today is compassion and love, it is, therefore, of the utmost importance that we cultivate kindly thoughts for others so that thinking fondly of their welfare becomes an ingrained habit of mind.

How to follow Buddhism?

The perfect practice of Buddhism is achieved not merely through superficial changes for example, through leading a monastic life or reciting from holy books. Whether activities in themselves should be called religious or not is even open to question; or religion should be practised in the mind. If one has the right mental attitude, all activities, bodily action and speech, can become religious. But if one lacks the right attitude, if one does not know how to think properly, one will achieve nothing even if one spends the whole of one's life in monasteries and in reading from the scripture. The first essential, therefore, is proper mental attitude. One should take the Three Gems-Buddha, Dharma and Sangha—as one's final refuge; one should take into account the laws of Karma and its fruits; and one should cultivate such thoughts as will benefit other beings.

If religion is earnestly followed by renouncing the world the follower finds great joy. There are many people in Tibet who have renounced the world in this way, and they possess an indescribable mental and physical satisfaction. The sum total of worldly pleasure, gathered through the motive of self-love and the effort to satisfy that love, is not comparable to a fraction of the higher happiness. People who possess this happiness are also of the greatest benefit to others, by virtue of their own inward state, which enables them to diagnose not only the true causes of the ills of mankind but provide also the true remedies for them. However, such renunciation of the world is not possible for everybody, because the sacrifices entailed are very great.

What sort of Dharma, what sort of religion can then be prescribed for people in ordinary walks of life? Immoral wordly activities, naturally, should be ruled out; these activities are never compatible with any religion. But morally justificable activities, such as helping to administer the Government of a country, or indeed doing anything useful and productive, taking any steps towards promoting the pleasure and happiness of others, can certainly go together with the practice of Dharma. In India and Tibet Kings and ministers have promoted Dharma. Salvation can be achieved, if one truly endeavours to find it, merely by leading a household life. We have a saying;: "People who make no mental effort, even if they remain in mountain retreats are like animals hibernating in their holes, only accumulating causes for a descent into hell."

Perhaps I may conclude with an old Tibetan story. Long ago there was a famous lama whose name was Drom. One day Drom saw a man walking around a stupa. "It is good that you walk around a stupa," he said. "But wouldn't it be better to practise religion?" "I had better read a holy book then," the man said to himself. And so he started a laborious course of reading.

One day Drom happened to meet him again. "Reading from a holy book is of course very good." Drom said, "but wouldn't it be better if you practise religion?

And the man thought: "It seems even recitation is not good enough. How about meditating?" Not long after, Drom saw him in meditation. He said : "I admit that meditation is good. But wouldn't it really be better if you practise religion?"

The man was bewildered. "What do you mean by practising religion?" he asked. "Tell me how it is done." "Turn your mind away from the forms of this wordly life" Drom told him" "Turn your mind towards religion."

13

Misconceptions and Realities of the Tibetan Issue

By
THE DALAI LAMA

RECENTLY A flood of articles on Tibet has appeared in the *New York Times* and many other newspapers throughout the world. Many of these articles contained patently false information about the situation in Tibet and the positions of the Tibetans in exile. I feel therefore, that it is time I myself contributed a brief article towards clearing up some of these misconceptions.

Tibet is geographically, racially and culturally different from China. Historically, too, Tibet has always been an independent country, and has never been "an integral part of China." The very fact that it has to be referred to now as "part of China" is a clear indication of its separate independent status in past. If it had always been a part of China what was the need of changing the boundaries in the maps of Central Asia prepared after 1959?

Another indication of Tibet's independent status is the great pain taken by the Chinese Communists in explaining to the Tibetans the status of Tibet. They make a distinction between China and "The Middle Kingdom." They have been stressing to us that Tibet isn't part of China, but that it is under the Middle Kingdom just as China is. Tibet and China, they explain, enjoy equal status and both are parts of the Middle Kingdom.

Second-Class Citizens

After the signing of the 17-point "Agreement" when the first Tibetan delegation, headed by Kalon T.T. Liushar, called on Mao Tse-Tung, the latter told Kalon Liusher: "Now that Tibet has returned to the motherland, Peking is your city, Shanghai is your city...". To this, Silon Lukhangwa my then Prime Minister, later remarked in Lhasa: "We do not want Peking or Shanghai, give us back Chamdo, the third largest city in Tibet, was kept under military administration by the Chinese since their invasion till the establishment of the Preparatory Committee for the Autonomous Region of Tibet.

In official documents, Tibetans enjoy the same rights as the Chinese, but when it comes to implementation the Tibetans are treated as second-class citizens in their own country. Tibetans have been forcibly recruited in labour gangs to construct roads, military installations and buildings. Hundreds of schools have also been built, but refugees who still manage to trickle out maintain that these cannot be called Tibetan schools as only a little Tibetan is taught in the beginning grades. The rest of the curriculum consist of Chinese language and history, basic arithmetic and manual labour. The thousands of kilometers of roads constructed since the Chinese takeover aren't of much use to the Tibetans since there isn't any public transportation.

Improvement has also been made in agricultural output, but according to refugees, at the time a harvest most of the grains is taken away by the Chinese as "Surplus Grain Sales," "State Grain Tax," "Commune Development Tax," "War Preparation Grain" etc., and the Tibetans are left with a meagre ration of between 90 to 120 kilograms of barley per person per year.

It is for these persons that the Tibetan Communists who had been most enthusiastic in the beginning, not only started to become disillutioned by about 1956 but eventually many of them openly resented the Chinese actions in Tibet. The result was that most of the Tibetan Communists were dismissed from their official posts and quietly deported to China.

We admit that the social and Governmental system of the past in Tibet was neither faultless nor suited to the changing times. But Tibetans were prepared to change of their own accord. Even before 1959 I brought about some reforms, but the Chinese weren't happy when we started to do these on our own. They didn't give their blessings. They wanted to reap the maximum benefit out of the reforms that they were planning to carry out, and our own action was endangering this prospect. Tibetans in exile are all for gradual modernity and change. With these aspirations in mind, I promulgated in 1963 the draft of a Constitution for a future Tibet. I have also said in an official statement a few years ago that the rule of the Dalai Lama may or may not continue in future Tibet and that we might even adopt socialistic systems. We are therefore, not against change of reform.

There isn't any doubt that China has made tremendous progress since the Communist take over. The masses have also benefitted from this. I admit that even in Tibet they have brought about many changes which were necessary, but which might not have been possible for us to carry out. But at what cost and sacrifice have they achieved this? In terms of human lives and freedom, that we cherish so sacredly, the sacrifices have been tremendous and terrible, to say the lest.

What has happened very often is this. In order to meet certain targets and to please higher authorities, Chinese officials have adopted every means, fair or foul, and completely failed to take into account the sufferings and feelings of the people, who in most cases have to pretend that they are happy even when they are not.

And the most unfortunate part of this whole process has been that the high officials were quite oblivious to what had actually happened on the spot, and accepted unquestioningly the reports of their subordinates even when they contained absolutely untrue statements. For example, while a certain section of the population might have strongly resented the implementation of a project, the report might say that the people whole heartedly jointed the PLA and the Party in its implementation.

About 50,000 Tibetans, including myself, who left the country in 1959, had already experienced nine years of Chinese rule in Tibet. All those years I tried to reach an amicable solution with them because the inevitable result otherwise would have been an open clash between the Tibetan people and the Chinese troops, in which case the former would unquestionably be in disadvantageous position. Unfortunately, the situation deteriorated so fast that all my efforts were in vain and the open clash did take place in March 1959, with predictable results.

Dividing to Conquer

The tragedy of Tibet is that a whole race, a people strongly opposed to foreign domination, has been subjugated, oppressed and gobbled up by China. This has happened not only to Tibet but also to Mongolia and Eastern Turkistan (Sinkiang). It may not sound right for me to speak of these two other countries.

Which are in a similar situation, but I happen to know the true feelings and the national aspiration of these people. Their feelings of resentment against Chinese domination are no less than those of the Tibetans.

To make it easier to devour the invaded nations, the Chinese try to cut them into pieces. They persist, for example, in dividing Tibet into two part: Inner and Outer Tibet. Historical facts and existing realities means nothing to them. In all their propaganda they only mean outer Tibet when they say "Tibet," or more officially, "The Autonomous Region of Tibet." This means the cutting away of about half of Tibet's territory, and about two-thirds of our population. In this part of Tibet—the Inner Tibet—we have the Amdo and Kham provinces, which traditionally were inseparable from the rest of Tibet. No Tibetan or learned scholar on Tibet can imagine Tibet or Tibetan without Amdo and Kham provinces. The whole of Tibet, without this mythical distinction has suffered under the invasion by the Communist China and has been determined in its struggle against the unjust foreign domination.

In fact, it was in the eastern part of Tibet, which the Chinese call Inner Tibet, that the initial sporadic revolts against the Chinese occupation took place. So much so that the Tibetan resistance movement has often been mislabelled as a Khampa resistance movement.

Even today, there are recent reports that desperate acts of fighting and sabotage have been carried out in these regions. Another clear indication of continued Tibetan resistance and failure on the part of the Communist Chinese to win over the Tibetans completely is the lack of any prominent Tibetan from among the younger generation to toe their line a generation that the Chinese had ample time to groom and indoctrinate since 1950.

It is well-known that the Chinese have made a similar arbitary demarcation in the case of Mongolia as well.

The struggle to free ourselves was and is a Tibetan initiative and a Tibetan movement. In the process of our struggle we have welcomed external help whenever it didn't go against our basic goal, and have shunned it whenever it did. And because our struggle is just and we believe in it, it could not and cannot be abandoned even if no help came at all.

Some parties persist in calling the Tibetans in exile "a handful of reactionary cliques" (some have given the figure 15,000). To me this need never be a subject of controversy. India and all other countries where there are Tibetan refugees are open societies. The truth or falsehood of claimes by "about 100,000 refugees" can easily be verified by visiting these places.

The world has seen how unpredictable and inconsistent the Chinese are through the vicissitudes in the lives of Liu Shaochi, Lin Piao, Teng Hsiao-Ping, and more recently the Gang of Four. These acts are unprincipled and conducted at the whims of few individuals. One can imagine how much the Tibetans have also suffered through such vicissitudes under the Chinese rule.

The Chinese have recently extended an "invitation" to the Tibetans in exile, including myself, to return home. When the offer became known a number of newspapers hinted that it might be "profitable" for me to return now. Some even informed its readers that some sort of secret and indirect negotiation was going on between my representatives and the Chinese leaders.

The Real Issues

These, rumours confirm that people in the West have totally misunderstood the true nature of our struggle. The issue isn't whether the Dalai Lama and the 100,000 refugees would be able to return to Tibet. The reason we appeal to other nations isn't because we want to go back and the Chinese arn't allowing us in. It isn't that I long for some of the privileges I used to enjoy and am bitter with the Chinese for having reduced me to the status of a refugee. The Chinese have been asking us to return since the end of 1963. Most of their offers have been regularly broadcast on Radio Lhasa and through printed leaflets. There has been no response from our side on this issue because this isn't the real issue. The real issues are the feelings and welfare of the six million Tibetans still left in Tibet. Why should an alien rule be forced upon them? Why shouldn't they have the choice of holding their own beliefs, traditions, culture and identity?

If those six million Tibetans there are really happy and contented, we would be prepared to return and accept whatever status the majority of them are prepared to grant us. But first it should be established to the total satisfaction of all Tibetans in exile that the Tibetans in Tibet are completely satisfied with their lot. This is only pre-requisite. There isn't any question of "secret negotiations" to make it possible for me to return.

So far what the Chinese have claimed either directly or through a few selected visitors hasn't succeeded in convincing us. Some of these visitors have always been uncritical admirers of the "Chinese Revolution." They make their living out of reporting first hand news from China and commenting on it. How can they be expected to say anything that would conceivably jeopardize their chances of obtaining more Chinese visas in future. Fortunately, some recent visitors have tried to give an objective accounts of their visits to Tibet and I hope there are more and more such visitors in future.

In spite of many difficulties, we have been getting information about the conditions in Tibet. We consider this to be of utmost importance, because we must act according to the wishes of this majority of our people.

In fact, it would be a reassuring sign to us if the Chinese government stopped being selective about whom to invite. It would also be encouraging if the visitors' itinerary weren't confined to Lhasa and its immediate vicinity. Some recent visitors have claimed to have travelled "throughout Tibet." But none of them mentions the name of other places, nor did they describe those regions. It is rather difficult for us to take their words for it.

In short, what is needed is what I have constantly been demanding an internationally supervised plebiscite both inside and outside Tibet to determine whether the Tibetans in Tibet are happy. The plebiscite should be conducted throughout Tibet and it should also include in its investigative body people who can understand and speak Tibetan, so that they don't need to depend solely on the Chinese interpreters. It might even include one or two Tibetans, who don't have to be selected or recommended by me. I am prepared to accept whatever verdicts and commendations such a plebiscite comes out with.

[From *Asian Wall Street Journal,* 25 August, 1977.]

14

To China: Open up Tibet

By

THE DALAI LAMA

THE RECENT developments in China indicate that the present Chinese leaders are following a moderate and pragmatic policy in their domestic as well as foreign affairs. As a result of this overall change, a certain amount of liberalization and leniency has been introduced in Inner Mongolia, East Turkistan and particularly Tibet.

This policy is certainly welcome, but it is difficult for us at the movement to be overly optimistic about these changes. It is yet too early to form a definite judgment on this. We view these recent changes with suspicion; something we had learned from the Chinese with our experience of having lived with them for nine years and having felt the impact of their policies in exile for almost two decades now. Chinese policies and the dramatic political changes in China have often been to unpredictable.

Teng Hsiao-ping was recently quoted as having said in Japan "If you have an ugly face, it is no use pretending to be handsome." I am impressed by this philosophy, particularly when it is adopted by a Chinese leader. This is definitely a correct and practical attitude, and if he means it sincerely it reveals his willingness to accept existing realities. There is always the danger for those who are powerful to be over-confident and be unaware of their faults or intentionally ignore them. This, in fact, is one the sources of many problems that we are confronted with in the world today.

The Chinese, through their official organs, have been saying that all is well and normal inside Tibet; that the Tibetan people are happy and contented under their rule.

We are far from being convinced and we cannot accept this propaganda for obvious reasons. We have in our possession, information and reports to the contrary. Therefore, we have two versions about the conditions inside Tibet: the Chinese version and the Tibetan version. I do not insist that the people of the world blindly accept the Tibetan version as the truth. I am simply demanding that the Tibetan people be given the opportunity of freely expressing themselves. So far the tendency in the world has been to regard only the Chinese version as authentic. There is a double standard to it.

While the world press diligently follows what the Chinese leaders have to say about China; about Tibet, and report matters of even the least importance if they come from the mouths of the Chinese leaders, they do not give credence to the ridiculous Chinese versions of the international situation, American "imperialism" Soviet "revisionism" or Indian "expansion." Just the history of the past 20 years should make the people outside China realize the extent of distortion of facts that comes from the Peking organs. When the Tibetans tried to tell the world in the 60's that conditions were bad inside Tibet, the world, by and large chose to call it refugee propaganda and accept the Peking version of a "socialist transformation" as authentic.

In the 70's, when sufficient evidence to support the previous refugee claims, has emerged, the world again turns to Peking for an official explanation. The new leaders in Peking now have to admit things were not rosy in the 60's as were printed at the time, but that is because the "gang of Four" was handling it at the time. This again is perfectly acceptable explanation to the world.

I have repeatedly said that the nature of our struggle is not anti-communist, anti-reform or even anti-Chinese. It is also not whether those of us in exile can return to Tibet. Fundamentally, the real issue is the happiness and welfare of the six million Tibetans inside Tibet. We are carrying out our freedom movements in accordance with the wishes of our people there. The majority of them, especially the young, are not at all happy with the Chinese and are not willing to live under their domination. But they are unable to do anything as the whole country is like a vast prison.

And as is the case with prisons of any size, not very many inmates succeed in effecting their released themselves. So they depend on us and we in turn depend on world conscience to support our cause.

Why should an alien rule be forced upon six million unwilling people? Why shouldn't they be given the right to choose for themselves? If the majority of people in Tibet are really happy and willing to live under the Chinese rule, it would be foolish and unreasonable on the part of the 100,000 Tibetans in exile to stubbornly act contrary to their wishes. It would not be right morally. But we must first know for certain that the Tibetans are completely satisfied and happy. So far it is only the Chinese publicity organs and their recognized spokesman in the West who claim that the Tibetans in Tibet are happy.

We do not have a single independent Tibetan support to this claim.

During the past 30 years there has been much propaganda about the tremendous progress made by China in virtually every field, contrary to what was actually happening in the country.

We now read that even the Chinese people are expressing their discontentment with the existing conditions and admiting failure to make adequate progress. If the Chinese themselves have suffered so much under their own leadership, one can imagine the extent to which the minorities have suffered, particularly the Tibetans, whose race, language, culture and way of life have no affinity whatsoever with the Chinese.

If the Tibetans are genuinely contented with the present state of affairs, there is a way in which the Chinese can easily convince us and the world of this. As I demanded in a statement on March 10, 1978, Tibet should be opened so that Tibetans within and without can freely visit each other.

If the rosy picture pointed by the Chinese is authentic and they have nothing to hide, we should be given the opportunity to see if for ourselves in a free and unrestricted manner.

Such an opportunity will help us in "seeking truth from facts," a popular slogan in China today.

And in this context I welcome the recent Chinese consent to allow a group of Tibetans in India to visit their relatives in Tibet.

The ultimate decision about the future of Tibet must be made by the majority of the people there. This is democratic; this is reasonable; and this is just. In order to be able to make that decision the people must have the freedom to express themselves without fear. The world must remember that the 1959 Tibetan revolt again the Chinese was ruthlessly suppressed by labelling it as counter-revolutionary, while it was, in fact, a popular people's uprising against the oppression and foreign domination of Tibet by Communist China.

[From *New York Times*, 3 February, 1979.]

15

China and the Future of Tibet

By

THE DALAI LAMA

DURING THE past few weeks I have visited many parts of the United States and spoken at universities, colleges and religious institutions and small centres of learning. I have also had the opportunity to address several organizations concerned with world affairs and foreign policy. In almost every situation I have taken the liberty to speak on love and compassion. I firmly believe that the promotion of these qualities can contribute to modern society's need for a balance against excessive material preoccupation.

I have spoken at length on these topics not simply as a Buddhist, but from a clear universal recognition that except for superficial differences all humans are in essence the same in that we all want happiness and do not want suffering and on this basis engage in various techniques to bring this about. Recognition of our fundamental aim and agreement is important.

The press, the general public and numerous individuals I have met have also indicated a keen interest in Tibet, the Tibetan people and their future. It is obvious that developments in China during the past few years have contributed to this interest and caused speculations of a quick end to my exile.

Therefore I think that I should express my thoughts on the subject and my views on what may possibly lie ahead.

One who is not politically motivated can easily understand that Tibet is a separate country different from China. This thought comes quite naturally because Tibet was and is infact different from China—racially, culturally, linguistically, geographically and historically. No knowledgeable person would for a moment think that Tibetans are Chinese.

In the past there existed a special patron-priest relationship between China and Tibet; a relationship which was spiritual rather than temporal. In those times, the three countries, China, Mongolia and Tibet, were referred to as separate countries. You ask a Tibetan what his nationality is and his answer will be "Tibetan." Similarly, when people discuss something Tibetan, it is always in the sense of something that is different and distinct from Japanese, Indian or Chinese. For example, when people talk about Tibetan Buddhism, it is never implied that Chinese Buddhism represents Tibetan Buddhism as well.

The word "China" is "Gya-nak" in Tibetan. Since the Tibetan word "Gya-nak" refers to a foreign land, it implies Tibet to be separate from China. The Chinese do not use this word. They use the vague term "our nation" and "motherland" instead of "China" in their official documents and publications in the Tibetan language. They explain to us that Tibet is not a part of Gya-nak (China), but that it is a part of Chung Kuo (Middle Kingdom), just as Gya-nak (China) also is! However, Chinese who are not politically oriented do not make this distinction for they refer to the Chinese language as Chung Kuo Hua (language of the Middle Kingdom). But politically motivated Chinese refer to it as Han Hua (language of Han) in order to justify their stand that Tibet is an integral part of the Middle Kingdom. Linguistic concoctions cannot hide the facts of life and history.

Because Tibet as well as Mongolia and east Turkestan are basically and historically different from China, the Chinese have established various autonomous administrative systems in these occupied areas. They also use the language of these countries along with Chinese, on their currency notes. Also, in the case of Tibet, because it was independent until 1950, the Chinese signed the 17-point Agreement with the Tibetan government. No other Chinese-occupied nationality has any such agreement, pact or treaty with China. Here again, the Chinese say that this is an "agreement" and not a "treaty," giving the unsatisfactory explanation that "agreements" are made only within a nation between the central and local governments.

It may be of interest that Sun Yat-sen, the father of the Chinese republic, considered Tibet, Mongolia, and Manchuria as foreign countries. Also, Mao Tse-tung, in the 1930s when he was carrying out his struggle and not yet in power, supported Tibetan independence. Many years later, in 1954 when I was in China, Mao told me that while we were poor and backward, China would help us, but that after 20 years we (Tibetans) would be able to help them (the Chinese). On another occasion he told me that the Chinese personnel then stationed in Tibet would be withdrawn when the Tibetans could manage by themselves.

Even after 30 years of occupation by the People's Republic of China-and in spite of China's world-wide propaganda projecting the picture of Tibet as an inseparable and integral part of China-nobody says that he has been to "China" when he has visited "Tibet," or that the "Chinese" have taken to socialism when he means that the "Tibetans" have.

During these past three decades the Chinese have placed great emphasis on the unity of their nation and have boasted much achievement in that direction. Speeches on this have been made on numerous occasions at public meetings and official receptions. If we are to go by the number of times this theme has been stressed, The Chinese should have by now achieved a rock-like, unshakable unity. But this has not happened, for it is an artificial unity that his being imposed unsuccessfully on different nationalities. Tibetans beings one of them.

To claim that Tibet is a part of the Chinese nation is both distorted and hypocritical. The Chinese seem to realise this, and one hopes therefore that they will change their policy and accept the reality of a Tibetan nation. If the Chinese really want understanding and friendship, Tibetans, Mongolians and East Turkestanis should be treated according to their real circumstances and given their inalienable national rights and fundamental freedoms in their own homelands.

The Chinese claim that they did not come to Tibet as imperialists or colonialist, but as "liberators." What sort of liberations is it that denies the people their birthright and the freedom to determine their own destiny themselves? Having deprived the Tibetan people of freedom, the Chinese talk about an imaginary "state of glorious happiness and progress" said to be existing in Tibet.

I am pointing out these facts not with any antagonism toward the Chinese. If one day all the countries of the world join together as one nation, I would welcome that, and Tibet would become a willing partner in such a movement. But as long as this does not happen, the six million Tibetans are entitled to all the rights that other free peoples have, including the preservation of their separate, unique identity and way of life. As long as the six million Tibetans remain under foreign military occupation, they will continue to struggle for genuine national liberation and for legitimate rights in their own country.

A Clear Account

I think it is important that we as Tibetans present a clear and factual account of the Tibetan Situation. This is particularly necessary now when the present Chinese leadership is reported to be following a more moderate and reasonable path. It remains to be seen whether Chinese leaders are prepared to recognize realities as they really exist, or whether they will continue to direct facts in order to draw conclusions that severe only China's interests.

I have always firmly believed that unless we act according to the real existing circumstances we can never achieve our true aspirations. To my great disappointment, ever since the invasion of Tibet by the people's Republic of China, owing both to a lack of understanding of the actual situation, and often because the truth was intentionally ignored by the Chinese, there has existed most unfriendly relations between Tibet and China. This is an unfortunate state of affairs between two countries who have been neighbours for centuries. The Chinese took advantage of the Tibetans whenever possible, and as a result the Tibetans have grown ever suspicious of them.

Unions or federations can take place only when there is mutual agreement and mutual benefits flow from such arrangements. But they have to be disbanded or discontinued when it is realized that the people do not support them. The uture of Tibet is not a matter of determination by the Chinese occupation force. Six million Tibetans obviously cannot be absorbed or integrated with China, and their identity cannot be destroyed.

Friendly relation between Tibet and China, which I dearly wish for, can be established only on the basis of equality, mutual respect and mutual benefit. I for one would gladly accept what ever destiny the six millions people of Tibet choose for themselves in a climate of genuine freedom and peace. The free will of the Tibetan people is the only true basis for determining their destiny. Until it flourishes, there will be no peace in the hearts and minds of my people. With boundless faith in themselves and in the righteousness of their own cause they will wait for the day, which must come, when they can fully and freely enjoy their legitimate national rights and at the same time enjoy a relationship with China on a new basis of mutual benefit and respect.

[From *The Wall Street Journal,* 8 November, 1979.]

Part B

LETTERS/SPEECHES/STATEMENTS

16

Appeals by His Holiness the Dalai Lama of Tibet to the United Nations

I

November 11, 1950, Kalimpong

THE ATTENTION of the world is riveted on Korea where aggression is being resisted by an international force. Similar happenings in remote Tibet are passing without notice. It is in the belief that aggression will not go unchecked and freedom unprotected in any part of the world that we have assumed the responsibility of reporting to the United Nations Organization, through you, recent happenings in the border area of Tibet.

As you are aware, the problem of Tibet has taken on alarming proportions in recent times. This problem is not of Tibet's own making but is largely the outcome of unthwarted Chinese ambition to bring weaker nations on its periphery under its active domination. Tibetans have for long lived a cloistered life in their mountain fastnesses, remote and aloof from the rest of the world, except in so far as His Holiness the Dalai Lama, as the acknowledged head of the Buddhist Church, confers benediction and receives homage from followers in many countries.

In the years preceding 1912, there were indeed close friendly relations of a personal nature between the Emperor of China and his holiness the Dalai Lama. The connection was essentially born of belief in a common faith and may correctly be described as the relationship between a spiritual guide and his lay followers; it had no political implications As a people devoted to the tenets of Buddhism, Tibetans had long eschewed the art of warfare, practiced peace and tolerance, for the defense of their country relied on its geographical configuration and on non-involvement in the affairs of other nations. There were times when Tibet sought but seldom received the protection of the Chinese Emperor. The Chinese, however, in their natural urge for expansion, have wholly misconstrued the significance of the ties of friendship and inter-independence that existed between China and Tibet as between neighbours. To them China was suzerain and Tibet a vassal State. It is this which first aroused legitimate apprehension in the mind of Tibet regarding China's designs on its independent status.

The conduct of the Chinese during their expedition of 1910 completed the rupture between the two countries. In 1911-1912, Tibet, under the Thirteenth Dalai Lama, declared its complete independence—even Nepal simultaneously broke away from allegiance to China—while the Chinese revolution of 1911, which dethroned the last Manchurian Emperor, snapped the last of the sentimental and religious bonds that Tibet had with China. Tibet thereafter depended entirely on its isolation, its faith in the wisdom of the Lord Buddha, and occasionally on the support of the British in India for its protection. No doubt in these circumstances the latter could also claim suzerainty over Tibet. Tibet, notwithstanding Anglo-Chinese, influence from time-to-time, maintained its separate existence, in justification of which it may be pointed out that it has been able to keep peace and order within the country and remain at peace with the world. It continued to maintain neighbourly good-will and friendship with the people of China, but never acceded to the Chinese claim of suzerainty in 1914.

It was British persuasion which led Tibet to sign a treaty which superimposed on it the nominal (non-interfering) suzerainty of China and by which China was accorded the right to maintain a mission in Lhasa, though it was strictly forbidden to meddle in the internal affairs of Tibet. Apart from that fact, even the nominal suzerainty which Tibet conceded to China is not enforceable because of the non-signature of the treaty of 1914 by the Chinese. It will be seen that Tibet maintained independent relations with other neighbouring countries, such as India and Nepal. Furthermore, despite friendly British overtures, it did not compromise its position by throwing in its forces in the Second World War on the side of China. Thus it asserted and maintained its complete independence. The treaty of 1914 still guides relations between Tibet and India, and China not being a party to it may be taken to have renounced the benefits that would have otherwise accrued to it from the treaty. Tibet's independence thereby reassumed *de jure* status.

The slender tie that Tibet maintained with China after the 1911 revolution became less justifiable when China underwent a further revolution and turned into a full-fledged Communist State. There can be no kinship or sympathy between such divergent creeds as those espoused by China and Tibet. Foreseeing future complications, the Tibetan Government broke off diplomatic relations with China and made a Chinese representative in Lhasa depart from Tibet in July, 1949. Since then, Tibet has not even maintained formal relations with the Chinese Government and people. It desires to live apart, uncontaminated by the germ of a highly materialistic creed, but China is bent on not allowing Tibet to live in peace. Since the establishment of the People's Republic of China, the Chinese have hurled threats of liberating Tibet and have used devious methods to intimidate and undermine the Government of Tibet. Tibet recognizes that it is in no position to resist. It is thus that it agreed to negotiate on friendly terms with the Chinese Government.

It is unfortunate that the Tibetan mission to China was unable to leave India through no fault of its own, but for want of British visas, which were required for transit through Hong Kong. At the kind intervention of the Government of India, the Chinese People's Republic condescended to allow the Tibetan mission to have preliminary negotiation with the Chinese Ambassador to India, who arrived in New Delhi only in September. While these negotiations were proceeding in Delhi, Chinese troops without warning or provocation, crossed the Di Chu river, which has for long been the boundary of Tibetan territory, at a number of places on October 7, 1950. In quick succession, places of strategic importance such as Demar, Kamto, Tunga, Tshame, Rimochegotyu, Yakalo and Markham, fell to the Chinese. Tibetan frontier garrisons in Kham, which were maintained not with any aggressive design, but as a nominal protective measure, were all wiped out. Communist troops converged in great force from five directions on Chamdo, the capital of Kham which fell soon after. Nothing is known of the fate of a minister of the Tibetan Government posted there.

Little is known in the outside world of this sneak invasion. Long after the invasion had taken place, China announced to the world that it had asked its armies to march into Tibet. This unwarranted act of aggression has not only disturbed the peace of Tibet, but it is also in complete disregard of a solemn assurance given by China to the Government of India, and it has created a grave situation in Tibet and may eventually deprive Tibet of its long-cherished independence. We can assure you, Mr. Secretary-General, that Tibet will not go down without a fight, though there is little hope that a nation dedicated to peace will be able to resist the brutal effort of men trained to war, but we understand that the United Nations has decided to stop aggression whenever it takes place.

The armed invasion of Tibet for the incorporation of Tibet in Communist China through sheer physical force is a clear case of aggression. As long as the people of Tibet are compelled by force to become a part of China against their will and consent, the present invasion of Tibet will be the grossest instance of the violation of the weak by the strong. We therefore appeal through you to the nations of the world to intercede in our behalf and restrain Chinese aggression.

The problem is simple. The Chinese claim Tibet as a part of China. Tibetans feel that racially, culturally, and geographically they are far apart from the Chinese. If the Chinese find the reactions of the Tibetans to their unnatural claim not acceptable, there are other civilized methods by which they could ascertain the views of the people of Tibet; or, should the issue be purely juridical, they are open to seek redress in an international court of law. The conquest of Tibet by China will only enlarge the area of conflict and increase the threat to the independence and stability of other Asian countries.

We Ministers, with the approval of His Holiness the Dalai Lama, entrusted the problem of Tibet in this emergency to the ultimate decision of the United Nations, hoping that the conscience of the world will not allow the disruption of our State by methods reminiscent of the jungle.

The Kashag (Cabinet) and National Assembly of Tibet, Tibetan Delegation, Shakabpa House, Kalimpong.

Dated Lhasa, the twenty-seventh day of the ninth Tibetan month of The Iron Tiger Year (November, 7, 1950).

II

New Delhi

September, 9, 1959

His Excellency Secretary General
United Nations
New York

Your Excellency,

Kindly refer to the proceedings of the General Committee of the United Nations General Assembly held on Friday, November 24, 1950, at which it was resolved that the consideration of El Salvador's complaint against "invasion of Tibet by foreign forces" should be adjourned in order to give the parties the opportunity to arrive at a peaceful settlement. It is with the deepest regret that I am informing you that the act of aggression has been substantially extended with the result that practically the whole of Tibet is under the occupation of the Chinese forces. I and my Government have made several appeals for peaceful and friendly settlement, but so far these appeals have been completely ignored. Under these circumstance, and in view of the inhuman treatment and crimes against humanity and religion to which the people of Tibet are being subjected, I solicit immediate intervention of the United Nations and consideration by the General Committee on its own initiative of the Tibetan issue, which had been adjourned.

In this connection I and my Government wish to emphasize that Tibet was a sovereign State at the time when her territorial integrity was violated by the Chinese armies in 1950. In support of this contention the Government of

Tibet urges the following:

First, no power of authority was exercised by the Government of China in or over Tibet since the Declaration of Independence by the Thirteenth Dalai Lama in 1912.

Second, the sovereign status of Tibet during this period finds conclusive evidence in the fact that the Government of Tibet concluded a many as five international agreements immediately before and during these years.

Third, the Government of Tibet takes its stand on the Anglo-Tibet Convention of 1914 which recognized the sovereign status of Tibet and accorded the same position to the Tibetan pleni-potentiary as was given to the representatives of Great Britain and China. It is true that this convention imposed certain restrictions on the external sovereignty of Tibet, but these did not deprive her of her internal position. Moreover, these restrictions ceased to have any effect on the transfer of power in India.

Fourth, there is no valid and subsisting international agreement under which Tibet or any other power recognized Chinese suzerainty.

Fifth, the sovereign status of Tibet is equally evident from the fact that during the Second World War Tibet insisted on maintaining her neutrality and only allowed the transport of non-military goods from India to China through Tibet. This position was accepted by the Governments of Great Britain and China.

Sixth, the sovereign status has also been recognized by other powers. In 1948 when the Trade Delegation from the Government of Tibet visited India, France, Italy, the United Kingdom, and the United States of America, the passport issued by the Tibetan Government was accepted by the governments of these countries.

Your Excellency, I and my government also solicit immediate intervention of the United Nations on humanitarian grounds. Since their violation of the territorial integrity of Tibet, the Chinese forces have committed the following offenses against the universally accepted laws of conduct:

First, they have dispossessed thousands of Tibetans of their properties, and deprived them of every source of livelihood, and thus driven them to death and desperation.

Second, men, women, and children have been pressed into labour gangs and made to work on military constructions without payment or on nominal payment.

Third, they have adopted cruel and inhuman measures for the purpose of sterilizing men and women with view to the total extermination of the Tibetan race.

Fourth, thousands of innocent people of Tibet have been brutally massacred.

Fifth, there have been many cases of murder of leading citizens of Tibet without any cause or justification.

Sixth, every attempt has been made to destroy our religion and culture. Thousands of monasteries have been razed to the ground and sacred images and articles of religion completely destroyed. Life and property are no longer safe, and Lhasa, the capital of the State, is now a dead city. The sufferings which my people are undergoing are beyond description, and it is imperatively necessary that this wanton and ruthless murder of my people should be immediately brought to an end. It is under these circumstances that I appeal to you and the United Nations in the confident hope that our appeal will receive the consideration it deserves.

The Dalai Lama

III

Swargashram,
Dharmsala, Cantt.
East Punjab, India
September 2, 1960

His Excellency
Dag Hammarskjold,
Secretary General of the United Nations,
New York.

Your Excellency:

Last year when I formally appealed to Your Excellency for the intervention of the United Nations on behalf of the people of Tibet, Your Excellency was kind enough to help my representatives with your inestimable advice and valuable support. I have, therefore, ventured to approach you once again in the name of the people of Tibet who are today groaning under an intolerable burden of terror and tyranny.

As Your Excellency in no doubt aware, the situation in Tibet has now become a grim tragedy. Hundreds of Tibetans have been arriving in India and Nepal to escape from merciless persecution and inhuman treatment. But there are thousands of others who find it impossible to seek asylum in the neighbouring countries and are, therefore, threatened with immediate death and destruction. I feel most strongly that something must be done immediately to save the lives of these innocent men, women, and children, and have accordingly sought the assistance and support of the governments of many member States of the United Nations. His Excellency the Prime Minister of the Federation of Malaya, and the Government of Thailand have generously responded to my appeal and have declared their intention to raise the Tibetan question at the next session of the General Assembly of the United Nations. It is in this connection that I have ventured to approach Your Excellency once again. As on the last occasion, I trust Your Excellency will find it possible to use your good offices and influence in devising a practical solution to the tragic problem of Tibet. Your Excellency, I hope, will permit me to express my own feelings in the matter. I firmly believe that the only effective and speedy way in which the United Nations can help the unfortunate people of Tibet is by way of mediation, either through an *ad hoc* body appointed for the purpose by the General Assembly or through Your Excellency's good offices. This is what I feel, and have also expressed this view to His Excellency Tunku Abdul Rahman and His Excellency Marshal Sarit Thanarat. This, however, is only a suggestion I am making for Your Excellency's consideration, and I would be most grateful if Your Excellency could see your way to favour me with your personal advice.

With assurance of my highest esteem and consideration.

I remain,
The Dalai Lama.

IV

Swargashram,
Dharmsala, Cantt.
East Punjab, India
September 29, 1960

His Excellency
Dag Hammarskjold
Secretary-General,
United Nations,
New York, N.Y.

Your Excellency:

1. May I convey to the United Nations and to Your Excellency my warm appreciation of the great work which has been and is being done in Congo under the auspices of the U.N.

2. Kindly refer to my letter of September 9,

1959, circulated by you as Note No. 2033, and also to my letter to Your Excellency of September 2, 1960.

3. I am happy to learn that the Question of Tibet has been inscribed on the agenda of the U.N. Assembly for this year at the instance of Malaya and Thailand to whom I am deeply grateful. I do hope that all the peaceloving countries will take head of the voice of my people and provide for them a ray of light in the night of subjugation and oppression through which they are passing.

4. I am happy to note that in his speech in the Assembly on September 24, 1960, H.E.N. Khrushchev called for the freedom of all colonial peoples. Unfortunately my country has been reduced to the status of a colonial country, and I hope that along with other countries the USSR will also raise its powerful voice in support of the restoration of freedom to my country.

5. I assert that long before 1911-12 there was no vestige of Chinese authority in Tibet, but it is not necessary for me to examine the historical aspect of this question for the purposes of this appeal.

6. Whatever the position of Tibet may have been prior to 1911-12, in any event, from the day that the Thirteenth Dalai Lama proclaimed the independence of Tibet, after the invading Chinese armies had been driven out of Tibet, Tibet was not only independent *de facto* but *de jure*.

7. In 1913 the Tibetan Government entered into a treaty with the Government of Mongolia. This entreaty was entered into under the authority of the Dalai Lama. By this treaty Tibet and Mongolia declare that they recognized each other as independent countries.

8. With a view to settle some outstanding questions, Tibet agreed to enter into tripartite discussions which commenced in 1913, at Simla. The parties to the discussion were the British Government, Chinese Government, and Tibetan Government. The representative of each government being a plenipotentiary on behalf of his government. This appears clearly from the text of the Convention which was initialed by the representatives of all the parties.

9. This fact is also emphasized by the White Paper No. 11 issued by the Government of India entitled "Notes, Memoranda, and Letters Exchanged between the Governments of India and China, September-November, 1959." This has been further emphasized in the note of the Government of India dated February 12, 1960 in the White Paper No. III issued by the Government of India.

10. Although the text of the Convention was initialed by the representative of the Chinese Government, the Chinese Government backed out and ultimately on the third of July, 1914, the signatures on behalf of the Dalai Lama, in his capacity as the head of the Tibetan State, and the British plenipotentiary were appended. At the same time the plenipotentiaries of Great Britain and Tibet, in view of the refusal of the Chinese Government, signed the following Declaration:

11. "We the plenipotentiaries of Great Britain and Tibet, hereby record the following declaration to the effect that we acknowledge the annexed Convention as initialed to be binding on the governments of Great Britain and Tibet, and we agree that so long as the Government of China withholds signature to the aforesaid Convention, she will be debarred from the enjoyment of all privileges accruing therefrom.

12. "In token whereof we have signed and sealed this declaration, two copies in English and two in Tibetan.

13. "Done at Simla this third day of July, A.D. 1914, corresponding with the Tibetan date—the tenth day of the fifth month of The Wood Tiger Year.

A. *Henry McMahon,*
British Plenipotentiary

(Seal of the British Plenipotentiary)

(Seal of the Dalai Lama)

(Seal of the Lonchen Shatra) *(Signature of the Lonchen Shatra)*

(Seal of the Drepung Monastery)

(Seal of the Sera Monastery)

(Seal of the Gaden Monastery)

(Seal of the National Assembly)"

14. The Chinese Government, never having adhered to the terms of the Convention, never became entitled to any of the advantages which they may have derived from the terms of the Convention.

15. In 1526 Tibet was represented at a Boundary Commission consisting of the representatives of Tibet, Tehri, and Great Britain which met at Nilang.

16. Between 1912 and 1950 there was not even a semblance of Chinese authority in Tibet. There was a Chinese mission in Tibet which arrived in 1934 to offer condolences on the death of the Thirteenth Dalai Lama. This Mission was permitted to continue to stay in Tibet on the same footing as the missions from Nepal and from the Government of India.

17. On numerous occasions after 1936 the officers of the Chinese mission to Lhasa used to travel via India to Tibet. On every occasion the Indian Government granted or refused transit visas after consulting the wishes of the Government of Tibet.

18. In 1949 even this mission was expelled from Tibet.

19. Tibet was not a party to the Sino-Japanese war, and even during the Second World War Tibet insisted on its position as a neutral and did not permit the transport of war material from India to China.

20. The Chinese claim that Tibetan delegates participated in the Constituent Assembly in 1946 and that they also sat in the Chinese National Assembly in 1948. This claim is absolutely false. Dzasak Khemey Sonam Wangdo, who was the leader of the Delegation which went to China says, "In 1946 The Tibetan Government had sent a good will Mission headed by Dzasak Rong-pel-lhun, Thubten Samphel and myself Dzasak Khemey Sonam Wangdo with assistants to offer victorious greetings to Britain, America, and the Kuomintang Government; we travelled via Calcutta to New Delhi, and offered the greetings to Britain and America through their Ambassadors; from there we went by air to Nanking and offered greetings. Due to illness and medical treatment we remained there for a few months. Then we toured several provinces and on our return to Nanking they were having their big assembly. We attended the assembly in order to study the behaviour of the Khamba and other Tibetan emigrants who attended the assembly as pretended Tibetan representatives. But we did not recognize or sign the new constitutional law *(Shenfa)* which was then made.

As for 1948, our mission in Nanking, namely the Khandon Losum, also attended the Chinese Assembly as visitors but no special representative was deputed from Lhasa, and they similarly did not recognize or sign the resolutions of the assembly.

21. In 1947 after India became independent, in reply to a communication from the Tibetan Government, the Government India replied as follows:

"The Government of India would be glad to have an assurance that it is the intention of the Tibetan Government to continue relations on the existing basis until new agreements are reached on matters that either party may wish to take up. This is the procedure adopted by all other countries with which India has inherited treaty relations from His Majesty's Government."

22. Between 1912 and till the Seventeen-Point Agreement was signed on May 23, 1951, Tibet continued to conduct its foreign affairs without reference to any outside authority. Tibetan delegations in 1946 and in 1948 traveled extensively on Tibetan passports.

23. Mr. H.E. Richardson, who was in charge of the British and later Indian Mission at Lhasa, stated to the Legal Inquiry Committee on Tibet, constituted by the International Commission of Jurists that, ... "The duties of the Officer in Charge of the British and later Indian Mission at Lhasa after 1936 were principally to conduct the diplomatic business of his Government."

24. The foregoing facts should suffice to show that Tibet was completely independent. Since, however, doubts were raised last year regarding the status of may country, the following facts may be usefully stated:

25. Sir Eric Teichmann in *Affairs of China* wrote: "Since (1912) no vestige of Chinese authority has survived or reappeared in Lhasa-ruled Tibet. In more than twenty years he (the Thirteenth Dalai Lama) ruled as undisputed master of autonomous Tibet, preserving internal peace and order and maintaining close and intimate relations with the Indian Government."

26. In 1928 Sir Charles Bell in *The People of Tibet* pointed out that Chinese authority in Tibet had ceased.

27. M. Amaury de Riencourt who was in Tibet in 1947, states, "Tibet ruled itself in all respects as an independent nation." He goes on to say that "Government's writ ran everywhere."

28. Tsung Lien-shen and Shen Chi-liu who were both members of the Chinese Mission in Lhasa, say, "Since 1911 Lhasa has to all practical purposes enjoyed full independence." In support of this they mention that Tibet had its own currency and customs, its own telegraph and postal service, and its own civil service different from that of China, and its own army.

29. In 1950 when the proposal of El Salvador to place the question of the invasion of Tibet on the agenda of the General Assembly was being considered, the Jam Saheb of Nawanagar, the representative of India said his government had given careful study to the problems raised by the proposal of El Salvador to place the question of the invasion of Tibet by foreign forces on the General Assembly agenda. That was a matter of vital interest to both China and India. The Committee was aware that India, as a neighbour of both China and Tibet, with both of which it had friendly relations, was the country most interested in a settlement of the problem. That was why the Indian Government was particularly anxious that it should be settled peacefully.

30. The claim of the Chinese to suzerainty over Tibet is based on the 1907 Convention between Great Britain and Russia. It may be pointed out that Tibet was not a party to that Convention and was in no way bound by that Convention.

31. As the head of the Tibetan government I say that what happened on October 7, 1950, was a flagrant act of aggression on the part of China against my country.

32. The Tibetan Government appealed to the United Nations for help. As a result of the defeat of the Tibetan army, and after the efforts of the Tibetan Government to get the help of the United Nations had failed, we were compelled to send a delegation to Peking. The delegation was compelled to sign what is known as the Seventeen-Point Agreement on May 23, 1951.

33. The events since then and till my

departure from Tibet in March, 1959, are too well-known to require any detailed recounting. Even now refugees are coming into Nepal, Bhutan, Sikkim, and India practically every day. The number of the refugees is 43,500. From the accounts of these refugees, the oppression and wholesale terror, to which I referred in my letter to you last year and also this year, have in no way lessened.

34. In this connection may I draw the attention of the United Nations to the excellent reports on the question of Tibet published by the International Commission of Jurists. In the second report, the distinguished Committee that closely examined the question come to the conclusion, *inter alia,* that Chinese authorities had been guilty of genocide within the meaning of the meaning of the Genocide Convention. I trust that the United Nations will carefully examine the facts on which this conclusion is based and will take appropriate action to deal with this matter. Genocide, even apart from the Genocide Convention, has been recognized as a crime against International Law.

35. As a result of a wholesale breach of all the important terms of the Seventeen-Point Agreement, the General Assembly (Consisting of officials and public, mainly the public) repudiated that Agreement, as it was well-entitled to do, and reasserted the independence of Tibet on March 10, 1959.

36. The fighting in Tibet against the occupiers and the oppressors is still going on. I appealed to the United Nations last year, and I am making this appeal again in the hope that the United Nations will take appropriate measures to get China to vacate its aggression. In my opinion, any measure short of this is not going to be of much help to my country where the Communist steamroller is every day crushing out the freedom of my people.

37. May I request Your Excellency to place this Appeal before the United Nations.

The Dalai Lama.

17

The Dalai Lama's Letters

The Letter sent to Dalai Lama on March 10 by General Tan Kuan-san

Respected Dalai Lama, it is very good indeed that you wanted to come to the Military Area Command. You are heartily welcome. Since you have been put into very great difficulties due to the intrigues and provocations of the reactionaries, it may be advisable, that you do not come for the time being.

Salutations and best regards

Tan Kuan-San

Dalai Lama's Letter of March 11

Dear Comrade Political Commissar Tan,

I intended to go to the Military Command to see the theatrical performance yesterday, but I was unable to do so, owing to obstruction by people, ecclesiastical and secular, who were instigated by a few bad elements and who did not know the facts. This has put me to indescribable shame. I am greatly upset and worried and at a loss what to do. When your letter (of the 10th) appeared before me, I immediately became overjoyed, you do not mind at all.

Reactionary evil elements are carrying out activities endangering me under the pretext of protecting me safety. I am taking measures to calm things down. In a few days when the situation becomes stable, I was certainly meet you. If you have any internal directives for me, please tell me frankly through this messenger (this refers to Ngapo Ngawang Jigme).

Dalai Lama

(Written by my own hand)

General Tan's of March 11

The reactionaries are now so audacious as to have openly and arrogantly carried out military provocations. They have erected fortifications and posted large numbers of machine-guns and armed reactionaries along the national defence highway (the highway north of Norbu Lingka) thereby seriously disturbing the security of the national defence communications.

Many times in the past, we told Kasha that the People's Liberation Army is duty-bound to defend the country and to protect the security of communication lines related to national defence, and, therefore it certainly cannot remain indifferent to this serious act of military provocations. Therefore, the Tibet Military Area Command has sent letters to Surkong, Neusha, Shasu and Pala asking them to tell the reactionaries to remove all the fortifications they established and to withdraw from the highway immediately. Otherwise, they will bear responsibility themselves for all the serious consequences. I want to inform you of this. Please let me know what your views are at your earliest convenience.

Salutations and best regards

Tan

Dalai Lama's letter of March 12

Dear Comrade Political Commissar Tan,

I suppose you have received my letter of yesterday (referring to March 11) forwarded to you by Ngapo. I have had the letter you sent me this morning. The unlawful actions of the reactionary clique break my heart. Yesterday I told Kasha to order the immediate dissolution of the illegal People's Conference and the immediate withdrawal of the reactionaries who arrogantly moved into the Norbu Lingka under the pretext of protecting me. As to the incidents of yesterday and the day before, which were created under the pretext of protecting my safety and have seriously estranged the relations between the Central Government and the Local Government. I am making every possible effort to deal with them. At 8.30 Peking time this morning a few Tibetan army men suddenly fired several shots near the Chinghai-Tibet highway. Fortunately no serious disturbances occurred. As to the questions mentioned in your letter (referring to the letter of the 11th sent by General Tan to the Dalai Lama), I am planning to persuade my few subordinates and give them instructions. Please tell me frankly any instruction you have for me.

Dalai

Letter to Dalai Lama by General Tan

Respected Dalai Lama,

I have the honour to acknowledge receipt of your two letters dated March 11 and March 12. The traitorous activities of the reactionary clique of the upper strata in Tibet have grown into intolerable proportions. These individuals, in collusion with foreigners, have engaged in reactionary, traitorous activities for quite sometime. The Central People's Government has long adopted an attitude of magnanimity and enjoined the Local Government of Tibet to deal with them seriously, but the Local Government of Tibet has all along adopted an attitude of feigning compliances while actually helping them with their activities with the result that things now have come to such a grave pass. The Central People's Government still hopes that the Local Government of Tibet will change its erroneous attitude and immediately assume responsibility for putting down the rebellion and mete out severe punishment to the traitors. Otherwise the Central People's Government will have to act itself to safeguard the solidarity and unification of the motherland.

In your letter, you said: "As to the incidents which were created under the pretext of protecting my safety and have seriously estranged relations between the Central Government and the Local Government, I am making every possible effort to deal with them." We warmly welcome the correct attitude on your part.

We are very much concerned about your present position and safety. If you think it necessary and possible to extricate yourself from the present dangerous position of being abducted by the traitors, we cordially welcome you and your encourage to come and stay for a brief period in the Military Area Command. We are willing to assume full responsibility for your safety. As to what is the best course to follow, it is entirely up to you to decide.

In addition, I have much pleasure in informing you that the Second National People's Congress had decided to open its first session on April 17.

Salutations and my best wishes

Tan Kuan-San

Dalai Lama's Letter dated March 16

Dear Comrade Political Commissar Tan,

Your letter dated the 15th has just been received at three o'clock. I am very glad that you are so concerned about my safety and hereby express my thanks.

The day before yesterday, the fifth day of

the second month according to the Tibetan calendar (March 14, 1959) I made a speech to more than seventy representatives of the government officials, instructing them from various angles, calling on them to consider seriously present and long-term interests and to calm down, or my life would be in danger. After these severe reproaches, conditions took a slight turn for the better. Though the conditions in here and outside are still very difficulty to deal with at present, I am trying skilfully to make a demarcation line between the progressive people and those opposing the revolution within the government officials. A few days from now when there are enough forces that I can trust, I shall make my way to the Military Area Command secretly. When that time comes, I shall first send you a letter. I request you to adopt reliable measures. What are your views? Please write to me often.

Dalai

18

His Holiness the Dalai Lama's Press Statements

STATEMENT ISSUED AT TEZPUR

18th April, 1959

1. IT HAS always been accepted that the Tibetan people are different from the Han people of China. There has always been a strong desire for independence on the part of the Tibetan people. Throughout history this has been asserted on numerous occasions. Sometimes, the Chinese Government have imposed their suzerainty on Tibet and, at other times, Tibet has functioned as an independent country. In any event, at all times, even when the suzerainty of China was imposed, Tibet remained autonomous in control of its internal affairs.

2. In 1951, under pressure of the Chinese Government, a 17-Point Agreement was made between China and Tibet. In that Agreement, the suzerainty of China was accepted as there was no alternative left to the Tibetans. But even in the Agreement, it was stated that Tibet would enjoy full autonomy. Though the control of External Affairs and Defence were to be in the hands of the Chinese-Government, it was agreed that there would be no interference by the Chinese Government with the Tibetan religion and customs and her internal administration. In fact, after the occupation of Tibet by the Chinese armies, the Tibetan Government did not enjoy any measure of autonomy even in internal matters, and the Chinese Government exercised full powers in Tibet's affairs. In 1956, a Preparatory Committee was set up for Tibet with the Dalai Lama as Chairman, the Panchen Lama as Vice-Chairman and General Chang Kuo Hua as the Representative of the Chinese Government. In practice, even this body had little power, and decisions in all important matters were taken by the Chinese authorities. The Dalai Lama and his Government tried their best to adhere to the 17-Point Agreement, but the interference of the Chinese authorities persisted.

3. By the end of 1955 a struggle had started in the Kham Province and this assumed serious proportions in 1956. In the consequential struggle, the Chinese Armed Forces destroyed a large number of monasteries. Many Lamas were killed and a large number of monks and officials were taken and employed on the construction of roads in China, and the interference in the exercise of religious freedom increased.

4. The relations of Tibetans with China became openly strained from the early part of February, 1959. The Dalai Lama had agreed a month in advance to attend a cultural show in the Chinese Headquarters and the date was suddenly fixed for the 10th of March. The people of Lhasa became apprehensive that some harm might be done to the Dalai Lama and as a result about ten thousand people gathered round the Dalai Lama's summer palace, Norbulingka, and physically prevented the Dalai Lama from attending the function. Thereafter, the people themselves decided a raise a bodyguard for the protection of the Dalai Lama. Large crowds of Tibetans went

about the streets of Lhasa demonstrating against the Chinese rule in Tibet. Two days later, thousands of Tibetan women held demonstrations protesting against Chinese authority. In spite of this demonstration from the people, the Dalai Lama and his Government endeavoured to maintain friendly relations with the Chinese and tried to carry out negotiations with the Chinese representatives as to how best to-bring about peace in Tibet and assuage the people's anxiety. While these negotiations were being carried out, reinforcements arrived to strengthen the Chinese garrisons in Lhasa and Tibet. On the 17th March, two or three mortar shells were fired in the direction of the Norbulingka Palace. Fortunately, the shells fell in a nearby pond. After this, the Advisers became alive to the danger to the person of the Dalai Lama and in those difficult circumstances it became imperative for the Dalai Lama, the members of his family and his high officials to leave Lhasa. The Dalai Lama would like to state categorically that he left Lhasa and Tibet and came to India of his own free will and not under duress.

5. It was due to the loyalty and affectionate support of his people that the Dalai Lama was able to find his way through a route which is quite arduous. The route which the Dalai Lama took involved crossing the Kyichu and the Tsangpo rivers, and making his way through Lhoka area, Yarlung Valley and Tsona Dzong before reaching the Indian Frontier at Kanzey Mane near Chuthangmu.

6. On the 29th March 1959, the Dalai Lama sent two emissaries across the Indo-Tibetan border requesting Government of India's permission to enter India and seek asylum there. The Dalai Lama is extremely grateful to the people and Government of India for their spontaneous and generous welcome as well as the asylum granted to him and his followers. India and Tibet have religious, cultural and trade links extending over a thousand years and for Tibetans it has always been the land of enlightenment, having given birth to Lord Buddha. The Dalai Lama is deeply touched by the kind greeting extended to him on his safe arrival in India by the Prime Minister Shri Jawaharlal Nehru, and his colleagues in the Government of India. The Dalai Lama has already sent reply to his message of greetings.

7. Ever since the Dalai Lama entered India at Kanzey Mane near Chuthangmu, he has experienced in full measure the respect and hospitality extended to him by the people of the Kameng Frontier Division of the North East Frontier Agency and the Dalai Lama would like to state how the Government of India's officers posted there had spared no efforts in making his stay and journey through this extremely well administered part of India as comfortable as possible.

8. The Dalai Lama will now be proceeding to Mussoorie which he hopes to reach in the next few days. The Dalai Lama will give thought to his future plans and, if necessary, give expression to them as soon as he has had a chance to rest and reflect on recent events. His country and people have passed through an extremely difficult period and all that the Dalai Lama wishes to say at the moment is to express his sincere regrets at the tragedy which has overtaken Tibet and to fervently hope that these troubles would be over soon without any more bloodshed.

9. As the Dalai Lama and the spiritual head of all the Buddhists in Tibet, his foremost concern is the well-being of his people and in ensuring the perpetual flourishing of his sacred religion and freedom of his country.

10. While expressing once again thankfulness at his safe arrival in India, the Dalai Lama would like to take this opportunity to communicate to all his friends, well-wishers and devotees in India and abroad his sincere gratitude for the many messages of sympathies and concern with which they have flooded him.

STATEMENT ISSUED AT MUSSOORIE

22nd April, 1959

On the 18th April, I issued a statement at Tezpur. I did not wish to follow it up with another statement at this stage. However, I have seen a New China News Agency report implying that I was not responsible for this earlier statement. I wish to make it clear that the earlier statement was issued under my authority and indicated my views, and I stand by it. I am making this bride statement to correct the wrong impression created by the New China Agency's report and do not propose to state anything more at present.

STATEMENT ISSUED AT THE PRESS CONFERENCE HELD IN MUSSOORIE

On 20th June, 1959

Ever since my arrival in India, I have been receiving almost every day sad and distressing news of the suffering and inhuman treatment of my people. I have heared almost daily, with a heavy heart, of their increasing agony and affliction, their harassment and persecution and of the terrible deportation and execution of innocent men. These have made me realise forcibly that the time has manifestly arrived when in the interests of my people and Religion and to save them from the danger of near-annihilation, I must not keep silent any longer but must frankly and plainly tell the world the truth about Tibet and appeal to the conscience of all peace-loving and civilised nations.

To understand and appreciate the significance and implication of the recent tragic happenings in Tibet, it is necessary to refer to the main events which have occurred in the country since 1950. It is recognised by every independent observer that Tibet had virtually been independent by enjoying and exercising all rights of sovereignty, whether internal or external. This has also been impliedly admitted by the Communist Government of China, for the very structure, terms and conditions of the so-called Agreement of 1951 conclusively show that it was an Agreement between two independent and sovereign States. It follows, therefore, that when the Chinese armies violated the territorial integrity of Tibet they were committing a flagrant act of Aggression. The agreement which followed the invasion of Tibet was also thrust upon its people and government by the threat of arms. It was never accepted by them of their own free will. The consent of the Government was secured under duress and at the point of the bayonet. My representatives were compelled to sign the Agreement under threat of further military operations against Tibet by the invading armies of China leading to utter ravage and ruin of the country. Even the Tibetan seal which was affixed to the Agreement was not the seal of my representatives but a seal copied and fabricated by the Chinese authorities in Peking, and kept in their possession ever since.

While I and my Government did not voluntarily accept the Agreement, we were obliged to acquiesce in it and decided to abide by the terms and conditions in order to save my people and country from the danger of total destruction. It was, however, clear from the very beginning that the Chinese had no intention of carrying out the Agreement. Although they had solemnly undertaken to maintain my status and power as the Dalai Lama, they did not lose any opportunity to undermine my authority and sow dissensions among my people. In fact, they compelled me, situated as I was, to dismiss my Prime Ministers under threat of their execution without trial because they had in all honesty and sincerity resisted the unjustified usurpation of power by the representatives of the Chinese Government in Tibet. Far from carrying out the Agreement, they began deliberately to pursue a course of policy which was diametrically opposed to the terms and conditions which they had themselves laid down. Thus commenced a reign of terror which find few parallels in the history of Tibet. Forced labour and compulsory exactions, a systematic persecution of the people, plunder and confiscation of property belonging to individual and monasteries and execution of certain leading men in Tibet,—these are the glorious achievements of the Chinese rule in Tibet. During all the time, patiently and sincerely I eneavoured to appease my people and to calm down their feelings and at the same time tried my best to persuade the Chinese authorities in Lhasa to adopt a policy of conciliation and friendliness. In spite of repeated failures, I persisted in this policy till the last day when it became impossible for me to render my useful service to my people by remaining in Tibet. It is in these circumstances that I was obliged to leave my country in order to save it from further danger and disaster.

I wish to make it clear that I have made these assertions against the Chinese officials in Tibet in the full knowledge of the gravity because I know them to be true. Perhaps the Peking Government are not fully aware of the facts of the situation, but if they are not prepared to accept these statements, let them agree to an investigation on the point by an international commission. On our part, I and my Government will readily agree to abide by the verdict of such an impartial body.

It is necessary for me to add that before I visited India in 1956, it had become increasingly clear to me that my policy of amity and tolerance had totally failed to create any impression on the representatives of the Chinese Government in Tibet. Indeed, they had frustrated every measure adopted by me to remove the bitter resentment felt by me people and to bring about a peaceful atmosphere in the country for the purpose of carrying out the necessary reforms. As I was unable to do anything for the benefit of my people, I had practically made up my mind when I came to India not to return to Tibet until there was a manifest change in the attitude of the Chinese authorities. I, therefore, sought the advice of the Prime Minister of India who has always shown me unfailing kindness and consideration. After his talk with the Chinese Prime Minister and on the strength of the assurances given by him on behalf of China, Mr. Nehru advised me to change my decision. I followed his advice and returned to Tibet in the hope that conditions would change substantially for the better, and I have no doubt that my hopes would have been realised if the Chinese authorities had on their part carried out the assurances which the Chinese Prime Minister had given to the Prime Minister of India. It was, however, painfully clear soon after my return that the representatives of the Chinese Government had no intention to adhere to their promises. The natural and inevitable result was that the situation steadily grew worse until it became impossible to control the spontaneous upsurge of my people against the tyranny and oppression of the Chinese authorities.

At this point I wish to emphasize that I and my Government have never been opposed to the reforms which are necessary in the social, economic and political systems prevailing in Tibet. We have no desire to disguise the fact that ours is an ancient society and that we must introduce immediate changes in the interests of the people of Tibet. In fact, during the last nine years several reforms were proposed by me and my Government, but every time these measures were strenuously opposed by the Chinese in spite of popular demand for them, with the results that nothing was done for the betterment of the social and economic conditions of the people. In particular, it was my earnest desire that the system of land tenure should be radically changed without further delay and the large landed estates acquired by the State on payment of compensation for distribution amongst the tillers of the soil. But the Chinese authorities deliberately put every obstacles in the way of carrying out this just and reasonable reform. I desire to lay stress on the fact that we, as firm believers in Buddhism, welcome change and progress consistently with the genius of our people and the rich traditions of our country, but the people of Tibet will stoutly resist any victimisation, sacrilege and plunder in the name of reforms, a policy which is now being enforced by the representatives of the Chinese Government in Lhasa.

I have attempted to present a clear and unvarnished picture of the situation in Tibet. I have endeavoured to tell the entire civilised world the real truth about Tibet, the truth which must ultimately prevail, however strong the forces of evil may appear to be today. I also wish to declare that we Buddhists firmly and steadfastly believe in peace and desire to live in peace with all the peoples and countries of the world. Although recent actions and policies of the Chinese authorities in Tibet have created strong feelings of bitterness and resentment against the Government of China, we, Tibetans, lay and monk alike, do not cherish any feelings of enmity and hatred against the great Chinese people. We wish to live in peace and ask for peace and goodwill from all the countries of the world. I and my Government are, therefore, fully prepared to welcome a peaceful and emicable solution of the present tragic problem, provided that such a solution guarantees the preservation of the rights and powers which Tibet has enjoyed and exercised without any interference prior to 1950. We must also insist in the creation of a favourable climate by the immediate adoption of the essential measures as a condition precedent to negotiations for a peaceful settlement. We ask for peace and for a peace settlement, but we must also ask for maintenance of the status and the rights of our State, and people.

To you, gentlemen of the Press, I and my people owe a great debt to gratitude for all that you have done to assist us in our struggle for survival and freedom. Your sympathy and support have given us courage and strengthened our determination. I confidently hope that you will continue to lend the weight of your influence to the cause of peace and freedom which the people of Tibet are fighting today. Gentlemen, I thank you, one and all, on behalf of my people as well as on my own behalf.

New York Times

Q. 1. Is His Holiness in favour of active rebellion by Tibetans against Chinese rule? If so, does he himself plan to take part in such a rebellion?

Ans. Tibet is a land of religion; although I and my people have no desire other than to solve our problems through peaceful means, the Chinese authorities by their extreme measures of suppression compelled my people through desperation to rise up and fight for their freedom.

Q. 2. Under what conditions would His Holiness return to Lhasa?

Ans. I will return to Lhasa when I obtain the rights and power which Tibet had enjoyed and exercised prior to 1950.

Q. 3. What does His Holiness think of the present Government in Tibet—the Preparatory Committee for Tibetan Autonomy headed by the Panchen Lama as acting Chairman? Does His Holiness think the Panchen Lama is willingly cooperating with the Chinese?

Ans. The Preparatory Committee for Tibet an Autonomy is nothing but nominal, with all the powers concentrated in the hands of the Chinese. The Panchen Lama has no alternative but to carry out the orders of the Chinese, for he had no actual power.

Q. 4. Does His Holiness plan any international appeal, e.g. to the United National on behalf of the Tibetan self-determination and against Chinese domination?

Ans. In case I am not satisfied by the terms of peaceful settlement offered by China, then shall consider my future plans.

Q. 5. Is rebellion against domination still going on in Tibet? What sections of the people are leading this rebellion?

Ans. Yes, the revolt is still going on. The leaders of the rebellion are all drawn from the various sections of the Tibetan people.

Q. 6. What does His Holiness feel is the ultimate Chinese aim as regards Tibet in terms of system of government and relationship to the Chinese Central Government?

Ans. The ultimate Chinese aim as regards Tibet, as far as I can take out from their present policies, seems to attempt the extermination of the religion, culture and even the absorption of the Tibetan race.

Q. 7. What is His Holiness' attitude towards the Nationalist Government in Taiwan?

Ans. Our attitude to all countries will be governed by their attitude to our problems.

Q. 8. If His Holiness does not return to Tibet in the immediate future, what are his plans?

Ans. At present I am not able to reveal any details of my future plan of action.

Q. 9. Does His Holiness consider himself the head of a Government in exile in view of the fact that most of his ministers are with him in India?

Ans. Wherever I am accompanied by my Government, the Tibetan people recognise us as the Government of Tibet.

Q. 10. Have any member of the Chinese Embassy or any other Peking emissaries discussed Tibetan affairs with His Holiness since he fled Lhasa?

Ans. No.

Press Trust of India —(1)

Q. 1. Would your Holiness welcome a suggestion, if it be made, for a summit meeting between Prime Minister Nehru and Prime Minister Chou En-lai, to discuss and find a solution of the Tibet question? Do you think that Tibet is a question which must draw world attention although China may not consider it to be so?

Ans. We will welcome such a summit meeting between Prime Minister Nehru and Prime Minister Chou En-lai, if the actual events of Tibet are considered in their true perspective. I certainly think that world's attention should be focussed on the question of Tibet.

Q. 2. Would you like to send an appeal to p.m. Chou En-Lai suggesting to him the convening of such a summit conference? Would you want to participate in such a meeting if it came through?

Ans. I have no such intention at present.

Q. 3. What, according to your Holiness, should be the status of Tibet now in the light of your past commitments and penetration of Peking's authority in Tibet already made?

Ans. Peking's authority in Tibet is one which has been established through military power. My statement fully explains this point.

Q. 4. Would your Holiness like world opinion to support Tibet's case or welcome negotiations with China either directly or through friendly countries like India for a rapprochement, if at all you think a rapprochement can be made?

Q. 5. Would your Holiness like Russia to understand Tibetan woes and bear and its influence with China for mutually agreed solution and compromise? Would your Holiness like that your emissaries go to New Delhi and meet the Ambassadors for the USSR and China for opening up negotiations or would you prefer to leave it to Shri Nehru to take the initiative?

Ans.(Combined Ans to Q. 4 and 5): We will welcome support from all countries in the world for Tibet's cause.

Q. 6. What is the feeling that your Holiness is having with the news coming from Tibetan sources about alleged cruelties suffered by your people in the hands of the Chinese armed authorities? Can you think that the spirit of your people would die like this?

Ans. The extreme measures adopted by the Chinese authorities have not only affected my feelings, but have also strengthened the spirit of the people.

Q. 7. Do you favour the raising of the Tibet question in the U.N.? Do you not think that the Western powers ought to allow China U.N. membership which alone would have made it possible for putting pressure of world opinion on Peking Government in cases like Tibet?

Ans. At present I have neither given thought to raising the Tibetan question in the U.N. nor weighed the prospects of China's U.N. membership.

Q. 8. Does your Holiness hope to be able to return to Tibet even if China should never bow down to world opinion?

Ans. It depend on the circumstances at that time.

Q. 9. Does your Holiness think that instead of armed rebellion, non-violent satyagraha by the entire Tibetan Nation would have achieved what they are unable to secure through armed uprising?

Ans. Until the last day I endeavoured to bring about a peaceful settlement, the failure of which resulted in the armed uprising of my people, who are compelled to fight for their freedom.

The Christian Science Monitor

Q. 1. According to an Indian report filed before the International Commission of Jurists, 65,000 have been killed in fights with the Chinese Occupation forces since 1956. The report also states that more than 5 million Chinese have been settled in Tibet. Will you comment on this?

Ans. The number of Tibetans killed in fights with Chinese occupation forces since 1956 is actually more than the Indian report filed before the International Commission of Jurists. The report of 5 million Chinese settlers in Tibet is correct and refers to those Chinese who have settled in North-Eastern and Eastern Tibet. According to recent reports, in addition to the 400,000 Chinese civil and military personnel already settled in U and Tsang provinces of Tibet (Central Tibet), they are planning to send another 4,000,000 (4 million) settlers to these parts.

Q. 2. The report also states that "a delibeıate and precise campaign has been conducted by the Chinese in Tibet against the Buddhist religion, the lamas and the Buddha Himself." Will you comment on this?

Ans. The report filed before the International Commission of Jurists is quite correct in stating that until 1958 over a thousand monasteries were destroyed, countless lamas and monks were killed and imprisoned and the extermination of religion was continuously attempted, and from 1959 onwards full scale campaign was conducted in the provinces of U and Tsang (Central Tibet) for the final extermination of the Religion. We have documentary proof to these acts and also accusation directed towards Lord Buddha Himself who had been named a "reaction ary element."

Q. 3. What is the culminating reason that made you decide to leave Lhasa?

Ans. On 17th March 1959, at 4 p.m, two

mortar shells were fired towards my residence as evidence of the Chinese intention to use military force, and although I had endeavoured to keep up friendly relations with them for the last 9 years, my hopes of rendering any service in the interest of my people by remaining in Tibet was finally shattered. Therefore, I and my Government had to leave for India secretly at 10 p.m. on March 17th, 1959 with a view to rendering more beneficial service to my people.

Q. 4. Do you accept Chinese suzerainty over Tibet unconditionally or do you feel this acceptance is tied up with Peking's acceptance of your country's autonomy? If the latter be the case, do you accept the condition of many Indians that the whole Indo-Tibetan Agreement now is null and void and that India, for one, should support Tibet's claim to sovereign independence?

Ans. We wish to remain in the same status which Tibet enjoyed prior to 1950.

Q. 5. Out of the last question, is there any possibility of your taking Tibet's case to the United Nations? If you, what other plans you have to support your people's struggle against Communist encroachments?

Ans. Please refer to *New York Times* Q. No. 4.

Q. 6. Do you feel that the Government of India is placing any restrains on your movements? If not, then are your contemplating any tours (a) in India, (b) outside it, in the immediate-failure?

Ans. The Government of India had not placed any restraint at all of my movements, and if the occasion arise, I intend to tour India and abroad.

Hindustan Times

Q. 1. Have you received any communication from Peking informing you of your recent re-election as Vice-Chairman of the Chinese People's Republic or invitation to Lhasa?

Ans. No.

Q. 2. What are your minimum terms of returning home with honour?

Ans. Please refer to the answer to *New York Times* Question No. 2.

Q. 3. Did the Chinese forces in Tibet attempt to intercept you while your were escaping? Would they have succeeded if they wished to capture you? Do they gain or lose by your being in exile?

Ans. The Chinese had no idea of my escape, or else they would certainly have tried to intercept. They would not have succeeded in capturing me because of the unity of purpose of the people and the National Voluntary Defence Army of Tibet. The Chinese may be able to answer the last point.

Bharat Press Service

Q. 1. May I know the story of your historic and thrilling escape from Tibet?

Ans. A detailed accounts will be issued in the near future.

Q. 2. Could you kindly enlighten us with your future plans in solving the ever-increasing Tibetan problem?

Ans. Refer to Question No. 8 of *New York Times.*

Q. 3. What further assistance do you expect from the Indian Government in solving your problem?

Ans. I hope the Government of India will give us the same support, if not more, as she has given to small countries like Algeria, Morocco and Tunisia, for our cause also.

The Himachal Times

Q. 1. Will His Holiness let us know if the revolt is still in progress in any parts of Tibet and if so, if any part in control of the Khambas?

Ans. As Tibet is a large country, there are

still some parts where fighting is going on. Moreover, there are several places in the East and north of Lhasa which are under the control of the Khambas.

Q. 2. Will the Dalai Lama kindly say if the genocide has been practised in his homeland by the Chinese?

Ans. Besides the civil and military personnel already in Tibet, 50,00,000 (five million) Chinese settlers have arrived in the Eastern and North-Eastern Tibet in addition to which four million Chinese settlers are to be sent to the U and Tsang provinces of Tibet (Central Tibet). Moreover, many Tibetans have been deported to China, thereby resulting in the complete absorption and extinction of the Tibetan race, which is being undertaken by the Chinese.

Q. 3. Will the Dalai Lama kindly comment on the statement made by the Panchen Lama that he was not given due respect during this tour with the Dalai Lama two years back?

Ans. At that time the Government and the entire people of India had extended both the Panchen Lama and myself the most cordial hospitality and respect. But the Panchen Lama having no freedom of will, may have had to make the statement.

Q. 4. Will the Dalai Lama kindly state if by his entry in India, Sino-Indian relations have been embittered later?

Ans. If both sides faced the actual events in Tibet in their true perspective, I don't see any reason why Sino-Indian relations should be embittered.

Q. 5. Will the Dalai Lama tell us his future plans and also what measures he suggests for the other 13,000 refugees to live by their own labour in India?

Ans. I am not able to comment on any particular future plan. But, I and my Government are also trying to make efforts for the refugees to start living by their own means.

Q. 6. Will the Dalai Lama like these refugees to go back or settle permanently in India?

Ans. They would like to go back when favourable circumstances arise in Tibet.

Press Trust of India—(II)

Q. 1. Now that you have rested, have you chalked out any future plans for yourself and in regard to regaining the autonomy of Tibet?

Ans. I am not yet able to comment on any particular future plans. My statement is clear regarding our aspirations.

Q. 2. Will your kindly explain what is exactly meant by the "autonomy of Tibet"?

Ans. The "autonomy of Tibet" is meant to be the right of self-government in internal affairs, but the existing autonomy of Tibet has no actual rights whatsoever for my Government is any affairs.

Q. 3. Will the Dalai Lama be pleased to state how the 1951 Agreement was honoured by the Chinese? If not, in what matters the Chinese interfered in the autonomy of Tibet?

Ans. This has been made known to you in my statement.

Q. 4. Will the Dalai Lama kindly explain what further atrocities have been committed by the Chinese in Tibet? (In this connection we refer you to your interview to the Correspondent of *The Statesman* wherein you are reported to have stated that further atrocities have been committed.

Ans. I will give a brief account of the recent events as reported to me by my people. The people of Lhasa, both men and women, have been classed into three groups. The first group is deported to China, where their fate is not known. The second group is imprisoned, interrogated and punished without limit in the various Chinese military headquarters in Lhasa. The third group is fed with the meanest food and driven to forced labour, each individual being made to carry 160 loads of earth daily failing which no food was given. Armed troops are posted in the streets of Lhasa, where two Tibetans are restricted to converse and where only aged men and women are to be seen. The Central Cathedral and all other places of worship are closed. In addition to all these, the reserves of the Tibetan Government and properties of private individuals are being listed by the Chinese, who are conducting an all-out propaganda for the formation of People's Communes.

Q. 5. Will the Dalai Lama kindly inform us about the state of the valuable Buddhist manuscripts in monasteries in Tibet? Have they been preserved or destroyed by the Chinese?

Ans. Many of the Buddhist manuscripts and printing blocks of unimaginable value have been destroyed, and many are transported to China.

Q. 6. Has any country invited your Holiness for staying either permanently or temporarily?

Ans. No. but I have received invitations from some Buddhist organizations abroad.

Q. 7. Both the Chinese and some of the Western newspapers have been persistently alleging that you are under duress. Are you a free agent in India or are you under any form of duress?

Ans. These rumours are baseless and unfounded.

Q. 8. Your elder brother has recently joined from the United States. Has the U.S. Government promised any support in regaining the autonomy of Tibet and is there are possibility of that country (U.S.A.) or any other country raising the Tibetan issue in the U.N. in the forthcoming General Assembly Session?

Ans. My elder brother, who has come to meet me as a brother, is not engaged in any political activities.

Q. 9. Will your Holiness kindly confirm that you wrote letters to the Chinese Military Commandant before you left? If so, under what circumstances you wrote those letters and subsequently made you leave your country? The Chinese say that there is an apparent contradiction between what you stated in your letters and the subsequent action that you took. They interpret this to mean that you left Lhasa under the influence of a few "Upper strata reactionaries".

Ans. Please refer to Q. No. 9 of the *Daily Telegraph*.

Q. 10. How will you reconcile your position as head of an autonomous state with the words "May I have your secret instructions" used in the last paragraph of your letter to the Chinese Military Commandant?

Ans. In many letter to the Chinese Military Commandant I have not used the words "Many I have secret instructions." My wording runs "May I have your intimate advice."

Q. 11. Will you kindly state if you are in favour of reforms being introduced in Tibet so that a socialist state is built up there?

Ans. I am in favour of introducing reforms in accordance with the traditions and customs of Tibet, the wishes of the people, and the system internationally practised. But I do not agree to such systems of reform are the people's communes being forced upon the people.

The Milap

Q. 1. Will the Dalai Lama kindly tell how long he intends to stay in India and what his future plans are?

Ans. At the moment I cannot tell the duration of my stay in India. As regards my future plans please refer to Q. No. 8 of *New*

York Times.

Q. 2. Will the Dalai Lama kindly state if the monasteries are safe and if the Lamas staying behind have not so far been indoctrinated?

Ans. Over a thousand monasteries have already been destroyed and still more are being destroyed. Monks by the thousands have been massacred and captured and the remaining are forced to be indoctrinated.

Q. 3. How far is this true that the younger generations of the Tibetans are being indoctrinated for Communism and that the Tibetan Community is being merged with the Hans?

Ans. Yes, it is true that the younger generation of Tibetans are being indoctrinated and their policy of colonisation practised.

Q. 4. Will the Dalai Lama kindly say that in India the people have shown him spontaneous affection and respect which is never possible in a regimented society like that of China?

Ans. As the people of India enjoy full freedom, they are at free will to show their affections and respect; but the people of China, though they may wish, they do not possess freedom of showing their affection.

Q. 5. Will the Dalai Lama as a religious man agree that the recent drought and damage to crops has been due to heinous crimes committed by the Chinese in Tibet and that God will further punish them for their misdeeds.

Ans. I am sorry to hear about the damage to crops in China. The crimes of suppression committed in Tibet are to be regretted, and we hope, better sense would prevail among the Chinese authorities.

The Daily Telegraph

Q. 1. Is it your holiness' intention to remain indefinitely in India as a religious refugee, or does your silence on the situation inside Tibet until now indicate that you have hopes of a settlement through the good offices of India and you do not wish during this period to embarrass your hosts?

Ans. We have no intention to stay in India indefinitely. We have no intention to unneccessarily embarrass the Government of India.

Q. 2. Failing any settlement of the Tibetan issue through India's diplomatic help is it your Holiness' intention to proceed to some other country where you will be permitted to take part in such political activity as may result in some help for Tibet?

Ans. At present I have not given any thought to this.

Q. 3. Is it true that your Holiness is considering going to the United States in order to make a personal appeal to the United Nations?

Ans. See answer to the 4th Question raised by the *New York Times*.

Q. 4. I understand that the Tibetan rebel groups in Tibet are disappointed at the lack of help and apparent lack of interest on the part of the Tibetan officials now in India and that it is their intention to form their own Government, make their own decisions and take the consequences. In view of this attitude does your Holiness consider that any possible negotiations or settlement agreed to by Tibetan officials in India, short of complete withdrawal of all Chinese personnel from Tibet, will be considered binding on the Tibetan rebel patriots?

Ans. What you have thought is fundamentally incorrect. Unlike in the past there is a strong unity among the entire people of Tibet.

Q. 5. Does your Holiness consider and *quid pro quo* that will be considered attractive enough by the Chinese to make them withdraw from Tibet? Or, do you simply hope that moral pressure from several countries, particularly Afro-Asian countries, will be enough?

Ans. The first question has been answered in my Statement. As regards the second question, I have every hope that all the countries of the world will support the truthful cause.

Q. 6. Has you Holiness any suggestion of your own which might satisfy both Chinese and Tibetans over the situation which has now arisen in Tibet, or has the matter gone so far that nothing short of Chinese withdrawal from Tibet or full scale war to a finish to the Tibet nation is unavoidable?

Ans. I cannot give a reply which could satisfy both the parties.

Q. 7. In the event of the above alternatives being accepted by the Tibetan people has your Holiness any intention of appealing for arms on behalf of the rebel patriots in order that they might not be annihilated without defence?

Ans. Although I have no intention to keep the National Defence Voluntary Army unaided, I am intending to help them by means of peaceful solutions rather than by military force.

Q. 8. Has your Holiness any idea of how many may have died since the revolt started in 1956, including the recent fighting in Lhasa?

Ans. The death casualties in the Eastern Khan of Tibet including Amdo since 1956 and that of the recent uprising in Lhasa is estimated at 65,000 at the least.

Q. 9. When your Holiness wrote the three letters to the Chinese authorities in Tibet what was in your mind? Were you stalling for time? Were you under pressure from your advisers to do so? Was it only a temporary ruse to keep the Chinese from indulging in some other drastic action against the Tibetans? Were you not aware of the possible effect of such letters on the world outside?

Ans. I wrote three letters to Chinese representative at a critical time when the lives and bodies of innumerable people were in the hands of the Chinese. This was a measure adopted in order to take a peaceful course of action. When the circumstances in which those letters were written are brought to the notice of the world, they could not have made any other impression rather than to expose the measure of Chinese oppression.

Q. 10. Is it true that there are now Russian troops in Tibet in addition to the technicians already known to be there?

Ans. I have heard such a report but I have no clear information yet as to how far it is true.

Q. 11. Will your Holiness give a personal account of details of the escape from Lhasa and subsequent journey to India?

Ans. I hope to give a detailed narrative of my escape from Lhasa to India later on.

Q. 12. Can your Holiness suggest what would be the most beneficial form of help which the various societies now being formed in several countries—such as the All-India Tibet Convention in India, shortly to be extended to Afro-Asian countries, the Tibet Society in Britain and others can offer? As these are not primarily political will your Holiness consider appointing some one to coordinate the activities of these many groups?

Ans. In view of the extremely difficult position in Tibet; the peoples of the different impartial countries of this world have been organising various conventions for the Tibetan cause for which we are cordially thankful to them. We hope these organisations will do a lot of good to Tibet.

Daily Mail

Q. 1. According to newspapers your Holiness is exceptionally tired by the journey from Lhasa. Is this correct?

Ans. Yes, that is a fact.

Q. 2. Since coming to Mussoorie has your Holiness been able to receive any news from Lhasa?

Ans. Yes, I received some news about which please refer to Q. No. 4 of *Press Trust of India* (II).

Q. 3. Why should it be necessary for Tibetans who have taken refuge in India to stay behind barbed wire?

Ans. Barbed wire is only for security and not for keeping Tibetan refugees under duress.

Q. 4. What were the relations between your Holiness and the Chinese General Tan before the Lhasa rising?

Ans. Uptil March 17th, I had tried my best to maintain good relations with the Chinese General Tan and the rest of their authorities.

Q. 5. Does your Holiness consider the treaty between Tibet and Chinese Government still in force?

Ans. The Sino-Tibetan Agreement imposed by the Chinese according to their own desire has been violated by the Chinese themselves, thus giving rise to a contradiction. Therefore, we cannot abide by this agreement.

Q. 6. After signature of that Treaty, how did Chinese treat religion in Tibet?

Ans. About extermination of religion in Tibet by the Chinese, has been answered in previous questions.

Q. 7. Does your Holiness and the Panchen Lama agree what is the best policy in Tibet?

Ans. Panchen Lama has been under Chinese influence ever since his boyhood and has never enjoyed any freedom.

Q. 8. On what condition would your Holiness consider returning to Tibet?

Ans. Please refer to Q. 2. of *New York Times.*

Q. 9. How could that be negotiated with the Chinese?

Ans. Unless there is a mediator from a foreign country, no direct negotiation will be useful because the terms and conditions will never be abide effectively.

Q. 10. What is your Holiness' opinion of the present form of Government at Lhasa?

Ans. The present form of Government at Lhasa is nothing but a deceptive Government with all the power in the hands of the Chinese. We, the people of Tibet, will never recognise it.

Q. 11. Is your Holiness planning to travel to other foreign countries?

Ans. When the right occasion arises I may go.

Timoleague

Q. 1. Is more help needed to the refugees reaching India from Tibet, or are the present facilities adequate? How can the overseas agencies best help the refugees?

Ans. At present the Tibetan refugees reaching India are being helped by the Government of India. Any help for these refugees from foreign countries will be welcomed.

Q. 2. Does Your Holiness approve of continued resistance in Tibet to conditions which caused His escape? Is the Chu-Shi-Kangdruk or Chul-Ka-Sum movement approved by His Holiness?

Ans. All are in unity with the uprising for freedom against the Chinese Communists by the people of Tibet Chul-Ka-Sum.

Q. 3. Is His Holiness satisfied that the world press has given an accurate picture of events in Tibet, and particularly his escape and the events which preceded and followed it?

Ans. Uptil now I have noticed a lot of comments in the world press about the events of Chinese Communists aggression in Tibet and my escape, but much more can be said about the Chinese suppression and I hope these accounts will be subsequently published by the world press.

Q. 4. Can His Holiness now make a statement of His future plans?

Ans. At present I am not able to comment of any future plans.

Q. 5. Does His Holiness desire to appear before the United Nations Assembly to plead the cause of Tibet? If this is not possible, does He anticipate any action to represent Tibet's cause to other nations?

Ans. Please refer to Q. 4 of *New York Times.*

Q. 6. If it is not possible to continue the resistance movement from India, out of consideration for India's political position in relation to China, would His Holiness consider moving elsewhere?

Ans. We have not carried out any resistance movement from India.

Q. 7. Is it true that eight Tibetans who desired to leave India to carry on anti-Communist activities from another country have been refused the possibility of re-entry into India?

Ans. I have no knowledge of this.

Q. 8. Will the Press have access more freely to His Holiness and His advisers in order to keep the Tibetan opinion before the world in an authoritative manner?

Ans. I will certainly consider this matter.

United Press International Inc.

Q. 1. Are you aware of the fact that the Dalai Lama's Mother's bedroom is being used by the Chinese officers as office? Have you any objection?

Ans. More than using my family's residence as their office is the fact that the Chinese have taken by force and ruined tens of thousands of homes belonging to my people.

Q. 2. The Chinese have denied that they have destroyed the monasteries. But other reports said they have. Are you planning to make my protest to the Chinese?

Ans. It is a fact that over a thousand monasteries have been destroyed by the Chinese and more are being reduced to ruins even today.

Q. 3. It is a fact that your treasure has been taken over by Chinese by breaking open the locks? Have they offered to return your jewellery etc.?

Ans. The Chinese have not only taken my treasures after breaking locks, but have also looted the reserves of my Government, the properties of the monasteries and people.

Q. 4. Are you in correspondence with Peking? If not, do you plan to meet any of their envoys here and talk peace with them?

Ans. No, I have not had any correspondence so far.

Kyodo News Service

Q. 1. What are His Holiness basic conditions for return to Tibet if invited by Peking?

Ans. Please refer to Q. No. 2 of *New York Times*.

Q. 2. Does His Holiness think that some kind of Cultural, Political and Religious revolution is necessary in Tibet?

Ans. I certainly have the thought of making all appropriate reforms in Tibet.

Q. 3. Will His Holiness be pleased to accept invitations from Buddhist organisations in Japan or Ceylon to visit those countries?

Ans. If I am invited I may go when the right occasion arises.

Times of India

Q. 1. What was your relationship of policy matters when you were in Lhasa with the Chinese Foreign Bureau, and Panchen Lama?

Ans. I do not interfere in policy matters of the Chinese Foreign Bureau and as my residence is in Lhasa, and that of the Panchen Lama in Shigatse, the relationship was as usual.

Q. 2. It is suggested in certain quarters that the whole Tibetan uprising was sparked off by Khambas who moved westward into Tibet proper from the adjacent Chinese province of Szechwan following the introduction of land reforms and other measures there. It is argued that there was no interference by the Chinese with the autonomy of Tibet under the terms of the 1951 Agreement and that it was these "outsiders" who formed an anti-Chinese Movement and forced your hands. Would you kindly comment on these views?

Ans. The Khambas are Tibetans and not Chinese. Therefore people from all parts of Tibet are united to fight for their independence.

Q. 3. What is the position with regard to your status as Chairman of the Tibetan Preparatory Committee and Vice-Chairman of the National People's Congress? Have you received any communication on this or any other subject from Lhasa or Peking?

Ans. I have received no communication.

Q. 4. According to your information, where do the autonomy of Tibet Region and the Sino-Tibetan Agreement of 1951 stand today? What are the changes introduced there since your departure in political, religious and social field?

Ans. This has been referred to in my Statement.

Q. 5. What are the conditions in which you would be prepared to return to Lhasa?

Ans. Please refer to the *New York Times* Q. No. 2.

Q. 6. If your stay in India is likely to be an extended one, are you thinking in terms of settling down in Mussoorie or do you envisage a change either in terms of visiting other parts of India or abroad?

Ans. I have made no decision yet.

STATEMENT ISSUED AT MUSSOORIE
30th August, 1959

On the 20th of June last I was impelled by the steadily deteriorating conditions in Tibet to break my silence and to give to the world a glimpse of the dark and dismal tragedy of my people. I also made it clear at the same time that I and my Government were fully prepared to accept a just and peaceful solution of the entire problem. Since then, the picture of Tibet has become immeasurably darker and gloomier and the sufferings of my people are beyond description. On the other hand, there has been no response to my appeal for peace and justice. In these circumstances I have no other alternative than to appeal to the United Nations for the verdict of the peace-loving and, conscientious nations of the world. I also take the opportunity to make a personal appeal to all civilised countries of the world to lend their fullest support to our cause of freedom and justice.

Dalai Lama

19

Chinese Reply to the Dalai Lama's Statement

ON APRIL 19, 1959 Peking Radio broadcast the Chinese reply to the Dalai Lama's statement. It came as a commentary and was later circulated by the *New China News Agency*. The following is an official summary:

The so-called Dalai Lama statement issued by Indian diplomatic officials on April 18th in Tezpur is a poorly composed document which contains constrained argument and is fraught with lies and loopholes. Disregarding the fact that China is a unified country formed by the Han, Mongolian and dozens of other nationalities, the statement begins by clamouring about the so-called independence of the Tibetan people.

As a matter of fact the political and religious systems in Tibet were all instituted successively by the Central Government in Peking in the course of several hundred years from the 13th to the 18th century. Even the title, status and functions and powers of the Dalai Lama were not instituted by the Tibetans themselves. The so-called Tibetan independence in modern history has all along been the scheme of British imperialism for aggression against China and first of all against Tibet.

The fact that the statement begins with so-called Tibetan independence proves that its author reflects the will of the imperialist aggressors and has all along been fundamentally opposed to the 1951 agreement on measures for the peaceful liberation of Tibet.

To start with, the 1951 agreement asserted that Tibet is a part of the People's Republic of China. There is not a single sentence in the statement which mentions this point. This fact in itself makes it utterly impossible to believe the statement's claim that the former Tibetan local government "tried their best to adhere to the 17-point agreement."

The statement alleges that the 17 articles of the 1951 agreement on measures for the peaceful liberation of Tibet were brought about under the pressure of the Chinese Government; since the entry of the Chinese People's Liberation Army into Tibet, the Tibetan Government did not enjoy any measure of autonomy and that even the Preparatory Committee for the Tibet Autonomous Region had little power; decisions on all important matters were taken by Chinese authorities. The truth is that the agreement was reached after prolonged talks and full consultations between the representatives of the Central people's Government and the Tibet Local Government from late April to late May in 1951. After the signing of the agreement the Dalai Lama in his message to Chairman Mao Tse-tung in October 1951 said that the agreement had been reached between the representatives of the two parties on a friendly basis. The Dalai Lama also said that the Tibet Local Government and the people of Tibet, both ecclesiastic and secular, unanimously supported this agreement.

Since entering Tibet, the People's Liberation Army has adhered to the 17 articles of the agreement with complete faithfulness. No changes have been made in the existing political system in Tibet, nor in the original status and functions and powers of the Dalai Lama. Officials at all levels, both ecclesiastic and secular, performed their duties as usual. Religious activities and the customs and habits of the local people have been respected and the Tibetan currency has continued to circulate. The stipulations in the agreement that the Tibet Local Government should carry out reforms on their own initiative and that the Tibet army should be incorporated step by step into the People's Liberation Army were not carried out by the Tibetan Local Government.

At the end of 1956 the Central People's Government informed the Tibet Local Government that democratic reforms need not be carried out before 1962. In short, during the past eight years the political, social and religious systems in the Tibet region have remained the same as before is peaceful liberation. Almost all the affairs within Tibet were handled by the former Tibet local government.

In order to carry out regional autonomy in the Tibet region, according to the constitution, the Central People's Government set up in April 1956 a Preparatory Committee for the Tibet Autonomous Region with the Dalai Lama as its head. The fact that the Preparatory Committee did not play much of a role was precisely due to obstruction by the former Tibet Local Government, because they did not want regional autonomy at all. What they wanted was the so-called independence of Tibet which was desired by the imperialists. They were bent on their plot for sabotaging the 17 article agreement and proceeded from directing the harassing activities of the Khampa rebels to the all-out armed rebellion which they themselves openly launched on March 10th.

The statement did not give a single instance of the efforts made by the former Tibet local government to observe the 17 article agreement; nor did it give a single instance of violation of the agreement by the Central People's Government. The only fact it cited was the putting down of the rebellion by the Central People's Government in the former Sikang area in 1955. But the whole world knows the Sikang area does not belong to Tibet at all. Previously it used to be Sikang Province and was later incorporated into Szechwan Province. As is known it was precisely in the summer of 1956 when the Dalai Lama and his party were passing through Szechwan on their way back to Tibet after attending the National People's Congress that the upper strata of reactionary clique in Tibet hastily conspired to start a conflagration and directed the Khampas to stage a rebellion right away. They plotted to use the Khampa rebellion to cover up their plot for driving out the Hans and their so-called independence in Tibet proper. They overestimated the combat strength of the Khampas. Therefore, they made a quick decision. They believed that to incite the Khampas to stage a rebellion first was quite a wise step. The facts, however, were contrary to what they conceived. This rebellion was rapidly put down. In the battle to put down the rebellion there were of course some casualties, and some buildings were damaged. Apart from this there were no such alleged incident in which many lamas were killed and many monasteries ruined.

The statement also distorts the facts when it speaks of the course which the rebellion took during the period from March 10th to 19th. As everybody knows March 10th was the date on which the rebellion was launched. The rebellious clique chose this date because the Dalai Lama himself had decided to go to the auditorium of the Tibet Military Area Command of the People's Liberation Army to attend a theatrical performance on that day, and the request to attend this theatrical performance had been made by the Dalai Lama himself one month earlier. The statement does not dare to deny this fact outright but deliberately says in a vague way that the Dalai Lama agreed to attend the performance, and the date of March 10th was said to have been suddenly fixed. As to who fixed the date the statement does not dare to explain. In his letter dated March 11th to the Acting Representative of the Central People's Government in Tibet the Dalai Lama said quite clearly, "I intended to go to the Military Area Command to see the theatrical performance yesterday (meaning March 10th) but I was unable to do so because of obstruction by people, lamas and laymen, who were instigated by some elements and who did not know the facts."

The statement avoids mention of the three letters sent by the Dalai Lama to the Central People's Government representative. This proves that the author of the statement dared not state the facts.

The statement alleges that the People's Liberation Army sent reinforcement to Lhasa and Tibet before March 17th and that on March 17th two or three mortar shells were fired in the direction of Norbu Lingka. This is out and out fabrication. Those responsible for the lie have opened the back-door for themselves saying that fortunately the shells fell in a nearby pond. But if the People's Liberation Army wanted to attack why did it fire only two or three mortar shells which, moreover, fell into a pond and why did it not fire more shells after that?

The way the statement speaks of the Dalai Lama's leaving Lhasa also calls for attention. It says that advisers became alive to the danger to the person of the Dalai Lama, and in these difficult circumstances it became imperative for the Dalai Lama, the members of his family and his high officials to leave Lhasa.

This paragraph shows that it was not the Dalai Lama himself but the so-called advisers that thought of leaving Lhasa. This is a naked revelation of the truth about the abduction of the Dalai Lama from Lhasa. The Dalai Lama said in his letter of March 11th to the Central People's Government Representative, "Reactionary evil elements are carrying out activities endangering me under the pretext of ensuring my safety." Again he said in his letter of March 12th, "Yesterday I told the Kashag to order the immediate withdrawal of the reactionaries who arrogantly moved into the Norbu Lingka under the pretext of protection." This shows that after March 10th the Dalai Lama was surrounded by armed rebels and was abducted on March 17th. The statement does not dare to deny these facts thus making it obvious that all the talk that the Dalai Lama would like to state categorically that he left Lhasa of his own free will and not under duress is a deceptive statement.

In the statement there are all kinds of signs which make one doubt whether after all it is a statement by the Dalai Lama himself. In the first place, the contents of the statement completely run counter to the many statements and articles by the Dalai Lama in the past eight years right up to the three letters in the Dalai Lama's own handwriting dated after the occurrence of the rebellion on March 10th. Even in 1956 when the Dalai Lama was in India and was surrounded by the reactionaries he had certainly not expressed during the conversations with Premier Chou En-lai such viewpoints as catering to foreign aggressors, as those contained in the present statement.

Secondly, although the present statement was issued in the form of a statement by the Dalai Lama himself, yet one cannot find mention of the first person "I" throughout the whole statement. In fact the third person "he" is used throughout. This is not the Tibetan style of writing at all, but some European or some quasi-European style of writing. Certain phrases in the statement are likewise foreign. For instance, the so-called suzerainty of China was initiated by the British imperialists and British aggression against Tibet was carried out precisely under the cover of recognising that it called China's "suzerainty over Tibet". Such terms have never been used in the documents of the Chinese Central People's Government, nor in the documents of the Tibet Local Government. The present gang of Tibetan rebels has been completely fostered by the British. Indian expansionist elements have inherited this in glorious legancy from Britain. And that is why members of this gang were of a mind to join foreign forces from within our country with their faces turned towards India and their backs to their motherland. Some phrases in the statement sound very similar to those used recently by certain foreign publications and statements when referring to the rebellion in Tibet, such as, "The Dalai Lama is the spiritual leader of the Buddists" and so on.

From what has been said one has reason to suspect that the statement was not made by the Dalai Lama himself but was imposed on him by others.

20

From a News Conference Held by the Dalai Lama on June 20, 1959, at Mussoorie, India

Q. YOUR HOLINESS, from the reports you have been getting from Tibet, what are the Chinese Communists up to?

A. The ultimate Chinese aim with regard to Tibet, as far as I can make out, seems to attempt the extermination of religion and culture and even the absorption of the Tibetan race.

Q. How?

A. Besides the civilian and military personnel already in Tibet 5 million Chinese settlers have arrived in eastern and northeastern Tso, in addition to which 4 million Chinese settlers are planned to be sent to U and Sung provinces of Central Tibet. Many Tibetans have been deported to China, thereby resulting in the complete absorption of these Tibetans as a race, which is being undertaken by the Chinese.

I will give a brief statement on recent events as reported to me by my people.

The people of Lhasa (the capital), both men and women, have been classed into three groups. The first group is deported to China where its fate is not known. The second group is imprisoned, interrogated and punished without limit in various Chinese military headquarters in Lhasa. The third group is fed with the meanest food and driven to forced labor. Each is made to carry 100 loads of earth daily, failing which, no food is given.

Armed troops are posted in the streets of Lhasa, where no more than two Tibetans are permitted to converse and where only aged men and women are to be seen. The central cathedral and other places of worship are closed. In addition, the reserves of the Tibetan Government and the properties of private individuals are being listed by the Chinese, who are conducting an all-out propaganda for the formation of people's communes.

Q. An Indian report filed with the International Commission of Jurists says that 65,0000 Tibetans have been killed in fighting with Chinese occupation forces since 1956. Is that correct?

A. The number of Tibetans killed in fighting the Chinese occupation forces since 1956 is actually more than the Indian report.

Q. Is it true, as this report says, that a "deliberate and precise campaign has been conducted by the Chinese in Tibet against the Buddhist religion"?

A. The report is correct in stating that, until 1958, over 1,000 monasteries were destroyed, countless lamas and monks killed and imprisoned, and the extermination of religious activity attempted. From 1955 onward a full-scale campaign was attempted in the provinces of U and Sung for the full-scale extermination of religion. We have documentary proof of these actions, and also of actions against the Buddha himself, who had been named as a reactionary element.

Q. Are younger people being indoctrinated in Communism?

A. Yes, it is true that the younger generation of Tibetans is being indoctrinated and the policy of colonization is being practiced.

Q. What made you finally decide to leave Lhasa?

A. On March 17, 1959, at 4 p.m., two mortar shells were fired toward my residence, as evidence of the Chinese intention to use military force, and, although I had endeavored to keep up friendly relations with them for the last nine years, my hopes of rendering any service in the interests of my people by remaining in Tibet were finally shattered. Therefore, I and my Government had to leave for India secretly at 10 p.m. on March 17, 1959, with a view of rendering more beneficial service to my people.

Q. Did the Chinese attempt to block your escape?

A. The Chinese had no idea of my escape or else they would have certainly tried to intercept. They would not have succeeded in capturing me because of the unity of purpose of the people and the national voluntary defense army of Tibet.

Q. Is the revolt still going on in Tibet? Is any part of the country under the control of the Khambas (rebel tribesmen)?

A. As Tibet is a large country, there are still some parts where fighting is going on. However, there are several places to the east and north of Lhasa which are under the control of the Khambas.

Q. Would passive resistance by your people have gotten better results than an armed uprising?

A. Until the last day, I tried to bring about a peaceful settlement, the failure of which resulted in the armed uprising of my people who were compelled to fight for their freedom.

Q. Is it true that there are now Russian troops in Tibet, along with the technicians already knows to be there?

A. I have heard such a report but I have no clear information yet as to how far it is true.

Q. Recently you wrote three letters to the Chinese authorities in Tibet. What had you hoped to accomplish?

A. I wrote the three letters to the Chinese at a critical time when the lives and bodies of innumerable people were in the hands of the Chinese. This was a measure adopted in order to take peaceful action. When the circumstances in which these letters were written were brought to the attention of the world they could not have made any other impression other than to expose the measure of Chinese oppression.

Q. What do you think of the Preparatory Committee for Tibetan Autonomy which the Chinese have set up, with the Panchen Lama as acting chairman?

A. The Preparatory Committee for Tibetan Autonomy is nothing but nominal, with all powers concentrated in the hands of the Chinese. The Panchen Lama has no alternative but to carry out the orders of the Chinese. He has no actual power.

Q. Is there any agreement between you and the Panchen Lama as to what is best for Tibet?

A. The Panchen Lama has been under Chinese influence ever since his boyhood and has never enjoyed any freedom.

Q. Do you consider the 1951 treaty between Tibet and the Chinese Government still in force?

A. The Sino-Tibetan agreement imposed by the Chinese in accordance with their own desires has been violated by the Chinese themselves, thus giving rise to a contradiction. Therefore we cannot abide by this agreement.

Q. Could you define the "autonomy of Tibet" that was supposed to be guaranteed by that agreement?

A. The autonomy of Tibet is meant to be the right of self-government in internal affairs, but the existing situation in Tibet gives no rights whatever to my Government.

Q. How much support is there for the present Government in Lhasa?

A. The present Government in Lhasa is nothing but a deceptive Government with all the power in the hands of the Chinese. The people of Tibet will never recognize it.

Q. Do Tibetans still recognize you and your ministers here with you as the Government of Tibet?

A. Wherever I am, accompanied by my Government, the Tibetan people recognize us as the Government of Tibet.

Q. Have any Communist Chinese diplomats talked to you about Tibetan affairs since you fled Lhasa?

A. No.

Q. Do you expect India's support in solving your problems?

A. I hope the Government of India will give us the same support, if not more, as she has given to small countries like Algeria, Morocco of Tunisia.

Q. Is India placing any restraints on your movements, as the Communists claim?

A. The Government of India has not placed any restraint at all on my movements, and if the occasion arises I intend to tour India and abroad.

Q. Do you plan an international appeal—for example, to the United Nations?

A. In case I am not satisfied by the terms of peaceful settlement offered by China, then I shall consider my future plans.

Q. Will you appeal for arms on behalf of the rebels?

A. Although I have no intention of keeping the national volunteer defense army unaided, I am intending to help them by means of peaceful solutions rather than military force.

Q. Under what conditions would you return to Lhasa?

A. I will return to Lhasa when I obtain the rights and powers which Tibet enjoyed and exercised prior to 1950.

[From *U.S. News & World Report*, 6 July, 1959.]

21

The Dalai Lama's Press Conference

"THE TIMES OF INDIA" NEWS SERVICE, MUSSOORIE, JUNE 20

AT A crowded two-hour conference this morning, the Dalai Lama made a number of pronouncements of far-reaching importance on the future of Tibet and her people. Obviously to avoid any further misunderstanding, each word uttered today was spoken by His Holiness in Tibetan rendered into English by an interpreter.

By far the most important observation made by the Dalai Lama was his commitment for restoration of the sovereign and independent status Tibet enjoyed before the Chinese invasion of 1950. He indirectly accepted the suggestion that he was now heading a Tibetan Government of exile; wherever he happened to be accompanied by His Ministers, the Tibetan people recognized him as the Government of the land.

He refused to commit himself on his future course of action though his reference to the possibility of an approach to the United Nations and of Tibet seeking UN membership constituted an important pointer.

In answer to a question the Dalai Lama said that he was in favour of a "summit" conference between Mr. Nehru and Mr. Chou En-lai, the Chinese Premier, on Tibet if it could be assured that the recent events in that country would be considered in their true perspective. He agreed the attention of the world needed to be focussed on the Tibet problem.

The Dalai Lama confirmed reports that during his 1956 visit here he had himself decided not to go back to Tibet, But he changed his mind after Mr. Nehru had conveyed Mr. Chou En-lai's assurance on the subject to him.

Today's press conference began delightfully on an informal note. Emerging from his room around 10 o'clock the Dalai Lama mixed freely with newspapermen gathered on the Birla House lawns. He greeted each correspondent in turn shaking hands with every one of them. Many autographs were taken during the half-hour preceding the question-answer session. Tea and biscuits were served on behalf of His Holiness. In all 92 questions were answered and the press conference was rounded off with a long 1,500-word statement reviewing the events in Tibet since the Chinese invasion of 1950.

Throughout his meeting with the press the Dalai Lama maintained his composure and indeed, despite strong denunciation of the Chinese policies and programmes, his serene expression was not disturbed for a moment.

Pre-1950 Tibet

As regards the demand for the restoration of the Pre-1950 status of Tibet, the Dalai Lama made it clear that all the territories taken away by the Chinese must be returned to the new greater Tibet. He defined the new territory as embracing all areas where people of Tibetan stock were resident.

Asked by "*The Times of India*" News Service

correspondent whether to seek an independent Tibet at this stage did not constitute a rather "large demand", the Dalai Lama replied, "There is truth in what has been stated (by you), but if we make necessary endeavours it may not prove a large demand."

Recalling the circumstances under which the Sino-Tibetan agreement was signed, the Dalai Lama declared that they were forced to acquiesce under threat of military force and out of a desire to save the country from total destruction.

As an example of deception practised by the chinese, he disclosed that the Tibetan seal affixed on the agreement was not genuine. It was forged and fabricated in Peking by the Chinese and "continues to be in their possession".

It was clear from the start, he said, that the Chinese had no intention of honouring the terms of the 1951 treaty. They began undermining the Dalai Lama's authority, and then followed a reign of terror which "finds few parallels in the history of Tibet".

The Dalai Lama said he was prepared to submit the charges of loot, plunder and murder by the Chinese to investigation by an international commission and to abide by its verdict.

He confirmed reports that large-scale slaughter of Tibetans had taken place, particularly during the revolt, and many more had been transported to China to be thrown into Chinese military jails.

Simultaneously, the Chinese were colonising vast areas with their own people. Some five million Chinese had already been settled in Tibet and about four million more were in the process of settlement. In addition about four lakh Chinese, civil and military officials, were at present in Tibet.

The Chinese game, the Dalai Lama said, was to exterminate the Tibetan religion and culture and to absorb the entire Tibetan race into China. He had documentary proofs of the atrocities committed by the Chinese, who had also hurled abuses against Lord Buddha himself, describing him as a "reactionary element."

Fighting Continues

Asked about the latest news of the fighting in Tibet, the Dalai Lama said in many fighting was still in progress. Several places around and near Lhasa continue to be under the control of the Khampas.

He said he and his Government were not carrying on any resistance movement from India. He intended to help the Tibetan "by all means of peaceful solution rather than by military force".

In another context, His Holiness expressed the hope that Tibet would receive at least the same support from the Government of India as had been extended by it to countries like Morocco, Algeria and Tunisia.

The Dalai Lama had no intention of staying on indefinitely in India or unnecessarily embarrassing the host Government.

Return to Lhasa

The Tibetan leader said he would return to Lhasa only when "I obtain the rights and powers which the Tibetan had enjoyed and exercised prior to 1950," added *Press Trust of India*.

The Dalai Lama said in reply to a question that he had not received any invitation from Buddhist countries for a visit, but he had received invitations from some Buddhist organisations.

He said the Chinese had looted the reserves of his Government and the properties of monasteries and the people.

About the working of the 1951 agreement, the Dalai Lama said: "While I and my Government did not voluntarily accept the agreement we were obliged to acquiesce in it and decided to abide by the terms and conditions in order to save my people and country from the danger of total destruction. It was, however, clear from the very beginning that the Chinese had no intention of carrying out the agreement.

"Forced labour and compulsory extractions, and systematic persecution of the people, plunder and confiscation of property, and the execution of certain leading men in Tibet are the glorious achievements of the Chinese rule in Tibet," he said.

He added he had tried his best to calm down the feelings of his people and persuade the Chinese to adopt a policy of conciliation and friendliness. It was only when he failed in this that he left his country.

Outside Support

The Dalai Lama said the revolt in Tibet was still going on. The leaders of the rebellion were drawn from various sections of the people. They would welcome support from all countries in the world for the Tibetan cause.

The number of Tibetans killed in the fight with the Chinese occupation forces since 1956, the Dalai Lama said, was actually more than what the report filed before the International Commission of Jurists had mentioned, namely, 65,000.

He also described as correct what the report to the Jurists Commission had said about the "destruction of Buddhism". Over 1,000 monasteries in Tibet had been destroyed by the Chinese until 1958, countless lamas and monks were killed or imprisoned, extermination of religion was continuously adopted and from 1959 onwards a full-scale campaign was conducted in two provinces for the final extermination of the religion.

Letters to Army Chief

The Tibetan leader admitted having written the three letters to the Chinese Military Commandant in Lhasa before leaving the Tibetan capital.

The Dalai Lama said that the present Government in Lhasa was nothing but "a deceptive Government with all powers in the hands of the Chinese. The people of Tibet will never recognise it."

Giving a brief account of recent events in Lhasa as reported to him by his people, the Dalai Lama said: "The people of Lhasa have been divided into three groups, the first groups is deported to China where their fate is not known; the second group is imprisoned, interrogated and punished without limit in the various Chinese military headquarters in Lhasa."

All-Out Propaganda

"The third group is given the meanest food and driven to forced labour. In the streets of Lhasa, two Tibetans cannot converse with each other. The central cathedral and all other places of worship are closed. In addition to the reserves of the Tibetan Government all properties of private individuals are being taken over by the Chinese who are conducting an all-out propaganda for the formation of people's communes."

On the question of reforms being introduced in Tibet, the Dalai Lama said that his Government was not opposed to reforms but these should be in accordance with international practice and the traditions and customs of Tibet and the wishes of the Tibetan people.

"I do not agree to such systems of reforms as the people's communes being imposed on the people."

Replying to a question regarding the allegations made by the Panchen Lama that due respect was not shown to him during his tour of India in 1956, the Dalai Lamas said: "At that time the Government and people of India had extended both to him (Panchen Lama) and me the most cordial hospitality and respect but the Panchen Lama, having no freedom of will, had to make the statement he made.

"The Panchen Lama has been under Chinese influence ever since his boyhood and has never enjoyed any freedom."

In reply to another question, the Dalai Lams said the Government of India had not placed any restraint on his movement.

22

Statements to the Legal Inquiry Committee by Dalai Lama and Officials

I

Report of the Interview with His Holiness, the Dalai Lama, on August 29, 1959, at Mussoorie

The Chairman of the Committee, Mr. Purshottam Trikamdas, accompanied by the Joint Secretaries, Messrs. G.B. Pai and I.N. Shroff, interviewed His Holiness, the Dalai Lama at Mussoorie on August 29, 1959. Besides His Holiness and his official interpreter, Mr. Kalon Surkhang Mangchen Geleg, a member of the Cabinet was present at the meeting.

Q. 1. A. Chinese ambassador of the Chiang Government now living in the United States has stated that a Tibetan Delegation took part in the Constituent Assembly convened by Chiang Kai-shek in 1946. Is this true?

Ans. Regarding this statement: In 1946 Tibet had sent a good-will mission on the conclusion of the Second World War to India and China to congratulate the Governments of Britain, America and China. When that mission was in China the Constituent Assembly was in session. The mission was not deputed to attend the Assembly and they went there only as visitors. They had no authority and they did not sign any papers.

Q. 2. Was the Government of Tibet requested to send any representatives?

Ans. There was no request.

Q. 3. Do you mean to tell me that when the mission was there they were asked to attend as individuals and not because they had any authority from the Tibetan Government?

Ans. Note at all with the authority of the Tibetan Government though the Kuomintang Government was making false propaganda to that effect.

Q. 4. Were they there as official observers?

Ans. They had no official part in the Assembly. When the propaganda came to the knowledge of our Government they were instructed by telegram not to attend.

Q. 5. Is the statement made by Tieh-tesng Li that Tibetans were seated in the National Assembly in 1948 true?

Ans. At that time there was a Tibetan mission in Nanking. They attend without authority. They simply witnessed the proceedings but did not take part therein or sign the constitution. One of them is here.

Q. 6. I would like his statement and details of what exactly happened in Nanking.

Ans. That gentleman is in Dalhusie now. But his statement will be sent to you. One of the leaders of the 1946 good-will Mission is here. You can have his statement.

Q. 7. Is it true that five million Chinese have been settled in Tibet? If so, in which part and when?

Ans. These Chinese settlements must have started about ten years back in Tsinghai. Such settlements have been quite an effect on the local Tibetan population; the language and customs have all changed considerably. At the same time on the eastern side of Tibet also there was a settlement. Since 1956 mass migration started into Chinopi and eastern Tibet until in the end it became twenty Chinese for every native Tibetan. In 1956, again on the frontier of inner Tibet, there were large settlements. In 1957 and later there were large settlements in Gyantse. Then at about the same time the Chinese started settling down in centres like Lhasa and Shigatse. Most of the Chinese who have settled down are in Tsinghai and Szechwan in Greater Tibet and the rest are in the Chambo area.

Q. 8. Is it true when you were in Peking a prominent Chinese leader mentioned colonization of Tibet by nine million Chinese?

Ans. In 1955 just before returning to Lhasa had been to see Liu Shao-chi. He mentioned to the Panchen Lama that Tibet was a big country and unoccupied and the Chinese had a big population which can be settled there. No figures, however, were mentioned then.

Q. 9. In 1958, were figures mentioned by Mao-Tse-Tung?

Ans. Maybe, But regarding the extermination of religion, something was mentioned. The day before we left Peking in 1955, viz., February 12, 1955, we had an interview with Mao. He told us that religion was something bad. He said two things had to be considered: (1) that the progress of the country would be set back; and (2) that the population would decrease. He considered that a poison had been instilled into Tibet by Machus by propagation of religion, I made no comment.

Q. 10. How many Chinese have crossed the effective boundary since 1950?

Ans. The total number of Chinese soldiers occupying the boundary since 1950, was 140,000, who along with their staff would come to 180,000. This excluded common people. The number of these people cannot be exactly mentioned. In the eastern province the number settled would amount to about 20,30,000.

Q. 11. The population of Tibet has been variously estimated as follows :

(1)	Sir Charlse Bell	15,000,000
(2)	Later census	10,000,000
(3)	Mao's estimate	12,000,000
(4)	At the time of the invasion	3,000,000
(5)	Latest estimate	1,200,000

Whis is correct?

Ans. The actual population of Tibet is 7-10,000,000 in greater Tibet inclusive of Smaller Tibet. In smaller Tibet it was a little over 3,000,000 on a rough Government census in 1947. The bigger figure of 7-10,000,000 was estimated from this smaller figure.

Q. 12. The 1951 agreement was signed by then Governor of Chamdo. Was he an authorized delegate? I am asking because he was captured.

Ans. Yet, he was authorized.

Q. 13. Were the other signatory delegated sent from Lhasa?

Ans. They were sent from Lhasa. They were not captured.

Q. 14 Your statement at Mussoorie mentions that the 1951 agreement was signed under coercion. Was there any public repudiation of this agreement?

Ans. Up to March 10, 1959, the Chinese were incomplete control of Tibet and there was no public repudiation. On March 10 there was public repudiation and this was done by the General Assembly consisting of the officials and the pubic, mainly the public.

Q. 15. Where did this meeting take place?

Ans. This meeting took place at the Norbulingka Palace for 3 days and later till the 17th at Shol. The outward policy of the officials was that they would seek a settlement with the Chinese. Inwardly they were with the people. Officials announcement of repudiation was made on the 17th.

Q. 16. Under what circumstances were the three letters written to the Chinese and for what purpose?

Ans. The main reason for writing these letters was the situation of the moment. A peaceful settlement could only be achieved by sending these letters. The *kashag* also wrote two letters.

Q. 17. At that time was there any pressure on you to place yourself under Chinese protection?

Ans. They had not asked us to surrender, but they had suggested to us to come to the military headquarters and stay there.

Q. 18. Would it be correct to say that these letters were written to gain time?

Ans. Yes.

Q. 19. Did you think that you would be held a prisoner if you went to the Chinese camp?

Ans. At the time the Chinese General had asked, it was quite impossible to go because people would have prevented this step. We were also afraid that we may be used as a tool to make statements to deceive our people.

Q. 20. What was the immediate reason for the bombardment of the palace.

Ans. The first shelling on the 17th took place because there was a large number of people on the highway who tried to intercept the Chinese who were in the trucks and to frighten them the Chinese resorted to firing. The second firing took place because the Chinese were apprehensive that there were armed people in the palace and they did not want them to gain contact with the people outside.

Q. 21. Was there any ultimatum given to you to surrender?

Ans. There were two warnings to the effect that unless we and the *kashag* came to the military camp and took the responsibility of quelling the uprising they would start bombardment.

Q. 22. What was the immediate reason for your leaving Tibet?

Ans. The reason for our leaving was a message we received through Norbu to the effect that the Chinese General wanted to know where we and our *kashag* were staying and also the information that the Chinese were determined upon the liquidation of the population inside those palaces. The two shells were fired in the morning of the day we left.

Q. 23. Were you afraid that you would be taken prisoner by the Chinese?

Ans. Yes, and also our life was in danger. Of course in Lhasa they would not declare openly that they (the Chinese) dislike us. In 1958 in the province where we were born, they had forcibly removed all my portraits from houses and had proclaimed their dislike for us in certain places.

Q. 24. In 1956 when you were in India it was stated that you did not wish to return to Tibet because of the attitude adopted by the Chinese. Did you ask for asylum in India?

Ans. Yes, we had mentioned to Prime Minister Nehru that the Chinese were not keeping to their promises and that therefore we had no desire to return to Tibet. We went back because of the advice of the Prime Minister.

He also had a talk with the Chinese Premier, Chou En-lai, and Mr. Nehru told us that the Chinese Premier had promised complete autonomy for Tibet and that he had stated that the Chinese had made a mistake in eastern Kham and they would not again make the mistake of thrusting reforms on Tibet against the wishes of the people. So Mr. Nehru advised us to return.

Q. 25. Was there mass sterilization by the Chinese?

Ans. Yes. In 1957.

Q. 26. Where can we have information about this?

Ans. The information is being put in a statement and will be sent to you.

Q. 27. Was it on a large scale?

Ans. Yes. On quite a large scale. Two or three villages were completely sterilised.

Q. 28. Was it because on any bad disease like leprosy or venereal disease?

Ans. No, not for any such reason.

Q. 29. You mentioned in the press statement about reforms which you contemplated and the Chinese obstruction to those reforms. What happened?

Ans. The Chinese wanted to have the reforms in their own way and did not want us to forestall them to carry out any reforms.

Q. 30. What reforms did you intend?

Ans. We wanted to bring about reforms in land holdings, in keeping with the Tibetan circumstances and traditions which would have been better than what the Chinese are attempting now. The Chinese were opposed to these. So we did not proceed further.

Q. 31. What land reforms were contemplated?

Ans. They were first contemplated in 1954. The first one was to reduce taxation. The second was debt-relief.

Q. 32. Were the lands in Tibet held by small peasant holders? I thought it was mostly held by monasteries.

Ans. There are four types of land holdings: Government, private and official, monasteries and peasant proprietors. The monasteries held most of the land. We cannot give you the exact percentage.

Q. 33. Would this amount to land reform when the percentage of peasant holdings was admittedly small?

Ans. The proposal was to take away the holding of private owners and officials after allowing them to retain sufficient for their maintenance and to compensate them appropriately.

It was further contemplated to distribute the land to the actual tillers of the soil.

Q. 34. Were there reforms publically proposed?

Ans. They were not publicly announced. They were discussed with the Chinese who objected to them.

Q. 35. Can it be said that after 1950 nothing could be done if the Chinese objected to it?

Ans. Yes, except for minor matters. All major policy decisions had to be taken with their approval.

Q. 36. In 1952 the Chamdo region was separated and put under the Chambo Liberation Committee. Does it mean that it was separated from the Lhasa Government?

Ans. In 1952 the Chambo region was separated from the Lhasa Government until the establishment in 1956 of the Preparatory Committee.

Q. 37. Was any area put under the Panchen Lama's Government?

Ans. The Panchen Lama's Bureau as such had no authority. But the Chinese tried to create a western region under the Panchen Lama. It was the intention to divide Tibet into three regions, with the central portion under Lhasa, the western under the Panchen and the eastern under Chamdo.

Q. 38. What did the Panchen Lama's Bureau represent?

Ans. The Panchen Lama had been assigned large areas of land. He had control over those and enjoyed certain powers in relation to those lands. But he had to consult the Central Government in all important matters.

Q. 39. Why were 10 members given to the Panchen Lama as opposed to only 15 given to the Lhasa Government?

Ans. That was the Chinese way to divide the rule.

Q. 40. Were the 15 persons allowed to the Central Government freely chosen?

Ans. The names had to be forwarded by the Central Government and the Chinese reserved the right to refuse the names.

But in this case all were accepted.

Q. 41. Were they nominated by you?

Ans. Yes, through a special committee.

II

Written Answers by the Dalai Lama in Response to Question

Q. 1. Between 1911 and 1934 what foreign representatives were in Tibet?

Ans. There was only the Nepalese representative who had been there previously, but no other representative staying permanently.

In the year 1934 the Kuomintang Government sent a Chinese official Huang Mu-sung to pay ceremonial tributes after the death of the 13th Dalai Lama. He had applied through the Eastern Governor (Dachi Tethong-pa) for permission to come to Tibet which was granted accordingly. When the Chinese official returned to China he left behind a representative in Lhasa on the pretext on continuing friendly talks between Tibet and China.

We can prove that this representative had no voice in Tibetan political affairs. Since the Chinese representative remained in Lhasa, Britain also left a representative in Lhasa according to the Simla Treaty. In 1949 when the Chinese Communists announced the new Government in China, we suspected that the communists might consider the Kuomintang representative in Lhasa as their own representative. So we expelled the Kuomintang representative from Lhasa.

In 1940 when the 14th Dalai Lama was installed to the throne, the Chinese official (Wu Chung-hsin) asked through the Indian Government if he may come to Tibet by sea to attend the installation ceremony. He was permitted accordingly. He returned to China after the ceremony. The Chinese had sent two representatives to Tibet. Britain had also sent representatives to offer ceremonial tributes to the late 13th Dalai Lama and to attend the installation ceremony of the 14th Dalai Lama.

Q. 2. (a) How far was the Preparatory Committee constituted in 1955 representative of the Tibetan people?

Ans. The representatives of the monasteries and well-known persons in the preparatory committee were selected by the Chinese according to their choice.

Q. 2 (b) Who are those persons?

Ans. According to our view there are only 15 appointed by the Tibetan Government and the rest were all selected by the Chinese.

It was decided in Peking in 1955 that the Tibetan Preparatory Committee should be formed; it was also decided that it should consist of 51 members. These members were mostly selected and appointed in Peking, wholly according to their voice, and they referred to us the appointments to show that the Tibetan Government had been consulted. The majority of the people of Tibet were not asked or given power to select according to their choice.

The announcement that the 51 members had the right to decide important matters in the Preparatory Committee was only fictional. The Chinese authorities used full power to purpose and plan according to their choice, and we just had to raise out hands to approve their proposals.

The 51 members of the committee were as follows: 15 from the Tibetan Government; His Holiness, Tutor Trichung Rimpoche, Surkhang, Ngabo, Shanka, Nayshar, Gatang, Lobsang, Samten, Khemey, Sampho, Khandrung Talama, Phala Denchi, Tsipon Namling, Monling, Rongpal Lhun;

10 from Tashi Lhunpo as follows : Panchen Rimpoche, Chigigme, Lhamon, Talama Nyagwang Jinpa, Dangchin Lasang Gyaltsen, Delekrubten, Rimshi Hawa Pawathon, Rimshi Danthun, Khenchung Daten, Dhonkhang Sonam Tobgyal;

5 Chinese members: Chang Kuo-hua, Wang Chi-mens, Tan Kuan-san, Fan Ming, Mu Shung-chung.

10 from Kham as follows : Phugcha, Takyup, Phuntsog Wangyal, Visit Gyattsen, Achok, Pomda Tabgyal, Karupon Tsewant Dorji, Pomi Sonum, Har Gyalsey Sonam Gyaltsen and Riche Phugchok.

The well-known persons nominated to the Committee were Yapshi Langdon, Tamnyen Thubeten Nima, Telhun Tengya, Yapshi Tsering Dalma, Dedhuwa Khensur Sirchi, Khemsur Lhunthub, Gaden Taksob Trulku, Tashi Lhunpo Tutar, Tsaubu Karma, Sakya Dakchen, Monling Chung Richpodi.

In order to deceive the foreign people and the Tibetan people that his Holiness really possessed the status, he was invited to attend the meetings. The decisions on the issue before the meetings were really arrived at beforehand by the Chinese; so His Holiness had no power except to approve and sign. Similarly to other Tibetan members and functionaries high or low, big or small, had no power at all in the work of the Preparatory Committee.

Q. 3. Is it correct to say that the Chamdo region was detached from the administration of Lhasa and put under the administration of the Chamdo Liberation Committee? If so, were any protests made by your Government against this step?

Could you give some idea as to what the Chambo Liberation Committee was and who the leaders of that Committee were?

Ans. In the year 1949, the Tibetan Earth-Ox year, Communist China began its careful preparation for the aggression of Tibet. Their first move was the concentration of large forces of Kedo, Denkhog, Derge Kamthog, Ba and Yuman. While full scape preparation for this invasion of Tibet was being carried out, to gain time, the Chinese Communists sent Getak Tilku to negotiate a peaceful settlement. But this was only to deceive the Tibetans, for soon after, although negotiation was being conducted, they suddenly launched an attack on Danchokargon, looted the Tibetan Government's wireless station and forcefully arrested the two operators.

In 1950 in the 3rd months of the Tibetan Iron-Tiger Year the Communists attacked our patrols and killed Rupon Bangargpa of the Gadang regiment and many soldiers and militarymen of Shotu Thosium district occupying all the Tibetan territory in Denkog area. Then in the eighth Tibetan month Tibetan territories namely Chaksamkha, Samsar Erponang, Lhathop, Denkag, Derge Kamthak, Markham, Tsachu and Tsawarong were simultaneously attacked by large number of Chinese forces. Consequently, the Commissioner of Domey (Eastern Tibet) province sent a special communication to Nangchen and Ba stating that further violation of the Tibetan territorial integrity should not be committed. The negotiation between Communist China's ambassador in New Delhi and the representatives of the Tibetan Government, namely Tsichag Khenchung Thubeten Gyalpo and Tsipon Shakapa were being carried out. But the Chinese would not listen and continued their aggression slaughtering thousands of Tibetans; unable to withstand the Chinese pressure the Commissioner of Domey and his officials fled to a stage of one day's journey from Chamdo only to be besieged and arrested there. Their arms and properties were all confiscated and they were indoctrinated with Communist political songs.

Soon after the Chinese announced that a Domey (Chamdo) Liberation Committee was to be formed and all prominent personnel under the jurisdiction of Domey such as Chamdo, Daya, Pasho, Dzogang, Langdyong, Langan, Markham, Gojo, Tsalko, Derge, Denma, Lhathog, Richi, Gyatuen, Shado, Zetho, Shodzong, Palbar, Pomey, and Hortso districts of Tenchen, Setsa, Lhonem, Trido, Nagsho Biru, Arzabesog, Dachen and Sakzong were instructed to attend the meeting where they appointed the heads and members of the Domey Liberation Committee. Although a few Tibetans were appointed as subordinates of the Committee they were people like Pangda Zoggyal who had been but a rebel to the Tibetan Government. The election was made entirely by the Chinese and the question of public opinion was completely ruled out.

Following the formation of such a Liberation Committee were set up branch office of this committee where Chinese officials accompanied by forces took charge of administration in all these districts while all existing offices of the Tibetan Government were abolished. There were a few Tibetans as members of the Liberation Committee but the factual situation was that they had no right to voice their opinion and the whole administration was functioned by the Chinese. The people of Kham soon perceived that the Chinese. The people of Kham soon perceived that the Chinese general policy was completely to exterminate the religion and the race of Tibet, hence the people both lay and monk, unable to bear such in human deeds, are even to this day fighting against it.

III

Oral answers by the Dalai Lama to questions put by the Legal Inquiry Committee at Mussoorie, India, on November 14, 1959

Q. 1. Chairman: The Chinese have stated that in 1950 they came to "liberate" Tibet from foreign Imperialists. Could you tell me how many foreigners were there in Tibet in 1950 before the invasion?

Ans. There were only very few foreigners at that time. This question has been answered in a detailed form by me already, but I would like to add a few words here. The Communist Chinese claim in 1950 that they were coming to "liberate" Tibet from foreign imperialist powers was merely an excuse. The charge that foreign imperialist powers were functioning in Tibet was totally baseless and untrue. There were no foreigners in Tibet at that time except a very few who were officially under the Tibetan Government's employment, and diplomatic representatives of the neighbouring countries Nepal and India. These two representatives have been in Tibet since a very long time ago. There were also Indian Trade Missions at

Gyantse, Yatung, Thoengari (Gartok, Western Tibet). The Trading Missions has been recognized by the Tibetan Government under proper agreements between them and the countries of the Trade Missions, viz. India and Nepal. Besides, there were accredited Nepalese officers at Shigatse, Gyantse, Nyarong and Kyitung. These officers were known as "Ditas" and were authorised to look after their own subjects only. In every country there are duly authorised representatives of various outside states. In Peking too there are representatives from many countries. Does Peking Government consider those diplomatic representatives as "foreign imperialists?"

Among the foreigners employed by the Tibetan Government were two Englishmen who were serving as Wireless Operators. They were Messrs R. Fox and Robert Ford (the latter was captured in Tibet by the Chinese Communists during their military occupation of Tibet). Then there was Mr. Nebiloff, a white Russian, who was employed by the Tibetan Government as an electrical engineer. The remaining two foreigners were Heinrich Harrer, an Austrian and Peter Aufschneiter, a German. The former was engaged for the construction of some irrigation canals in the southern part of Lhasa, and the latter was employed as Chief Adviser for a new powerhouse project in Lhasa. The Chinese have been carrying on a great deal of propaganda regarding their work in constructing power projects in Lhasa. This was really nothing more than a continuation of the work which the Tibetan Government themselves were unable to do after, and because of, the Communist Chinese invasion. A large quantity of equipment for the power-house had been ordered from England by the Tibetan Government and had actually arrived before the Chinese army marched into Tibet and occupied the country.

Q.2. Chairman: In your Holiness' Appeal to the UN dated September 8, 1959, you state "First, they have dispossessed thousands of Tibetans of their properties...". According to Chinese sources very few Tibetans possessed any properties, the majority of them being serfs. Could you, therefore, elaborate your statement?

Ans. It is unfair and untrue for the Chinese Communist Government to state that the majority of the Tibetan people are serfs and that very few Tibetans possessed and properties. I do not mean to say that there is no poverty in Tibet; indeed there is, as there is poverty in many countries of the world, but the number of destitutes is not so large. The Communist Chinese Government have grossly exaggerated the number of the poor people in Tibet. Considering the population of Tibet, I feel that the number of poor people there will constitute only a very small percentage. Many Tibetans may appear to be in straitened circumstances outwardly, because they, due to the rough condition of living, the climate the terrain, are not well-dressed. Their shabby outward appearance does not necessarily prove that they are either poverty-stricken or are serfs. Some of these persons may be reasonable well-off. There was an instance of a very shabbily-dressed person actually having made donations to a group of almost 20,000 monks.

I shall briefly refer to the living conditions of the common mass of the people of Tibet. Almost every Tibetan engaged in agricultural occupation, however poor he may be relatively, has his the possession a minimum of 5 to 6 cattle and about 30 sheep. The land that is available to him for cultivation is of an extent that would give him an annual yield of 100 to 150 "khaes" of barely, approximately equivalent to 40 to 60 maunds (2-1/2 khaes are approximately equal to one maund). The well-to-do farmers obtain an annual yield of a few thousand khaes of barley and cash savings of about 10 to 20 thousands rupees in Indian currency. A Tibetan who may be commonly described as a "nomad" may possess anything up to 1,000 yaks and 10,000 sheep. There is no need for me to mention the living standards of the Government officials, the lamas, business people, "nomad" chiefs, village heads etc., all of whom are in a position to have a comfortable living. If China claims that the majority of Tibetans are utterly poor, then I would like to state truthfully that since about 1955, no less than ten thousand Chinese Communist military personnel and about forty thousand Chinese civilians have depended on the Tibetans for their livelihood.

Q. 3. Chairman: In the same document you state : "Third, they have adopted cruel and inhuman measures for the purpose of sterilizing Tibetan men and women with a view to the total extermination of the Tibetan race." Could you furnish us with details of these measures and the extent and areas in which they were used?

Ans. My statement regarding the Chinese Communists having sterilized Tibetan men and women is true, although these measures have not yet been practised in all parts of Tibet. Chuni (population 2,000) in Amdo province, is one of these places where these cruel acts were committed for so-called experimental purposes. The Communist Chinese adopted these measures under the pretext of preventing certain epidemic diseases. They administered certain injections on men and women in order to make them impotent. They also forced upon them certain other treatment to make the male and female reproductive organs functionless. As evidence of this we have about 10 persons among the Tibetan refuses in India who had personally experienced such treatment. The treatment had resulted in several deaths in Chuni.

Q. 4. Dr. Thompson: There is a difference in law between knowledge and belief. Therefore (a) is it possible to interrogate any of these people; (b) are you in touch with any of these people who can furnish information?

Ans. Yes. It will be possible to produce some of the men concerned from amongst the refugees for medical examination. Unfortunately, it will not be possible to produce any women as there are none among the refugees.

Q. 5. Dr. Mookerjee: Will it be possible to produce more than two or three with evidence as the particulars?

Ans. Yes.

Q. 6. Chairman: In your News Conference on June 20, you stated that five million settlers arrived in Eastern and North-Eastern Tso. Since when did this settlement commence? How could such large numbers be settled on land which we understand is far from productive?

Ans. I admit that technologically and industrially our country is very backward; but this does not mean Tibet is short of foodstuffs. In the matter of food we are completely self-sufficient. Until recently, foodstuffs were not included in our import list. Due to the high altitude and the cool dry climate to Tibet, we can preserve foodgrains in good condition for long periods, even 25 to 30 years. Because of the vast area of Tibet and the scanty population, food is only a minor problem for the Tibetan.

Chinese settlement in Tibet started a few years ago. They had no problem in feeding these settlers because they have confiscated large quantities of foodstuffs which has been stored by Tibetans in various parts of the country. It is true that 5 million settlers cannot all depend on Tibetan food stocks permanently. Therefore, these settlers have already begun intensive cultivation in the Kulmuk area with modern farming equipment. As for the meat, the northern parts of Tibet have vast resources of yaks, sheep, goats and wild animals. In the lakes fish is available in abundance. Tibet has sufficient potentialities which, if developed can easily yield food for five million people. There are several large areas in Tibet which are very fertile.

Q. 7. Dr. Thompson: What conclusion do you draw from such a large number of settlers?

Ans. As I have stated in my written statement, I feel that since the country is scarcely populated, such large scale immigration of Chinese will be dangerous to the Tibetan race.

Q. 8. Mr. Seni Pramoj: Could you give us the number of Chinese emigrants before 1950 and after 1950?

Ans. It is not possible for me just now to give figures but the majority of these settlements were between 1955 and 1956.

Q. 9. Mr. Pramoj: How did the settlers behave with the Tibetans? What attempt has been made to assimilate the Tibetans? In order words, did they bring their women or did they marry Tibetan women?

Ans. The Chinese have brought in both men and women and they have also tried their best to inter-marry.

Q. 10. Mr. Pramoj: Of the children deported to China, have they been indoctrinated and sent back or have they disappeared?

Ans. Some of the children completely disappeared, whilst some came back.

Q. 11. Mr. Chatterjee: Could you give the total number deported and the total parts of Tibet.

Ans. I cannot give the exact number, as the children were sent from all parts of Tibet.

Q. 12. Dr. Mookerje: Could you give us approximate figures?

Ans. To my knowledge about 10,000 children were taken to China. To give a particular place, about 3,000 to 4,000 were taken from Lhasa alone. Of these about 500 have returned and there is no news as to the rest.

Q. 13. Mr. Pramoj: Were they taken forcibly? What do the 500 who returned do now?

Ans. Of the children taken to China and majority of them were taken against their will. Among the 500 who returned are two classes. The majority of these are resisting the Chinese.

Q. 14. Dr. Mookerjee: Are they available to be questioned?

Ans. Yes, there are many in India and they will be available.

Q. 15. Dr. Mookerjee: Since when were they sent to China? In 1950 or after that? Has the number increased afterwards?

Ans. There were quite a large number sent in 1953 but since the March 10, 1959, their number has increased considerably.

Q. 16. Dr. Alafriz: Have you got any official Chinese documents, decrees, etc., to prove genocide or violation of human rights? Could you place it before the Committee?

Ans. Yes, I have got documents relating to extermination of religious rights.

Q. 17. Dr. Alafriz: Could you give us details of the revolt in February 1956? Was poisonous gas used by the Chinese?

Ans. In 1956 in Eastern and North-eastern parts of Tibet children and women were massacred. I am not sure of the poisonous gas, but I am still investigating the fact.

At that stage, the Chairman informed the Committee that Mr. Lukangwa, one of the leaders, has been addressed on the subject for details.

Q. 18. Mr. Chatterjee: What was the danger that the Dalai Lama expected?

Ans. Happenings round about the frontiers

and the happenings in Lhasa up to 17th March, 1959 led me to expect danger to my person.

Q. 19. Chairman: Were Communist "reforms" carried out or attempted to be carried out in any part of Tibet? If so please give us some details.

Ans. The Chinese Communists certainly attempted through every means available to them to carry out their so-called "reforms' in the whole of Tibet. They did not succeed fully because of Tibetan resistance. The Tibetan became aware, seeing the results of the Communist regime in China, that these "reforms" instead of improving their condition, would cause a deterioration in it and bring misery and suffering to them instead of supposed happiness. No doubt, the Chinese forced their "reforms" in various places including Eastern Tibet, Amdo, and Kham, to a great extent, but the Tibetans continued to resist.

In the first stage of the "reforms", every weapon including even kitchen knives were confiscated from the Tibetan of the area concerned, in order to prevent any armed rebellion. Secondly, every item of individual property such as houses, sheep, horses and other cattle, etc., were confiscated. Thirdly land was taken under Chinese control and "People's Cooperative Communes" were established whereby land was divided into various sections and tillers were forced to labour in an inhuman way. The labourers were not permitted to enjoy the fruit of their labour. All the produce of the land was collected by the Chinese and the tillers were given totally inadequate rations. The only reward which the tillers got for their ceaseless toil was empty name sand worthless medals. Fourthly, in the name of the "Struggle against Oppression" students were induced to beat up their teachers, children their parents, monks their tutors, and servants their masters. The so-called "reforms" did not in any way help the poor. They resulted only in lowering the living conditions of the richer people to the same level as those of the poor. The final outcome was that everyone, either rich or poor, found himself living in a state of constant fear and suffering.

Q. 20. Chairman: According to Chinese sources, the Chinese in 1956 decided that no communist reforms would be carried out for a period of six years. Is it a fact that as a result of this "reforms" were postponed?

Ans. It was stated in the 17-Point Agreement of 1951, Article 11, as follows:

"In matters related to various reforms in Tibet, there will be no compulsion on the part of the Central Authorities. The Local Government of Tibet should carry out reforms of its own accord and, when the people raise demands for reforms they shall be settled by means of consultation with the leading personnel of Tibet."

This agreement was violated by the Chinese Communists themselves. "Reforms" were introduced in Kham and Amdo by force where no Tibetans had asked for those reforms. Harsh methods adopted by the Chinese, drove the Khambas and Amdos into revolt, and the uprisings in those areas caused much difficulties for the Chinese. Fearing similar consequences in the 'U' and Tsang provinces into if Communist "reforms" were introduced by force, the Chinese authorities officially announced in 1956 that "reforms" would be postponed for six years.

Q. 21. Chairman: Could you tell us the policy followed there in respect of these reforms after your departure from Tibet?

Ans. My information is that since the events of March last my escape from Tibet, the Chinese Communist policy regarding 'U' and Tsang provinces has changed. Through the medium of a few specially chosen Tibetans, the Communist Chinese having announced that "reforms" would be carried out. There is now no question of asking for the consent of the Tibetans themselves. "Reforms" are apparently taking place. Everyone is suffering except the few persons who are under the spell of Community indoctrination. The personal properties of all those who are not under such influence have been listed and confiscated by the Chinese who have punished these people on totally false charges. The Punishments were in many cases death through torture. In other cases, the so-called "upper strata" people were subjected to beating by mobs. Some were exiled to China and others to unknown places. The majority of these people have, I understand, been sent for forced labour. Severe punishments have been meted out regardless of the sex or the age of the unfortunate people, whose suffering is indescribable.

Q. 22. Chairman: It was stated by Shri V.K.K. Menon, the Defence Minister of India, in the General Assembly of United Nations on October 22; 1959, that even now you continue to be one of the vice-presidents of the People's Republic of China. Is this correct?

Ans. In 1954 when the first session of the Chinese People's Congress was held in Peking, I was elected as one of the Vice-Chairmen of its Standing Committee. It seems that the Chinese have retained my name in the capacity during the Second Session of the Chinese People's Congress held in April 1959.

Q. 23. Mr. Bentsi-Enchill: May I take it that the Chinese operations in Tibet were progressively increasing?

Ans. Yes.

Q. 24. Mr. Bentsi-Enchill: Was there some measure of cooperation from the Tibetan Government?

Ans. The Tibetan Government tried to conciliate as much as possible.

Q. 25. Mr. Bentsi-Enchill: Did you find any Chinese authorities sympathetic towards Tibetans.

Ans. None.

Q. 26. Mr. Bentsi-Enchill: Concerning the removal of young Tibetans was the Tibetans Government asked to render assistance? Did they write any letter to the local Tibetan Government explaining why they want to remove the children to China?

Ans. In some areas the Chinese forcibly removed them. In some areas, they wrote to us to send this children through the Government.

Q. 27. Mr. Bentsi-Enchill: Can we see those letters or copies of them?

Ans. None of those documents are with us.

Q. 28. Mr. Bentsi-Enchill: What was said in those documents?

Ans. I cannot remember the details, but I can get everything recorded about what they indicated in the letters.

Q. 29. Mr. Bentsi-Enchill: Did they indicate the age groups?

Ans. No.

Q. 30. Mr. Bentsi-Enchill: When did they start Chinese settlements?

Ans. 1952

Q. 31. Mr. Bentsi-Enchill : Where there are Chinese Settlements in Tibet before 1952?

Ans. There were one or two Chinese traders in Lhasa, and some Chinese Tibetan.

Q. 32. Mr. Bentsi-Enchill: Did the 500 children return to their families? Did they intend to make them communists?

Ans. Some have been returned to their families and some worked with the Chinese.

Q. 33. Mr. Fernando: Are there any documents available proclaiming orders put out in public places by the Chinese Army?

Ans. I am not sure if I have understood the question correctly.

Q. 34. Mr.Fernando: Before the period commencing March 1959, were any decrees or orders posted by the invading armies in market places, etc., threatening consequences for disobedience?

Ans. Yes.

Q. 35. Mr. Fernando: Are the originals or copies of such decrees available?

Ans. No.

Q. 36. Mr. Fernando: Could the Committee then have at least the gist of such proclamations in the form of a statement?

Ans. Yes. I can produce the gist of the proclamation by the Chinese.

Q. 37. Dr. Thompson: Could His Holiness tell us about the Chinese Buddhist Association which is flourishing in China? Did the Tibetan monks agree with the views of the Chinese Buddhist Association?

Ans. This is a religious association in China. This association is only to make propaganda under the pretence that it had religion in China. For instance, in the monasteries in Peking there had been about 100 to 200 monks before but to-day there are only one or two left. So this association is nothing else but a communist front.

They have established a branch of this association in Tibet in 1956. I doubt the bonafides of the Association and its members.

Q. 38. Dr. Thompson: Has it a religious purpose?

Ans. I doubt whether it has any religious purpose. This association does not make any distinction between the Chinese and Tibetans. This association is a Communist front.

Q. 39. Dr. Thompson: Is it correct that the Chinese Buddhist Religious Association is Communist, whilst Tibetan Buddhists are not?

Ans. That is so, but they are increasing the Chinese Buddhist Religious Associations in Tibet.

Q. 40. Mr. Chatterjee: Was the 1951 agreement made under pressure?

Ans. That is true.

Q. 41. Mr Chatterjee: What sort of pressure?

Ans. It is better is one of the signatories who is here answers this. (A written statement was received).

Q. 42. Mr. Chatterjee: Are you continuing to be the Chairman of the Preparatory Committee?

Ans. The Chinese are still continuing my name.

Q. 43. Dr. Thompson: Could you give us some details about forced labour? In what conditions people had to work?

Ans. Some of the refugees who were involved will be made available for examination by the Committee.

Q. 44. Dr. Mookerjee: Please see the report of the Interview of His Holiness with the Chairman of the file. Are there any documents available about the destruction of monasteries?

Ans. Yes. I have got the documents about the extermination of religious activities, and they will be sent to the Chairman as soon as possible.

Q. 45. Dr. Thompson: The Chinese

Government says that the people involved in the rebellion were reactionaries and imperialists agents. Were people involved in the recent uprising? Had it any mass appeal?

Ans. The recent uprising was not an accident. People were suppressed for the last so many years. It was not instigated from outside. It has mass support.

Q. 46. Dr. Thompson: Was it instigated by the vested interests?

Ans. No.

23

Statement of the Dalai Lama to the Legal Inquiry Committee at Mussoorie, India, on November 14, 1959

MR. CHAIRMAN and Members of the Legal Inquiry Committee,

I am glad to meet you this morning. I have carefully studied the Preliminary Report on the Question of Tibet published by the International Commission of Jurists. It is a matter of satisfaction to me that the Commission has gone to all this trouble to place before the civilized world not only the aspects relating to the position of Tibet under International Law but also the events and facts that lead to my being compelled to leave my beloved people and my country in the hope and expectation that by doing so I might be able to seek and obtain justice against the terrible oppression to which my people and my country are being subjected at the hands of the Red Chinese conquerors. I thank the Commission on the admirable and substantially accurate statement of the case of Tibet.

In spite of the painstaking accuracy of the statements in the report, a slight inaccuracy crept in. At page 98 it is mentioned an agreement between Tibet and Mongolia. The gist of the agreement is correctly set out. It is further stated on the authority of Sir Charles Bell that the authority of Dorgieff whose Tibetan name was Tsenshap Geshe Ngawang Dorgi (his name is not mentioned in the report) to enter into such an agreement with Mongolia on behalf of the Tibetan Government was repudiated by the Dalai Lama. I am sorry to say that the latter statement is not correct. Dorgieff was an accredited representative of the Dalai Lama. He, is fact, was also the negotiator on behalf of the Dalai Lama at St. Petersburg at the court of the Tsar in 1906.

Since the 13th Dalai Lama formally declared the Independence of Tibet in 1912 till the invasion in 1950, there was not even a semblance of Chinese authority in Tibet. I want to ask the world through you, gentlemen, as to how long it takes for a country to be considered independent. Is not forty years enough, after the last vestige of a past conqueror disappeared?

I also want to refer to the statements. . In the last paragraph the Chinese version as put forward by Tieh Tseng Li is set out. According to this in 1946 Tibetans participated in the Chinese National Assembly which drafted a constitution and in 1948 Tibetans were seated in the National Assemblies.

The fact is that a Tibetan Delegation was sent to India which later on proceeded to China. The purpose of the Delegation was to offer congratulations to the British Government and to the American Government on their victory in war. This they did in New Delhi and thereafter proceeded to China for a similar purpose. During the time when they were in Nanking the Constituent Assembly was meeting and the members of the Tibetan Delegation attended some sessions as visitors. It is not correct to say that they participated in the proceedings of the Assembly, nor did any authorised Tibetan sign the constitution when it was finalized. Similarly it was not true that any authorised Tibetan representative attended the National Assembly as a member. The representatives of the Tibetan Government, Khendom Losum, at Nanking attended some of the meetings again as visitors.

I also want to mention the fact that the delegates of 1946 travelled on Tibetan passports. In March-April 1947 when the Asian Conference was held in New Delhi, Tibet participated as an independent country. Thechi Sampho Tsewang Rigzin and Khenchung Lobsang Wangyal represented Tibet. The Tibetan National flag was flown at the Conference. Our representatives attended on the same footing as those of other countries. This fact is well-known to everybody.

In 1948 again a Trade Mission headed by Tsepon Shakabpa visited U.S.A., U.K. and other European countries. The original passport of Shakabpa was produced before you, Mr.Chairman, and photocopies were taken by you. This passport of Shakabpa was issued in 1950 when he and Tsechak Thupten Gyalpo were sent as Tibetan delegates to proceed to China for negotiations, prior to the invasion by the Communist Chinese.

I understand that in this inquiry you have undertaken, you are mainly concerned with investigating how far there has been a violation of human rights by the Red Chinese occupies and whether there is any evidence to show that there has been an attempt at genocide.

I am not a man learned in law and therefore you will forgive me is my understanding of the term "genocide" is not accurate. As I understand it, it is not necessary for the perpetration of genocide to destroy the major portion of the population. It is enough if an alien power, by such things as mass killings, deportations and immigrations, so changes the face of the country that the people become a minority, if such a policy is persisted in, and their religionis exterminated, their culture destroyed and even their identify. In my News Conference held on June 20th, 1959 (see report page 200) I stated this was happening in Tibet.

As stated in that conference more than 65,000 were killed in fighting against the Red Chinese occupation forces. This happened between the end of 1955 to 1959. The Chinese Communists invaded Tibet in the name of "liberating" Tibet. Liberation has come to those brave countrymen of mine who died fighting in the cause of Tibetan freedom. The rest of my country is enslaved by a foreign power known for its ruthlessness and expansionists policies. The heavy casualties were largely due to aerial bombing of areas where the freedom fighters were active.

There was a feverish highway building programme in 1952-54. A highway between Kham and Lhasa, a distance of 2,255 kilometers, was planned. The labour needed for this was forced Tibetan labour. On a section 229 kilometers long between Lhasa and Kongpo alone 15,300 Tibetans were forced to work. This can give you some idea of the magnitude of forced labour on road construction work. Much other highway construction was also going on. From among the Tibetan workers large numbers perished and numbers of them committed suicide to unbearable conditions.

In the attempt to impose reforms, there have been wanton killings, often of individuals and on many occasions large numbers of vertiable massacres, in regions not readily accepting Communist China propaganda or resisting to be converted, with a view to terrorizing the people into submission. I understand that large numbers of refugees are submitting statements to your committee. I have not seen these statements. I am, however, confident that these statements will bear out what I am placing before you.

It has been reported to me that with a view to destroy the Tibetan race, sterilization of men and women has been resorted to.

Before my departure the Red Chinese have sent thousands of my countrymen to China by force.

Large scale settlement of Chinese has taken place in Eastern and North-Eastern Tibet as stated by my in the News Conference, and millions were proposed to be settled in U and Tsang provinces of Central Tibet. It was clearly stated to me while I was in Peking in 1955 that Tibet was a vast country with scarce population and China has a large population with insufficient land, so land and people should be exchanged. I understand that during the past few months this is being done on a considerable scale in Central Tibet. Once this is achieved my people will become a hopeless minority in my country.

Starting almost from 1956, there was a virulent propaganda against the Buddhist Religion. When there was resistance to the propaganda they destroyed monasteries. Destruction or looting of sacred religious objects, burning religious books; public humiliation, and imprisonment or killing of venerated religious leaders, large scale destruction of monasteries and dispersal of monks who were compelled to forced labour. Even Lord Buddha was not spared from vulgar propaganda. Several Chinese Communist officials openly stated that religion is poison. In the report an example of this has been cited. Such propaganda had become widespread.

(A) The report have been set out several heads dealing with the utmost seriousness and with all the authority at my command that every aspect of Human Rights has been violated by the Communist Chinese. I have already dealt with heads (a) and (b), part of (c) (h) (m) and (n). Perhaps in the statements submitted to you, you will find evidence of inhuman acts and torture inflicted one those who are unwilling to submit to the Chinese Communists. Such things were reported to me while in Tibet and on some occasions I had drawn the attention of the Chinese Communist authorities but to no purpose. I could only chafe under helplessness.

(B) Regarding (d) and (g) numerous instances have occurred when Tibetans have been turned out of their homes unceremoniously because accommodation was needed by the Communist Chinese for their troops, officials and officers, very often without compensation. Arbitrary confiscation for land, herds and other property became the rule of the day as the Red Chinese spread their tentacles over Tibet.

(C) Regarding (f), large numbers of monks were turned out of monasteries and forced to marry. Many of them were taught communist doctrine instead of religion.

(D) Regarding (i) and (j), Tibetans could only listen to Communist propaganda. The Mimang (the Tibetan people) in 1952-53 which grew in opposition to Communist Chinese occupation was suppressed and their leaders were jailed or deported. As stated by me in the News Conference, in Lhasa this year after the uprising no more than two Tibetans were permitted to converse in the streets in Lhasa.

(E) Regarding (k) there existed in Tibet a National Assembly representative of the various sections of the people. After the Red Chinese occupation such as assembly met only on such occasions as the Chinese wanted a ratification of their policies; which the Assembly had no choice but to ratify. As an example, the dismissal of Setsap Lukhangwa and Lobsang Tashi (acting Prime Ministers) which the Red Chinese demanded took place on an apparent demand of such an assembly. The last time such an assembly met was between the 10th and 17th March, 1959, this time not on Communist Chinese demand but spontaneously. This Assembly called for the repudiation of Communist Chinese authority and reassertation of Tibetan independence.

(F) As for (q), the only cultural life that a Tibetan could enjoy was such as that provided by the Chinese in their Communist propaganda, meetings and shows. Such schools as were opened were for the purpose of indoctrinating children and Chinese language was made compulsory.

Mr.Chairman and gentlemen, in this short statement I have endeavoured to tell you briefly the aspects of the question with which you are concerned. The chairman has sent me a detailed questionnaire. Answers to some of the questions have already been submitted and answers to be the rest are being prepared. The Chairman had a long interview with me and some of my ministers at Mussoorie at which various questions were also answered. I am willing to answer any questions you may desire to ask and also to send the Committee such further information as may be within my power to give.

It seems that events in Tibet concern the world at large and particularly Asia. For example, how is it possible for a person infected with a contagious disease to avoid its contamination unless healthy persons, for their own safety, help the diseased persons to recover? Moreover, it is possible for the healthy persons to be infected. There is no other way than legal and moral means of stopping inhuman acts in the world except by justice and peaceful means.

The world knows this and I hope your painstaking endeavour to bring in justice and fair play will be highly appreciated by the justice and peace loving people of the world.

I still request Mr. Chairman and members of the Committee for more thorough investigation and deeper understanding of what is happening in Tibet so that it may be conveyed clearly by the honourable members of the International Commission of Jurists to the people of the world.

May I hope that Tibet be restored its lost independence and the racial and cultural integrity of its people may be preserved in accordance with human rights.

Finally I want to thank you for taking the trouble to come here all the way and for listening to me patiently. I intended, as you know, to meet you in Delhi but circumstances prevented me from doing so. I am sorry for not being able to come down and save you the trouble.

I pray for peace and prosperity of the people of the world.

24

Speech Delivered by His Holiness the Dalai Lama at the Civic Reception given by the Mayor of Delhi, 3rd September, 1959

MR. MAYOR, Members of the Delhi Corporation, Ladies and Gentlemen,

When I had the privilege of visiting this illustrious crade of culture and cioilisation in 1956, I was-greatly impressed by the zeal, the enthusiasm and patriotic fervour of the people of the new Republic of India. But what was more naturally welcome to me was the kindness and the friendly feelings you showered upon me during my stay in this great country of yours. The great honour which you have done me this afternoon is an unmistakable evidence of friendly feelings which you all entertain for my people and I offer you my sincerest thanks. The relation between my people and the people of India go back to the very dawn of History, and we, the Tibetans, owe a great deal of gratitude to the people of India for the inspiration and encouragement which we had derived from their culture, their religion and their tradition. We are passing through a most sorrowful period in the history of our country, but I believe most firmly, that ultimately the truth must prevail. As your ancient and illustrious Scripture says, "Satyameva Jayate Na Anritam"—the truth must triumph and not untruth. I fervently hope that one day in the near future, the people of Tibet will be granted the opportunity of fostering and promoting the relations of friendship and amity which have always existed between our two countries. I thank you once again, ladies and gentlemen, for the great honour you have done me this afternoon.

New Delhi

Dalai Lama

25

Speech Delivered by His Holiness the Dalai Lama at Delhi, 5th September, 1959

MR. PRESIDENT, Ladies and Gentlemen,

This is an occasion on which I feel the barrier of language appears to be almost insurmountable. I wish I could speak to you in your own language so as to be able to give you a correct picture of my feelings. I have heard and read about the splendid work which you have been doing to help my people in their grim struggle for survival. It is your courageous efforts and your unstinted sympathy and support which are the source of inspiration and encouragement to the people of Tibet, who are confronting today an almost undendurable tragedy of suppression and suffering. I and my people are particularly grateful to your President and other members who are giving us so much help in these dark days of despair and frustration. I must therefore, take this opportunity to offer you our sincerest thanks. The relation between our two countries have subsisted for several centuries, and the bonds of culture and religion have knit us together at all times, whether of peace or of stress and storm. The noble endeavour which you are making on behalf of the people of Tibet offers the finest evidence of this time-honoured relationship. I have no doubt that whatever be our future, whatever be the outcome of the efforts you and I and all of us are making today, the relationship, the bond, which exists-between us will survive every test and ordeal.

I do not wish to inflict on you today any detailed statement on the tragic situation of Tibet. All that I wish to make clear is that since my country embraced Buddhism, we have been wedded to the doctrine of peace and goodwill. We have lived for centuries to friendly relations with all our neighbours. We have had no unholy desire for expansion of conquest. We have lived in peace and our earnest desire is to live in peace. The long and honoured relations between India and Tibet have always been on a friendly basis. Ideas and concepts of religion and culture have brought us together and cemented this relationship. We have also lived on terms of friendship and amity with the British Government in India. We have also had diplomatic relations with the Government of Russia. As early as 1901, a Delegation from the Dalai Lama was received by the Head of the Russian State. Cultural and religious ties have always subsisted between the people of Tibet and the great Russian people. We have had, therefore, no feeling of enmity or hatred against any foreign country. Even today we do not cherish any ill-feelings against the people of China. It is no doubt true that the recent happenings in Tibet have created the deepest feelings of hatred and resentment against the Chinese authorities in Lhasa, but the fact remains that we are peace loving people and cherish no ill-will or danger against any other people or nation. We are wedded to the policy of peace and today we are fighting not only for our freedom, but also for the peace of our country. It is for this reason that in my statement of 20th June I made clear to the world that I and my Government are fully prepared to accept a just and peaceful solution of the Tibetan problem. But our appeal has found no response, and the people of Tibet are continuing to suffer from inhuman cruelty and torture. It is in these circumstances that despite the advice which we have received from the Government of India, we have decided to appeal to U.N. It is our cherished hope and our fervent faith that whatever be the result of this appeal, the cause of truth and humanity will ultimately triumph.

26

Speech Delivered by His Holiness the Dalai Lama at the Reception given by the Indian Council of World Affairs New Delhi, 7th September, 1959

MR. PRESIDENT, Ladies & Gentlemen,

I greatly appreciate the honour you have done me by giving me this opportunity to speak to you very briefly on one or two aspects of the tragic problem of Tibet. Mr. President, I am personally grateful to you for the active interest you have evinced in this matter and for the earnest efforts made by you to arouse the conscience of the world. I am not a statesman or politician. I am not a student of international law. I am only a priest wedded to the dharma of peace and freedom and dedicated to the cause of the welfare of my people who have been entrusted to my care by Divine Providence. It is in this spirit that I propose to make a few observations on the grave tragedy which confronts today the people of Tibet. It is needless for me to emphasize that I have been prompted purely by the desire to help the cause which is nearest to my heart; and if in making these observations I have to differ from the views expressed by some great and distinguished statesmen, I do so with the greatest regret and in all humanity.

Ladies and Gentlemen, it is our firm conviction that Tibet was a separate and sovereign State at the time when her territorial integrity was violated by the Armed Forces of China. Several weighty arguments can be urged in support of this contention. In the first place, it should be remembered that no power or authority was exercised by China over Tibet between 1894, when the 13th Dalai Lama assumed reins of Government, and 1950 when the Chinese Forces marched into Tibet under the orders of the Peking Government. This fact is clearly admitted by the People's Government of China in the preamble to the Agreement of 1951, which was drafted by the Peeking Government and thrust upon Tibet under threat of further military action against her people. It is clearly acknowledged in the preamble that Tibet and the Tibetans have been outside the pale of the authority of China for several decades. In their note of 16th November 1950, to the Government of India, the Peking Government have implicitly endorsed this position. They have stated : "when the Chinese Government actually exercised its sovereign rights, and began to liberate the Tibetan people and drive our foreign forces and influence to ensure that the Tibetan people will be free from aggression and will realise regional autonomy and religious freedom, the Indian Government attempted to influence and obstruct the exercise of its sovereign rights in Tibet by the Chinese Government." This statement clearly shows that the so-called sovereign rights claimed by the Government of China had not been exercised by them prior to the invasion of Tibet. The Chinese authorities did not, however, disclose the source of such sovereign rights, because there is none from which such extravagant claims could be derived. However, whatever be the nature of the claim advanced by China, it is perfectly clear that during this period the Government of Tibet was not subject to any control by the Chinese Government. This *de facto* independence became legally valid and effective when in 1912 the 13th Dalai Lama issued a proclamation declaring the complete independence of Tibet and denouncing the Chinese claim to suzerainty. It is our considered opinion that this Declaration had the same effect in international law at the Declaration made by Bulgaria in 1908, terminating the rights of suzerainty vested in the Government of Turkey. This declaration, although unilateral, was accepted by the concert of powers which had previously recognised Turkish suzerainty under the Treaty of Berlia of 1878. Our position is, therefore, clear and unambiguous. So far as China was concerned, during this entire period Tibet was completely independent and not subject to any control by the Government of China.

In the second place, according to the best advice available to me, one of the essential ingredients of the sovereign status of a State is the right to conclude treaties with other international persons. If this be the criterion of a sovereign State, surely the Government of Tibet was in full possession of external sovereignty, for during this period they entered into as many as five international agreements. The first was the Treaty of 1856 between Tibet and Nepal which bound the Government of Nepal to render assistance of the Government of Tibet in the event of invasion of Tibet by a foreign power. As regards China, the treaty expressly stated that, "both states pay respect as always before to the Emperor of China". In other words, the High Contracting Parties acknowledged the nominal suzerainty of China as had always been the case since the installation of the First Dalai Lama. The second treaty was between Outer Mongolia and Tibet and recognised the independence and sovereignty of the two contracting States. Then came the Lhasa Convention of 1904 between the British Government and the Government of Tibet. This Convention expressly speaks of "the relations of friendship and good understanding which have existed between the British Government and the Government of Tibet." This was indeed a clear recognition of the sovereign, status of Tibet at the time. It should also be pointed out that under this Convention, the Government of Tibet engaged that without the previous consent of the British Government, no foreign power would be permitted to intervene in Tibet affairs and that no representatives of any foreign power would be admitted to Tibet. This provision was applicable to China as well as to other foreign powers. It follows, therefore, that even if Chinese suzerainty did survive the assumption of power by the 13th Dalai Lama, is ceased to have any effect after the conclusion of the Convention. It should also be pointed out that the provisions of this Convention were accepted by the Government of China under the Peking Convention of 1906. The next important international agreement was the Simla Convention of 1914 Article 1 of the Convention stipulated that the British Government recognized the suzerainty of China whereas the Government of China undertook to recognise the autonomy of Tibet. It was, however, expressly made clear that the suzerainty of China did not authorize her to interfere in the administration of Tibet or to convert Tibet into a Chinese Province. There was a further prohibition on the Government of China restricting them from sending troops into Tibet, or stationing civil or military officers or establishing Chinese colonies in the country. The Convention also continued the restrictions which were imposed on the authority of the Chinese Government under the Lhasa and Peking Conventions. However, the Convention, although initiated by the Chinese representative, was not ratified by the Government of China. It is, therefore, manifestly clear that no claim to Chinese suzerainty, much less a claim to sovereignty, can be founded upon the provisions of this Convention. As the Chinese Government did not ratify the Convention, the Article recognising the suzerainty of China was null and void and had no effect. There is, therefore, no international agreement under which the Government of Tibet acknowledges and recognises Chinese suzerainty. The position was made clear beyond doubt by the British Foreign Secretary in his memorandum to the Chinese Prime Minister in 1943, where he stated that the British Government were prepared to recognise the suzerainty of China over Tibet only if China, on her part, recognised the autonomy of Tibet. Since there has been no such recognition of the autonomy of Tibet by the Chinese Government, there is no valid international agreement giving due recognition to Chinese suzerainty. However, the point of paramount importance in connection with the Simla Convention is that the representative of the Government of Tibet was recognised by the Government of Great Britain and China as a plenipotentiary and accorded the same status as the representatives of the other two Governments. This is amply borne out by the preamble to the Simla Convention. There cannot be any clearer and more unmistakable evidence of the international status of Tibet. This was followed by the Anglo-Tibetan Agreement relating to trade regulations. Here, again, the representative of the Government of Tibet occupied the same position and status as a plenipotentiary as the representative of His Majesty the King of Great Britain. In the face of this clear and positive evidence, it is difficult to see how it can be contended that Tibet did not possess and enjoy international status before the Chinese invasion of 1950

I should like to invite your attention, Ladies and Gentlemen, to an extremely important question which arises in this connection. The Government of India contend that the boundary between Tibet and India has been finally settled according to the McMhona Line, but this frontier was laid down by the Simla Convention and this Convention was only valid and binding as between Tibet and the British Government. If Tibet did not enjoy international status at the time of the conclusion of the Convention, she had no authority to enter into such an agreement. Therefore, it is abundantly clear that if you deny sovereign status to Tibet, you deny the validity of the Simla Convention and, therefore, you deny the validity of the McMohan Line. On the other hand, if the McMohan Line is valid and binding, the Simla Convention must be valid and binding. And, therefore, it follows as a logical corollary that Tibet did possess sovereign and international status at the time when she concluded the Simla Convention. And if she did possess sovereign status in 1914, nothing happened subsequently to impair that status in any manner.

Ladies and Gentlemen, this is then the position which Tibet occupied according to valid and duly concluded agreements of an international character. Can this unimpeachable testimony be discarded merely because the powerful Government of China have advanced unfounded and baseless claims? I believe that the conscience of the civilised world will not permit such violations of the universally accepted principles of law and justice. In this connection I wish to bring to your notice another point of great importance. There is considerable confusion in the minds of people regarding the two concepts of sovereignty and suzerainty. I am advised that there are fundamental differences between them. Sovereignty signifies complete and absolute control. Suzerainty, on the other hand, does not necessarily imply the loss of the international personality of the vassal State. Thus, for instance, Bulgaria enjoyed all rights of external sovereignty while under Turkish suzerainty. She attended the Hague Conference in 1899 as an equal member with her suzerain, and took a decision regarding the covenant which emerged from the Conference different from the decision taken by Turkey. Similarly, Morocco and Tunisia concluded treaties with the Republic of France, while still remaining under Turkish suzerainty. This was also the position of Serbia.

Our contention is that Chinese suzerainty legally came to an end when the Declaration of Independence was made by the 13th Dalai Lama. Even if it be accepted for the sake of argument that Chinese suzerainty survived this Declaration, it is clear beyond doubt that the Anglo-Tibetan Convention completely deprived the suzerainty of China of all legal effect and consequence; and this Convention, as we have already pointed out, was accepted by China under the Peking Convention of 1906. Moreover, Article I of the Simla Convention which purported to recognise Chinese suzerainty did not come into operation as the Convention was not ratified by the Chinese Government. There was, therefore, no foundation for the Chinese claim that China was exercising her sovereign rights when her Armed Forces violated the Tibetan territory.

But this is not the whole story. Ample evidence of the sovereign status of Tibet is to be found in other indisputable facts and circumstances. Thus, for instance, in 1942 the Chinese Government pressed for the opening of communications through Tibet. As it was imperative at the time to do everything possible to bolster up Chinese morale and Anglo-Chinese relations, the British Government joined with the Government of China to bring pressure on the Tibetan Government. The proposal was stoutly resisted by the Government of Tibet, but eventually they gave in to the advise of the British Government. They, however, made it clear that they would only allow non-warlike goods to pass through Tibet from India to China in order to preserve their neutrality in a war in which both China and Great Britain were involved. This position was accepted by the Governments of China and Great Britain. If Tibet could thus maintain her neutrality, there can be no doubt that at that time she did possess and enjoy international status. Moreover, during this entire period of Government of Tibet had diplomatic relations with various foreign powers. In 1901 a diplomatic delegation from the Dalai Lama was received by the Head of the Russian State. Similarly, Tibet had treaty relations with Great Britain throughout the period. She also had diplomatic relations with Outer Mongolia and the neighbouring States of Nepal and Bhutan. It is inconceivable that a State which did not enjoy international status could have such direct relations with other States. Similarly, in 1948, a Trade Delegations from Tibet visited the countries of the United Kingdom, the United States of America and France, an the passports issued by the Government of Tibet were duly accepted by the Governments of these countries. The right to issue its own passports can only be claimed by a State of international status, and this fact alone fully endorsed the position which had been accorded to Tibet under international agreements. For these reasons it is our firm conviction that Tibet was in full possession of external sovereignty and, therefore, enjoyed international status at the time when her territory integrity was violated by the Chinese forces. The conclusion is, therefore, irresistible that the Chinese invasion of Tibet in 1950 was a flagrant act of aggression in defiance of all principles of law and the comity of nations.

Our position is that the act of aggression committed by the People's Government of China has not come to an end. On the contrary, the area of aggression has been substantially enlarged, and today practically the whole of Tibet is under the complete domination of the Chinese Forces. Dire consequences have followed. A reign of tyranny and oppression prevails over the whole country. Innocent men, women and children have been massacred *en masse* and are being daily massacred, to enable the Chinese authorities to achieve their objective of total extermination of the Tibet race. Crimes against humanity are being daily committed. Equally rampant are crimes against religion. Thousands of monasteries have been razed to the ground and sacred images and articles have been ruthlessly destroyed. Dispite these atrocities, I and my Government are prepared to accept a just and peaceful settlement, and in my statement to the Press on the 20th June last, I made a clear and emphatic appeal for peace and justice. So far my appeal has evoked no response. In these circumstances we have no alternative but to ask the United Nations to take up the consideration of the Tibetan issue which is already pending before the General Assembly. Our decision to appeal to the United Nations has received a great deal of criticism. I wish to make it perfectly clear that we are and have always been prepared but to accept any other reasonable remedy which might be available, at the present moment no other course is open to us, and I would be failing in my duty if I did not take every possible measure to assist my people in their bitter and grim struggle for survival. It has been argued that our appeal to the United Nations may not produce any immediate or practical result, but this does not and should not afford us sufficient justification for discarding the instrument of peace which has been evolved by the peace-loving nations of the world. In these circumstances, ladies and gentlemen, I make an earnest appeal to you, one and all, to lend your fullest support to our cause. I also appeal to the peoples and Governments of all nations to come to the succour and assistance of the tortured and oppressed people of Tibet.

27

Press Statement, 13th October, 1959

It is a matter of gratification to me that my appeal to the United Nations Organisation in connection with the terrible happenings in Tibet during the last nine years of Chinese occupation and the horrors which are being daily perpetrated in Tibet by the Chinese occupies in the name of liberation and progress, has not gone unheeded by the World Organisation.

I wish to express my sincere thanks to Irehand and Malaya for taking up the cause of my country and moving for the inscription of the question of Tibet on the agenda of the U.N. Assembly.

I also thank the Steering Committee for voting the inscription and the distinguished representatives of the many countries who expressed their sympathies and concern over happenings in my country.

I am also deeply grateful to the General Assembly for having accepted the Steering Committee's recommendation and decided to debate the question of Tibet. To all those countries whose support has made this possible. I extend my renewed thanks.

It would be less than human on my part if I did not express the hope that when the question is debated by the Assembly, my appeal would be considered in all its aspects and that the august Assembly will take or recommend appropriate measures to alleviate the terrible travail of my country and people whose very existence is at present in peril.

Dalai Lama

28

Speech at the National Press Club, Washington Delivered by Mr. Gyalo Thondup, Representative of His Holiness the Dalai Lama of Tibet, 30th October, 1959

Mr. President, Ladies and Gentlemen,

I greatly appreciate the honour you have done me by inviting me to be in your midst today and to speak to you regarding the grim tragedy which confronts the people of Tibet.

Ever since the violation of the territorial integrity of Tibet by the Chinese armed forces under instructions from the Peking Government, every effort has been made by His Holiness, the Dalai Lama, to arrive at a peaceful settlement of the complex problem. The Agreement of 1951 which was forced upon the Government of Tibet at the point of the bayonet did purport to recognise the position and status of the Dalai Lama and the internal autonomy of the Government of Tibet. Although this agreement seriously affected the status which Tibet had enjoyed for a period of 50 years, the Government and people of Tibet were obliged to accept the agreement under duress. However, soon after the agreement had been signed under compulsion by the Tibetan representatives the real objective of the Communist Government of China began to emerge. It was clearly evident from the very beginning that the primary purpose of the Chinese authorities was to exterminate the people of Tibet. Thus began a nightmare of massacre and oppression which finds few parallels in the history of the world. The spontaneous upsurge of the people which directly resulted from these atrocities was ruthlessly suppressed. These tragic events placed the Dalai Lama, in an increasingly embarrassing position, and his efforts to maintain peace and tranquility in the country were deliberately frustrated by the Chinese authorities. It is in these circumstances that the Dalai Lama was compelled to leave his country and seek asylum in India. Since then the policy of persecution, and oppression has been continued with increasing vigour, and the people of Tibet are groaning under an unbearable burden. His Holiness has made repeated appeals for a just and peaceful solution but these personal appeals have been completely ignored. Consequently the only remedy which was available to the Government of Tibet was to appeal to the United Nations for the active support of the peace-loving nations of the world.

The people of Tibet owe a deep debt of gratitude to the distinguished representatives of the Malayan Federation and the Irish Republic for placing the entire Tibetan Question before the General Assembly of the United Nations. They are also sincerely grateful to all those members of the United Nations who have readily come forward to give their fullest support to the Tibetan cause. The resolution passed by the General Assembly has endorsed the views repeatedly expressed by His Holiness the Dalai Lama. It will, I am sure, be a source of encouragement and inspiration to all my countrymen who are engaged in the grim struggle for regaining their peace and freedom. I must honestly admit that the resolution does indeed fall short of our expectations in so far as it does not provide for any positive action for restoring the freedom and liberty of the people of Tibet. Nevertheless, His Holiness the Dalai Lama has welcomed it as it is an unmistakable acknowledgement on the part of all peace-loving nations of the world of the tragic situation which exists in Tibet today. We also hope that in the near future it will be possible for the members of the United Nations to initiate measures of mediation and conciliation for the settlement of the entire Tibetan problems.

There are, however, two aspects of the Tibetan Question which I should like to emphasize. In the first place, I must honestly confess that I have been gently surprised to find so much ignorance and misunderstanding regarding the exact status of Tibet from the point of view of international relations. For instance, the Soviet delegate to the United Nations recently asserted that "for centuries Tibet has been inseparable part of the Chinese State." May I respectfull point out that nothing could be further from the truth. The Soviet delegate has not only ignored the history of his own country but has also conveniently forgotten that both Russian and Mongolia have in the past treated Tibet as a separate and sovereign State and dealt with her on a footing of equality. Thus, for instance, in 1901 a diplomatic delegation from the Dalai Lama was received by the Head of the Russian State. Similarly Mongolia entered into a treaty with Tibet recognising her independence and sovereignty. Moreover, under the treaty concluded between Russia and Great Britain in 1907, the Government of Russia, while recognising Chinese sovereignty over Tibet, accepted as binding the Anglo-Tibetan Convention of 1904, and this convention, it should be remembered, placed China, inspite of her sovereignty, in the same position as any other foreign State so far as Tibet was concerned. The sovereign status of Tibet was also accepted by the Government of China at the conference held in 1913 at which the Tibetan plenipotentiary was accorded the same status as the representatives of the Governments of Great Britain and China. It was also recognised by the Government of China when, during the Second World War, the Government of Tibet refused to allow any warlike materials to pass through their territory from India to China so as to maintain and preserve her neutrality. The sovereign status of Tibet has also been acknowledged by the Government of Great Britain in the treaties concluded by them with the Government of Tibet as well as in the dealings between the two Governments. The Government of Great Britain had, therefore, maintained a diplomatic representative at Lhasa until the transfer of power in India in 1947. The present Government of India also accepted this position and continued to maintain a diplomatic representative at Lhasa after India became independent. Similar representatives were sent by the neighbouring States of Nepal and Bhutan. The international position of Tibet was also recognised by the governments of other countries like the United States, France and Italy when in 1948 they accepted the passports issued by the Government of Tibet in favour of their trade delegation visiting these countries. Indeed, in the so-called agreement of 1951 the Communist Government of China have themselves admitted that Tibet had been outside Chinese jurisdiction and authority for several decades, and this admission categorically belies the assertion now made by the Soviet delegate. The indisputable facts clearly establish that the violation of the territorial integrity of Tibet by the Chinese Communists in 1950 was a flagrant act of aggression.

Secondly, as you are no doubt aware, the Dalai Lama also sought the intervention of the United Nations on the ground of flagrant breaches of human rights by the Chinese authorities in Tibet. These charges have been set forth in His Holiness' appeal and have also been examined by the Commission of International Jurist in their first report. The question is being further examined by the commission and their final report will be available in the near future. His Holiness has repeatedly pointed out that we-Buddhists are wedded to the doctrine of peace, and our only desire is to live in peace and freedom as we did in the past before the Chinese invasion. We have not, therefore, come here to carry on a hostile propaganda against the Communist Government of China. All that we want is a just and peaceful settlement, and I shall, therefore, refrain from commenting on the various breaches of human rights which have been committed by the Chinese authorities in Tibet. There is, however, one point which I should like to bring to your notice. Atrocities and inhuman persecutions in Tibet have not yet come to an end. In a statement which His Holiness issued after his arrival in India he made the suggestion that if the Chinese authorities were not prepared to accept the charges made against them, they should agree to the appointment of an international commission to investigate these charges on the spot. So far there has been no response to this suggestion. On the other hand, the Soviet delegate has now boldly claimed that these charges are more "congeries of specially invented, fabricated and utterly unfounded allegations". Therefore, I take this opportunity to make a personal appeal to him that if he believes that these allegations are unfounded he should welcome the appointment of an international commission for investigation and persuade the Communist Government of China to agree to the proposal made by the Dalai Lama. We, on our part, are prepared to accept the verdict of such an impartial tribunal.

In the course of the discussion of the Tibetan question in the Steering Committee of the General Assembly certain disparaging observations were also made by the representative of the Soviet Union. These have come as a great surprise to me, as they were based merely on the propaganda of the Communist Government of China and have no foundation whatsoever. I was all the more surprised as the people of Tibet have no quarrel with the people of Russia. They have long had cultural and historical relations with various communities of the Soviet Union. They have had diplomatic relations with the Russian Government in the past. They did not, therefore, expect to hear from the representative of the Soviet Union such uncharitable and baseless observations. It has, therefore, become necessary for me to examine these allegations. In the first place, it is not correct to assert that and kind of serfdom exists in Tibet. It is true that ours is an ancient society and its time-honoured traditions and customs have survived because we have lived in complete isolation for several centuries. The system of land tenure obtaining in Tibet is, therefore, feudal in character. This does not, however, mean the laws of Tibet recognise any form of serfdom. On the contrary, every family in Tibet owned and cultivated its own plot of land, however small it might have been. The family was not required to pay any rent but had to place the services of one member at the disposal of the landlord, either as a domestic help or as a cultivator of the land. The other members of the family were free to follow any profession or calling. The rights which is peasant possessed under this system were well protected, for he was entitled to appeal to the Central Government at Lhasa against the decision of his superior landlord. It must be admitted that this system had worked well in the past, but the Dalai Lama was fully aware of the difficulties and hardships which such a system entailed. It was for this reason that he proposed as soon as he assumed the reins of Government that the system of land tenure should be reorganised and all large estates in the possession of private individuals or monasteries should be acquired on payment of compensation and distributed amongst the actual cultivators of land. But this just and reasonable proposal could not be brought into force because of the obstructive attitude of the Chinese authorities.

A great deal has also been said in the recent discussions in the United Nations about the reforms introduced by the Chinese authorities. It must, therefore, be pointed out that for a period of nine years the Chinese Communists did not introduce any measure for the improvement of the economic or social conditions of the people of Tibet. On the contrary, every attempt made by His Holiness to improve the standard of living of the people of Tibet was steadfastly resisted by the Chinese authorities. Indeed, if we were to examine carefully the record of Chinese achievements in Tibet, it would present a sorry spectacle of the total disregard of the needs and demands of the people. The reforms introduced by the Chinese authorities were these: dispossession of all Tibetans, whether landlords or tenants, of their immovable properties, leading to death and starvation; compulsory exaction of labour without any payment; and the settlement of considerable number of Chinese colonists on lands previously belonging to the Tibetans. These so-called reforms have naturally brought about circumstances in which it has become impossible for the Tibetans to struggle for their survival. In this connection I must briefly refer to the reforms which the Dalai Lama attempted to introduce soon after his assumption of power. I have already spoken about the changes which His Holiness wanted to bring about in the system of land tenure. A special organisation was also created by His Holiness for the purpose of introducing other far-reaching and necessary changes. A system of democratic government has always existed in Tibet, and the National Assembly has always been composed of representatives of all classes and communities in the State. Although its sessions were held only at intervals, the Assembly has exercised considerable influence in the hoping of the policies of the Government, particularly in regard to matters of importance to the people. It was His Holiness' intention that the National Assembly should be reorganised on a broader basis and given every opportunity to work for the benefit of the people. But these reforms could not be carried into effect, because the Chinese authorities adopted an attitude of obstruction and did not desire that His Holiness's Government should introduce any measure for the improvement of the social, economic and political condition of the people of Tibet.

Ladies and gentlemen, this is a brief but unvarnished statement of our position and of the conditions which prevail in Tibet. I hope, I have been able to give you a clear picture not only of the existing situation in Tibet but also of our aims and purposes.

The press of the world has rendered a great service to the people of Tibet in their grim struggle for survival. I am therefore taking this opportunity to appeal to you to lend us once again your fullest support and assistance. The people and Government of the United states of America have always fought and fought hard for the freedom of the small nations of the world. We are all fully aware of what you have done for the self-determination of various peoples, and recognising your earnest efforts in the behalf, we have come to you, to seek, not only your sympathy, but also your active support for the people of Tibet who are living today under a reign of tyranny and terror.

29

Statement of His Holiness the Dalai Lama on the 2nd Anniversary of the Tibetan People's National Uprising Day of 10th March, 1959

(MARCH 10, 1961)

ON THE 10th of March 1959 the Tibetan people reasserted their independence suffering almost nine years of foreign domination. Foreign rule, alas, still continues in Tibet but I know that I am proud to know that the spirit of our people remains uncrushed in their resolve to fight on till independence is regained unshaken. I know that the struggle which began a few years ago is still being waged in Tibet against the invader and the oppressor who masquerades under the name and guise of 'liberator'. I can confidently assert that the civilised world is, every day, becoming more and more aware of those, who, in the name of liberation, are crushing out the freedom of defenceless neighbours.

The world has been made aware of the terrible happenings in Tibet by the two illuminating reports of the International Commission of Jurists. These reports have pointed out that the Chinese have, ruthlessly, trumpeted on the elementary Human Rights of our people, that thousands of our people have been killed for the only reason that they asserted their right to live in the manner they desired to do, following their cultural and religious heritage. The reports have further point out that the Chinese have been guilty of genocide by reason of their killing many Tibetans with the intent of destroying the Tibetan religion and by deporting thousands of children to China.

The sympathy aroused in the world was evidence by the fact that the United Nations by their Resolution in 1959 appealed for the cessation of practices depriving the Tibetan people of their fundamental Human rights and their traditional autonomy. I assert that it is now autonomy but independence of which we have been deprived. Anyway, so far as the Chinese are concerned, the appeal fell on deaf ears. Things have become worse as is clear from the steady and unceasing flow of refugees from Tibet.

As further evidence of that sympathy, we had in new Delhi in April 1960, a Convention by the representatives of 19 nations, convened by the respected Indian leader, Shri Jayaprakash Narayan. This Convention brought to the notice of the world the happenings in Tibet. The Afro-Asian Council, established by the Convention, sent its representatives to New York to support the Tibetan appeal in World Assembly in 1960. On behalf of the Tibetan people, I express my sincere thanks to the Afro-Asian Council for the great interest they have taken in our cause and the valuable help they have rendered. I am glad to learn that the Council is deputing Shri Purshottam Trikamdas to be in New York when the Assembly reconvenes.

Shortly the Question of Tibet will come up for discussion in the plenary session of the U.N. Assembly. I appeal to our sponsors and to the Assembly to get the Chinese to vacate their aggression and to help restore the independence of Tibet. Any half measures will be of little avail. Our gratitude is due to the federation of Malaya, Thailand, Ireland and E1 Salvador for sponsoring our cause. May I appeal to India, our great neighbour, which has given refuge to thousands of us, to lend its powerful support to our cause.

Recently the United Nations passed a resolution on the declaration of the grant of Independence to colonial possessions. Our country, which was till recently independent, has been reduced to the status of a colonial possession. We cannot in any event be denied the right to self-determination.

I am aware that the Tibetan people, inside Tibet, are undergoing the travail, that foreign rule brings in its wake. I appeal to them to keep up their spirit and their resolve to regain their independence. On my part, I need hardly say, I am far from happy to be away from my country and my beloved and brave people. I want to tell them that I share with them their hopes and their agony.

To the thousands of my countrymen in India. Nepal, Bhutan and Sikkim, I want to say that a heavy responsibility devolves on all of us to prepare ourselves for the day when we can return to our country and build and greater independent Tibet. New Tibet will need thousands of trained and skilled men and women, necessary to bring Tibet in consonance with the spirit of democracy without losing our cultural and religious heritage or our soul.

During the Chinese occupation before I was compelled by circumstances to leave Tibet, the Kashag and myself made efforts to introduce land and other reforms in Tibet but as is well-known our efforts were blocked by the Chinese. The Communists are today forcing what they call reforms down the throats of our people. I have given careful consideration to these so-called reforms and I have come to the conclusion that at the end of the reforms the Tibetan people will be reduced to the state of mental and economic serfdom.

Such reforms are not is consonance with the Charter of the U.N. nor with the Universal Declaration of Human Rights. The reforms that I visualise must, while preserving the intellectual, moral and religious freedom, bring about an equitable distribution of the wealth of the country. In this connection I shall repeat what I said sometime back in Dalhosie: "In order to make Tibet a rich, strong and vigorous nation, the special privileges and the large estates enjoyed, whether by monasteries or the aristorcratic families, will have to go and every one will have to learn to live with the help the common people." I further said, "changes must come in all sphereds. The government structure will also have to undergo far-reaching reforms so that the people are more intimately associated with the policies of the government and the administration of the country. The task and responsibility of establishing improved political and religious institutions lies upon all of us."

I am preparing a draft of the constitutional and economic structure, which I visualise for our country and I shall place it shortly before the representatives of the Tibetan people in India and the neighbouring countries for their consideration. Ultimately it will be the whole Tibetan people who will have no decide.

The world has been very rightly concerned by recent murders in the Congo. I join my voice in condemning these murders whether in the Congo or in Algeria or elsewhere. I would, however, ask the world not to forget that thousands of Tibetans have been and are being killed for the only reason that they refused to accept f eign domination.

I want to remind my countrymen inside and outside Tibet that God's ways are inscrutable and the travail of Tibet cannot be to no purpose. The cause of Truth and Justice must prevail and our of this night of horror and suffering a bright day for Tibet and its people is bound to drawn.

I want to express my deep gratitude to India, Bhutan, Sikkim and Nepal for the hospitality and the kindness which we have received from these neighbours of ours. I must also express my gratitude to the various international and Indian institutions and individuals, who have given generous aid for the relief of our refugees. Since refugees are still pouring in I shall appeal to everyone to continue to help us in the same generous way they have done so far.

Finally I request my people to join me in my prayer for peace in the world.

30

Statement of His Holiness the Dalai Lama on the 3rd Anniversary of the Tibetan People's National Uprising Day of 10th March, 1959

(MARCH 10, 1962)

THIS DAY, three years ago, the unarmed and peaceful people of Lhasa rose against the armed might of their conquerors. No sacrifice was too great for them, and they gladly laid down their lives in defence of their land and liberty. The reign of terror still continues; and every day that passes more and more refugees are fleeing to the neighbouring states to escape from inhuman treatment and persecution. But the spirit of the people has not been and cannot be crushed. Those who cannot escape are still offering passive resistance to the unwelcome measures of the authorities in military occupation of Tibet. The heroic struggle of the Tibetan people still goes on. Their courage and determination still inspire them to defend their hearths and homes against the ruthless attacks of the invaders. Their belief in the future destiny of Tibet is still unshaken, and they still remain proud of their cherished heritage. Today, in his grim hour of tragedy, our heart naturally turn towards them. To them we all Tibetans in exile how in gratitude and admiration. To them I send my blessings. For them I lift my voice, this day as on other days, and pray that the great Lord of Mercy may grant them succour and sustenance to enable them to face their ordeal with unflinching courage and devotion.

We, here in exile, cannot materially help our people in Tibet, who are confronting destruction of all that they love and cherish. We can only pray with all the strength of our hearts that their nightmare of agony and terror will disappear in the not too distant future. A heavy responsibility lies on all of us to do all that is possible to hasten the end of this sad plight of our people. On this day we must not fail to remember that our first obligation is to the people whom we have left behind and who cannot escape from the trails and tribulations of foreign dominations. We must be united as we have always been. A great task lies ahead of us. The events and circumstances during the last three years which forced me and my people to be exiled from our own country have already aroused the conscience of the civilized world. The sufferings of my people were such that there was no alternative for us but to give at least some indication of their full truth. As a result of these sustained efforts, not only by us but also by means friendly States, a resolution was passed last year by the General Assembly of the United Nations. I consider that this resolution is a distinct advance in the furtherance of our cause. It not only expresses grave concern of the world authority at the unfortunate events which are taking place in Tibet but also sets out two definite objectives for the future. It clearly lays down that the fundamental rights and freedoms of the Tibetan people must be restored. It also recognises for the first time the right of the people of Tibet to determine and shape their destiny. I am fully conscious of the fact that the passing of the resolution cannot immediately lead to the cessation of the oppressive policies and measures of the conqueror. However, I earnestly hope and pray that the appeal of the United Nations will not go unheeded by the great Chinese people. The Government of China was a party to the declaration made at the historic meeting of Afro-Asian Powers at Bandung which reaffirmed the fundamental principles of the Charter of the United Nations and the Universal Declaration of Human Rights. The Government of China has also affirmed that the subjection of peoples to alien domination and exploitation constitutes a denial of fundamental human rights, offends against the Charter of the United Nations and is an impediment to the promotion of world peace and co-operation. If these declarations have any meaning at all, the Chinese Government must realise that the measures which has been adopted by its representatives in Tibet constitute total negation of these principles. It must also realise that there must be an end to the policy of force and intimidation which it is pursuing in Tibet and that the only solution to the Tibetan problem is a peaceful settlement consistent with the fundamental rights and freedoms of the Tibetan people. I, therefore, take this opportunity to appeal to the Chinese people to create immediately the persecution and oppression of my people.

The resolution of the General Assembly of the United Nations also calls upon the member States to take appropriate measures for achieving the purposes of the resolution. I hope, therefore, that even if the appeal to the Government of China is ignored, the leading peace-loving nations of the world will not hesitate to mediate on behalf of the poor and unfortunate people of Tibetan freedom. We are all deeply grateful to the States which have espoused our cause and taken a lead in persuading the United Nations to interest itself in the restoration of Tibetan freedom. We have every confidence that, as in the past, they will continue to endeavour to promote the cause of peace and freedom in Tibet.

So far more than 70,000 refugees have sought asylum in the neighbouring States of India, Sikkim, Bhutan and Nepal. They have been driven by the gravity of the situation in Tibet to save themselves from death and destruction despite the hardships and difficulties they have had to encounter on the way. This mass exodus of refugees clearly shows the intolerable conditions under which the people of Tibet are living today. But what is more important is that something must be done, and done now, to help these refugees and the rehabilitate them in suitable places in India and elsewhere. A great deal has already been done by the Government of India and by the other organizations, both national and private, have come generously to our assistance. I am deeply grateful to the Government of India and the organizations concerned. But a great deal remains still to be done, and the continuous influx of refugees is increasing our task. I have no doubt that all men and women all over the world, who love peace and freedom must be gravely concerned at the unfortunate situation in which my people find themselves today. I, therefore, appeal to them once again to come forward with whatever help they can give us and assist us in improving the lot of these unhappy and destitute refugees from Tibet.

May God's blessings be upon all mankind, and may truth and justice prevail.

31

Statement of His Holiness the Dalai Lama on the 4th Anniversary of the Tibetan People's National Uprising Day of 10th March, 1959

(MARCH 10, 1963)

A YEAR has rolled by since I spoke to my beloved people on this memorable day to mark the spontaneous upsurge of the peace-loving and devout people of Tibet against their ruthless and insensate conquerors. Since then there has been no respite in the struggle of my unfortunate people for peace and freedom. The night of terror still continues. Hundreds of people are being massacred to satisfy the greed and impious ambition of the Chinese military leaders. The revered places of worship are being destroyed or converted into arsenals for conquest and oppression. Famine and starvation stalk our beloved land. Refugees are fleeing to the neighbouring States to escape from cruel and inhuman persecution. The passive resistance of our people still continues. Vivid accounts of unspeakable misery are still being brought to us in exile. The situation continues to be desperate and hopeless. But those of our unfortunate brothers and sisters who remain in Tibet must not lose their faith in the ultimate victory of truth. I believe and believe firmly that the faith and spirit of my people cannot be broken. I believe and believe firmly that evil cannot last forever. It is my earnest faith and hope that the time will come when our struggle for freedom and independence will bring about the end of this vicious and barbarous rule. This memorable day as on other days, I pray with all earnestness and fervour that the great Avaloketswara may grant my beloved people courage and determination to enable them to continue their passive struggle against tyranny and oppression.

In my message last year I referred to the Resolution of the General Assembly of the United Nations and expressed the hope that the appeal of the World Assembly not go unheeded by he great Chinese people. I also ventured to state that the Chinese Government must realize that the inhuman measures which have been adopted by its representatives in Tibet constitute a total negation of the principles of humanity and justice which it has done more than once publicly accepted and endorsed. I also stated that the present leaders of China must realize that there must be an end to the policy of tyranny and oppression which it is pursuing in Tibet. Unfortunately, the voice of the people of the world has fallen on deaf ears, and my earnest appeal has evoked no response. We have already seen the dire result of their insensate ambition. Without any rhyme or reason they defied the basic principles of international justice and poured hordes into Indian territory, carrying death and destruction to the innocent people of the frontier areas of India. Their naked aggression has been condemned by the whole world, including almost all the countries of the Communist bloc. I hope and pray that the leaders of China have learnt their lesson from this vicious adventure. I hope and pray that they have realized that they cannot defy the conscience of mankind and the opinion of the civilized peoples. I, therefore, once again appeal to them to bring about a change in their policy in Tibet and realize that the only solution to the Tibetan problem is a peaceful settlement consistent with the fundamental rights and freedoms of the Tibetan people.

Today in this modern world, when colonialism in every form is being eliminated and the equal right to freedom for all people is being realized, I think it is a grave mistake one the part of China to believe that she can forcibly occupy and claim Tibet to be a part of her territory. She must realize that history has proved, in many instances, a country no matter how powerful, can never continue to dominate another country forever. I, therefore, earnestly appeal for the complete withdrawal of the Chinese from Tibet.

I take this opportunity to express once again our deepest gratitude to the States which have been moved by the tragic situation in Tibet and taken an active part in persuading the United Nations to interest itself in the restoration of the freedom and liberties of the Tibetan people. The last Resolution of the General Assembly of the United Nations appealed to every member state to use its good offices and best endeavours to bring to an end the practices which deprive the Tibetan people of their fundamental human rights and freedoms. I have no doubt that all these peace-loving States will not fail to respond to this appeal and do their best to bring peace and freedom to my unfortunate people.

We must all therefore, with unshaken faith, continue to struggle for the not too distant day of regaining freedom of our country. To build and prepare for the future is one of our primary responsibility. For this purpose, I have prepared a future Constitution for Tibet which is consistent with the teaching of Lord Buddha and with the rich spiritual and temporal heritage of our history and democracy. This Constitution provides for effective participation by the people and also for securing social and economic-justice. I have decided that on Tibet regaining freedom the Constitution shall immediately come into force but later my be suitably recast on the advice of the elected representatives of the people.

I invoke the blessings of Divine Providence on all mankind.

32

Statement of His Holiness the Dalai Lama on the 5th Anniversary of the Tibetan People's National Uprising Day of 10th March, 1959

(MARCH 10, 1964)

FOR OVER nine years the peace-loving people of Tibet had tried their utmost to come to an amicable settlement with their invaders; but nothing that they could do would satisfy the ambition and avarice of the Chinese conquerors. Tyranny and oppression prevailed over Tibet, and finally the unarmed citizens of Lhasa rose in a body against the violence of the Chinese Communist authorities, and the torch of freedom was lit once again in every corner of Tibet. Since then my unfortunate people have made great sacrifices. Thousands of them have been massacred. Thousands of them have been rendered homeless. Thousands of them have escaped to neighbouring States. But the barbarous atrocities, even to the extent of exterminating the race and religious belief of the Tibetans, still continue, and the struggle of the people still goes on. Today, which marks the fifth anniversary of the spontaneous upsurge of my people, we must pay our humble tribute to all those stalwart champions of liberty and faith who have fallen victims to the armed might of the Communist Government of China. Today I sent my special blessings to all those who are engaged in a bitter campaign against the enemy. I congratulate all my people for their courage and determination in their struggle for political and religious freedom and pray for their success. Our way may be a hard and long one, but I believe that truth and faith must ultimately prevail.

Many thousands of our people have found refuge and shelter in the neighbouring States, particularly in India which we have always regarded as our Holy Land. The problem of the refugees has been extremely difficult, but with the ready assistance of the Government of India and other friendly countries we have been able to solve their difficulties to a large extent. However, a great deal still remains to be done, particularly for the unfortunate children who have been deprived of the love and care of their parents. But I hope and trust that with the help and encouragement of many of our friends here in India and elsewhere we shall be able to arrange for their proper education and up bringing. On this occasion I would like to impress on all those who have been fortunate enough to escape from the persecution of the Chinese authorities not only to strive for their own benefit but also for all those friends and relations who have been left behind. At this critical juncture in our history it is our duty to do all that we can do to help our fellow countrymen in Tibet and to render them every possible assistance in their ceaseless struggle for freedom and justice.

I must also take this opportunity to express on behalf of my people our deepest sense of gratitude to all those freedom-loving States which have so generously espoused our cause in the United Nations. I would particularly mention the representatives of Malaysia, Thailand, Ireland and El Salvador. The first resolution which was passed by the General Assembly called for respect for the fundamental human rights of the Tibetan people and for their distinctive cultural and religious life. The second resolution renewed the call for the cessation of practices which deprived the Tibetan people of their fundamental human rights and freedoms including their right to self-determination. It also expressed the hope that member States of the United Nations will make all possible efforts towards achieving the purposes of the resolution. I have myself also made appeals to the Chinese Government to bring to an end the inhuman persecution of the people of Tibet and to agree to a peaceful settlement of the Tibetan problem. But I deeply regret to say that these appeals have failed to have the slightest effect on the attitude and policy of Communist China. On the contrary, in order to enlist the opinion of the world in support of their pretensions, they have come forward with a proposal against imperialism and colonialism. I, therefore, consider it necessary to point out that the present Chinese regime in Tibet has been described by an eminent statesman as "the worst form of colonialism". The free nations of the world have rightly condemned the suppression of the coloured people in South Africa, but the form of oppression and persecution which the Chinese invaders have adopted against the people of Tibet are a thousand times worse that the system of apartheid. Nowhere in the world, even under colonialism of the worst type, has a government ever used public torture as a political deterrent as the Chinese have done and are still doing in Tibet. In this connection, I would like to emphasize the fact that the Tibetans are a distinct people, speaking a language unrelated to Chinese and possessing a religion and culture of their own. Moreover, before the Chinese invasion, the Tibetans had remained free and independent for decades. In the circumstances, I, with respect, fully beg of all progressive and freedom-loving countries of the world not to be misled by the propaganda of the Communist Government of China, and, in all fairness and justice, to continue to help the unfortunate people of Tibet.

I pray for the blessings of the Lord Buddha upon all peoples and communities of the world.

33

Statement of His Holiness the Dalai Lama on the 6th Anniversary of the Tibetan People's National Uprising Day of 10th March, 1959

(MARCH 10, 1965)

ONCE AGAIN we solemnly remember the day when the innocent and unarmed people of Tibet rose in spontaneous revolt against the Chinese (Imperialist) conquerors. Six years have rolled by since that memorable date, but the grim specter of tragedy still stalks our holy land; tyranny and oppression still continue, and the sufferings of our people cannot be described in words.

The General Assembly of the United Nations has twice called for the cessation of the inhuman practices against the people of Tibet. I have myself on several occasions appealed for a just and equitable settlement of this tragic problem. But, as the International Commission of Jurists has recently pointed out, "neither the Resolution of the General Assembly nor the call of human conscience have had any effect upon Communist Chinese policy. The Commission, which comprises of eminent and outstanding jurists of international reputation, has also asserted that most of the liberties proclaimed by the Universal Declaration of human rights, including those fundamental civil, religious, social and economic rights with which the Rule of Law is concerned, do not exist under the Chinese rule in Tibet." But it is not only the grant breaches of human rights and fundamental freedoms from which the people of Tibet are suffering to day. What is still more grave in the fact that the Chinese authorities in Tibet are virtually denying that Tibetans are human beings and cherish and entertain the feelings and sentiments of human beings. Thus the Tibetans are being driven from their lands to make room for Chinese settlers. They are being systematically deprived of their only sources of livelihood. in Chinese calculations, the life of a Tibetan has no value at all. It is true that the Chinese authorities vehemently deny all this. But there exists overwhelming evidence against such details. In the first place, thousands of Tibetans have braved the hazards and rigours of a long and troublesome journey and sought refuge in the neighbouring States, Surely, if their life had been tolerable at all they would not have left their hearts and homes for an uncertain future. Secondly, the recent events in Tibet also clearly demonstrate that the declarations of the Chinese authorities are totally unfounded. For instance, the recent public denigration of the Panchen Lama by the Chinese authorities in Peking provides impeachable evidence of the gravity of the situation of Tibet. It should be remembered that he Panchen Lama was born in Chinese-occupied territory and was educated and trained in China. He owed his position to Chinese support. But no Tibetan worth the name could fail to protest against the oppression and tyranny of the Chinese conquerors. Hence it is that the Panchen Lama is now being branded by the Chinese authorities as a stooge of the Imperialists, for it is the invariable practice of the Chinese authorities to condemn,.anyone who criticizes their measures and policies in the interest of humanity as a puppet of the Imperialist powers, however mild fair such criticism might be.

This being the situation today, it is necessary for us, Tibetans and other peace-loving people alike, to rouse the conscience of the world and to enter a strong protest against the barbarous and inhuman treatment of the Tibetans by the Chinese conquerors. Today, I wish to call upon all Tibetans to renew their faith and once again determine to do that lies in their power for the restoration of peace and freedom to their beloved motherland. Today in the name of humanity I call upon all the peoples of the world to come to the rescue of the unfortunate and unhappy people of Tibet.

I also wish to take this opportunity to emphasize the extreme danger of the present situation. We all know of the naked and brutal aggression by the Chinese armies against the territorial integrity of India despite the repeated attempts made by the government of India to befriend the Chinese Republic. The naked aggression should provide the evidence, if any evidence were necessary, of the threat to the Peace of Asia posed by China. I firmly believed that as long as the Chinese remain in occupation of Tibet, there will always be a threat to the peace and progress of the countries in Asia and South-East Asia. The gravity of the situation has been aggravated by the recent nuclear test by the Government of China. So far, the nuclear powers have shown considerable restraint because they fully realize that the use of nuclear weapons would be disastrous to mankind. Would the Chinese authorities exercise a similar restraint once they are in possession of fully developed nuclear weapons? I fear, such a restraint could not be reasonably expected from a Government whose insensate and godless ambition knows no bonds. I, therefore, sincerely hope and pray that the peoples of the world will foresee the danger and threatens us all.

On this day as on other days I pray for the peace and happiness of all beings.

34

Statement of His Holiness the Dalai Lama on the 7th Anniversary of the Tibetan People's National Uprising Day of 10th March, 1959

(MARCH 10, 1966)

IT CAN now seven years since that historic day when the people of Tibet rose in spontaneous revolt against the tyranny and oppression of the Chinese Communist military occupation. Against fearful odds and in utter self-sacrifice, our people stood up as one against the might of their conquerors. Many died in the struggle and others suffered torture and humiliation before being killed. It is to the memory of these martyrs of Tibetan nationalism and the cause for which they have made their supreme sacrifice that we dedicate this day. Tibetan all over the world will remember this as an historic day and strengthen their firm determination that these noble patriots have not sacrifice their lives in vain.

Since the invasion of Tibet by the Chinese Communist in 1949, our people were reduced to the status of a subject race under the shackles of an alien conqueror bent on wiping every vestige of our national and cultural heritage. In flagrant violation of the truth the Chinese have tried to cover up their inhuman and brutal treatment of the Tibetan people under the names of 'liberation' and 'progress'. They have killed and tortured our people; they looted the ancient treasures of Tibet; they have deprived our people of even the smallest traces of fundamental freedom and have made the Tibetans into a second-class citizen existing only to serve the Chinese. In short the Tibetans have become the victims of Han imperialism. And yet the Chinese Communists have accused the Tibetans as fighting for the forces of reaction and resisting progress. The fact that the Tibetan people are firmly determined to forge ahead with the times, that we do not defend any archaic and unjust social system, and that we welcome progress from all quarters, are brushed aside. What we oppose are the imperial and colonial policies of the Chinese and their dogmatic assertion of greater Han nationalism and their Han chauvinistic attitude beyond the slightest trace of reason of justification.

The Chinese Communists, however, continue to camoulage their imperial policies behind empty slogans and impressive facades. Last year, for example, they have utilised the full force of their vast propaganda machinery to publicise the inauguration of Tibet as an Autonomous Region. This charade cannot, however, hide the fact that the so-called Autonomous Region of Tibet comprise of only a part of Tibet and that other regions are carved into separate parts following the old imperial policy of 'divide and rule'. Nor can it be denied that one third of the members of the Council of the Autonomous Region of Tibet are Chinese and that Tibetan members are recruit mostly from what the Chinese themselves call the 'feudal landlord class.' Moreover, all key posts are in the hands of the Chinese and the Tibetan members exist only as a rubber stamping apparatus. With the exception of a few quisling and opportunists the people of Tibet are united in their firm determination to build a free Tibet. The very Tibetans trained and educated by the Chinese to act as collaborators are among those in the foremost ranks of the national resistance front. The desire and determination of the Tibetan people to regain their national freedom cannot be overcome and the will of our people to be free will ultimately prevail over the forces of tyranny and oppression.

On behalf of those of our people who have given up their lives for freedom, those who heroically continue to resist the Chinese in Tibet and those in exile, I would like to think the government of EI Salvador, Ireland, Malaysia, Malta, Nicaragua, the Philippines and Thailand for sponsoring the resolution calling for the immediate cessation of oppression and the restoration calling for the immediate cessation of oppression and the restoration of fundamental freedom in Tibet at the General Assembly of the United Nations. I would also like to thank the Governments who supported the resolution. In particular we are grateful to the Government and people of India for their support and for their wholehearted and warm sympathies to us, and for the large scale programmes in rehabilitation and education of the Tibetan refugees.

To us Tibetans these are hard and tragic times. And it is only natural that we realise and feel the full anguish and sorrows of our brothers who are also victims of brutality and aggression. I fervently hope and offer my ardent prayers that peace may be restored in all the areas of conflict and that humane consideration will prevail over all forms of oppression, injustice and aggression. If mankind is to survive there is only the path of peaceful co-existence and this can be achieved through mutual understanding and respect for the rights of others.

35

Statement of His Holiness the Dalai Lama on the 8th Anniversary of the Tibetan People's National Uprising Day of 10th March, 1959

(MARCH 10, 1967)

ON THIS day, eight years ago, the people of Tibet rose in spontaneous uprising against the armed might of China in a heroic bid to free themselves from the mounting oppression and tyranny of the Chinese Communists, unarmedmen, women and children paraded in the streets of Lhasa calling for the restoration of Tibet's independence and the rights of the Tibetan people. In the brutal repression that followed, thousands of innocent Tibetans were massacred and countless others were imprisoned, tortured and killed or deported to forced labour camps. It is therefore fitting that while we solemnly dedicate this day to the memory of these martyrs of Freedom we recall the cause for which they made their supreme sacrifice and strengthen our determination to reach the goals for which they gave up their lives.

The sixteen years of Communist Chinese armed occupation of Tibet in one long catalogue of untold miseries and sufferings. Farmers and herdsmen are deprived of the fruits of their labour. Large groups of Tibetans on a meager ration are forced to construct military roads and fortifications for the Chinese. Countless numbers have been victims of 'public trials' and 'purging sessions' during which all manner of public humiliation and brutalities have been inflicted. The wealth of Tibet, accumulate over the long centuries, have been taken to China. There is a persistent campaign of 'hanization' of the Tibetan population by forcing the Chinese language in place of Tibetan and by changing Tibetan names into Chinese. This is 'Tibetan Autonomy' in the Chinese Communist fashion.

Recent developments indicate that the reign of terror of Han imperialism has, if anything, increased. The persecution of Buddhism and Tibetan culture has reached a new pitch of intensity with the advent of so -called Cultural Revolution and its by-product, the Red Guard movement. Monasteries, temples and even private homes have been ransacked and all religious articles found have been destroyed. Among the countless number of images destroyed was one of Avaloketesvara built in the 7th century. Two severed and multilated heads of this image have been secretly brought out of Tibet and recently exhibited to the press in Delhi. This image has not only been deeply venerated throughout the centuries but also constitutes an important and irreplaceable historical monument of the Tibetan people, and its destruction is a great loss and a source of profound sorrow to all Tibetans. The recourse to such barbarous methods by frenzied mobs of immature school children let loose on an orgy of senseless vandalism instigated by Mao Tse-Tung under the so-called Great Proletarian

Culture Revolution' is a clear evidence of the depth to which the Chinese rulers have fallen in their efforts to wipe out all traces of Tibetan culture. Mankind and history will surely condemn the savage on slaught by the Chinese against the enslaved people of Tibet and against their cherished cultural heritage.

The Chinese have also started dropping their former proteges and collaborators. The Panchen Lama has long since come out in open rebellion. And now lives in disgrace after being subjected to brutal treatment by the Chinese. The Tibetan students carefully trained in China to 'act as the vanguard of a new army of Tibetan Communist Cadres' have soon realised to brutal treatment of their own people once they returned to Tibet and many of them have joined the foremost ranks of the national liberation front. Even the handful of prominent Tibetan collaborators who till now have proved to be faithful henchmen of Peking have been recently denounced and disgraced.

While we look with the profound sorrow at the abject misery and suffering of our people in Tibent we cannot but renew our firm determination to regain the freedom of our people. During the period of our exile in these past eight years we have made every effort to prepare ourselves for the day when we can return to a free Tibet. To this end we have drawn and promulgated a provisional constitution for Tibet based on the principles of justice, equality and democracy as laid down by Lord Buddha which was warmly received by all Tibetans, particularly by the elected representatives of the Tibetans in exile. We have also undertaken various programmes in the field of resettlement and education made possible by the keen sympathy and extensive assistance of the Government of India. Indeed my people and I are deeply grateful to the Government of India for all their assistance to us not only in rehabilitation and education but also in our cultural and religious programmes. We would also convey our grateful thanks to the various Indian and international organizations which have given without stint to us Tibetans. We still need their support and we confidently hope that it will be forthcoming as before. We are also grateful to the Government of India and the other Governments who supported the cause of Tibet in the United Nations. However, in view of the flagrant denial of even the smallest trace of fundamental rights to our people by the Chinese for which the United Nations appealed more than once and in view of the mounting sufferings in Tibet we believe that the time has come when we should ask the Government of India for more positive support including political support.

We firmly believe that for the lasting peace of Asia and the world the two great nations, India and China, should remain at peace. But we also believe that unless Tibet is restored her freedom and created into a demilitarized Zone that peace will not be achieved. Above all we believe that with her important position in world affairs and the respect she enjoys in the world at large as the largest democracy and the constant champion of justice, peace and freedom, the mighty voice and support of India will hasten the day when the anguish of the people of Tibet will come to an end and freedom, dignity and peace restored to a long-suffering people.

36

Statement of His Holiness the Dalai Lama on the 9th Anniversary of the Tibetan People's National Uprising Day of 10th March, 1959

(MARCH 10, 1968)

THE COMMEMORATION of this day become sacred to all Tibetans and is an important landmark in the historic struggle of men to free themselves from their oppressors. For it was on this day, nine years ago, that the people of Tibet made a very brave attempt to free themselves from their Chinese rulers who in 1950 had forcefully occupied our country under the guise of an ambiguous and obsolete claim to suzerainty. Thrown against the superior size of the Chinese forces, our resistance that day was doomed and resulted in the large scale massacre of thousands of our countrymen. But the spirit of a people who believe in the dignity of man and in the freedom of all nations large or small cannot be quelled by the might of an aggressor. It was that fateful day which united the whole country in defiance of the Chinese and redeclared our sense of nationhood in no uncertain terms to the outside world, and that struggle to assert ourselves as a people still continues today both inside and outside Tibet.

For those of our countrymen remaining in Tibet the struggle is both physical and moral. The Chinese have used every ruse and to force to beat down the resistance of the Tibetan people. The fact that they have not succeeded is admitted by China and evidence by the number of Tibetans who escape into India and other neighbouring countries every year in spite of increasingly stringent border controls imposed by the Communist Chinese. Only recently almost 500 Tibetans died trying to flee to India. They knew that chances of their bid for escape as well-neigh impossible, and yet they preferred to face this risk. Is it conceivable that a people who the Chinese Communists claim are content with the regime under which they live would resort to such drastic measures?

With every year that passed the Chinese have successively tried to indoctrinate the thousands of Tibetan children by forcefully separating them from their parents and sending them to China where they are alienated from everything that is Tibetan and are taught the doctrines of Mao and made to deride and ridicule the Tibetan way of life. But contrary to the Chinese expectations a great majority of these are now resisting the Chinese rule in Tibet. As long as men have the capacity to think and as long as they seek after truth, the Communist Chinese will not completely succeed in indoctrinating our children. There is no doubt that the Chinese treatment of the conquered minority nationalities is a clear cause of Han chauvinism. However, far from succeeding in their aims the Chinese are only adding fuels to the flame of nationalism. It is for this reason that even young Tibetan

Communists are solidly lined up with the rest of the country against the Chinese.

Cultures and religious belief in our country have been one of the major targets of Chinese Communist oppression. The destruction of monastic Universities, cultural centres and other allied institutions which was undertaken from the very beginning of the Chinese takeover was intensified with the recent Cultural Revolution and Red Guard Movement. The remaining monks, nuns and scholars have been driven out from the monasteries and cultural institutions and, with many of the local populace, are forced to build a vast net-work of strategic roads linking Tibet which has now been turned into a huge military base, with the borders of its neighbouring countries, thus posing an ever increasing threat to the peace in those regions.

In 1996 drastic changes have taken place in Tibet. While the Chinese continue to suppress the Tibetan people, the Chinese themselves have been engaged in a long struggle amongst themselves. The total bankruptcy of Chinese policy in Tibet is evidenced by the fact that all the 301 so-called elected representatives of the Tibet Autonomous Region Council have been dismissed. Likewise practically the Tibetan cadres have disappeared. Tibetans who have been trained for years in China have been trained for years in China have been accused of "regional nationalism" and removed from their post for 're-education' in forced labour camps. Since September last year the military has taken up every apparatus of the administration and the country today is entirely in the hands of the Chinese occupation forces without even a semblance of civilian administration.

It now remains for those of us who have been fortunate to escape from under the Chinese Communists to take up the noble task for which so many of our patriots have laid down their lives on this memorable day. Our people living in exile are conscientiously striving to prepare for the day when we can return to a free Tibet. For instance, Tibetan children, whom I look upon as the future foundation of a free and independent Tibet, are being provided with the best possible opportunities of development, of growing mentally and morally into men and women, deeply rooted in their own culture, belief and living habits, as well as acquainted with modern civilization, enriched by the greatest achievements of world culture, and thus becoming sound and creative Tibetan citizens, capable of serving our nation and the whole of mankind. There are 85,000 Tibetans living in exile outside Tibet. Of these, we are in the process of rehabilitation 20040 in agricultural settlement, animal husbandry, small-scale industries and handicraft centres in India, Bhutan, Nepal, Sikkim and Switzerland. This would not have been possible without the generous assistance, both financial and otherwise, in particular of the Indian Government, of the governments of the respective countries, and of the voluntary Agencies, and I take this opportunities to express my personal gratitude and that of my people to them. There are still 20,000 refugees who are yet to be rehabilitated and it is up to us to work hard to help expand and improve on what has been done so that we may not only contribute to the prosperity of our host country and our benefactors but also that a truly Tibetan culture may take root and flourish outside Tibet until such time as we are able to return.

That we will able to return someday is a hope which will always be with us and for which we must always work. Many countries have supported our cause in the United Nations and have condemned Chinese aggression in Tibet. We are very grateful to them and hopeful that they will continue to support us both in the United Nations and elsewhere, for we firmly believe that the Chinese occupation of Tibet poses a threat to Asia and more particularly to those countries which share a common frontier with it. In this light as also from the humanitarian standpoint of support of a just cause, we would once again request the Government of India for increased political support; for it is only the voice of India which, we believe, can lead the way in championing our cause, not only because of her position in the Asian world but also because of its cultural and physical affinity with Tibet and its role in sheltering the thousands of Tibetans who have been forced to flee their homeland. We believe that this support must come as long as men believe in freedom. As Tibetans, let us work for this and renew our resolve to continue the struggle for what is truly our heritage.

In conclusion, I wish to offer my prayers to invoke the blessings of the Triple Gems for peace and happenings to all the sentient beings.

37

Statement of His Holiness the Dalai Lama on the 10th Anniversary of the Tibetan People's National Uprising Day of 10th March, 1959

(MARCH 10, 1969)

THE TENTH of March is a day of special significance to us. It is so not only for the Tibetans but for all those who cherish freedom and peace as the hall-mark of the highest human values. The historic revolt of the Tibetan people which has come to be a symbol of the tenacious determination of the Tibetan people to re-achieve the sovereign freedom of Tibet is a decade old. A decade is a long time indeed if we just pause to recall the harrowing experiences of naked terror, sufferings and nightmarish hardships undergone by those of our countrymen left in Tibet. With each passing year, the anguish and sufferings brought about man's cruelty to man perpetrated on the roof of the world, has increased in magnitude and intensity. Each new movement, whether it be "three-antis", or "proletarian cultural revolution" or evolutionary committee, or "thought propaganda team" has only been an instrument of destruction under a different grab to wipe out the totality of Tibetan identity. The situation is deteriorating at an accelerating pace, spelling of all the character, of a grave crisis.

The Chinese Communist propaganda machinery constantly boasts of a new life of prosperity and happiness enjoyed by the Tibetans. This is what they want to world to believe. This is nothing but the stereotyped Chinese Communist pattern of distoring the true facts in their bid to deceive the people of the outside world, and to create public opinion which would lend support to their garbled version. But, the reality of the situation and the facts such as we find in Tibet repudiate these shameless assertions.

In fact, there is a surging tide of dissatisfaction and opposition to be seen in all spheres of activities—in words, thoughts and actions. Increasing number of Tibetan youths trained and indoctrinated in China are publicly denouncing the very present of the alien rulers, and participating in acts of sabotage and other anti-Chinese activities.

To the Chinese Communists, Tibetan lives are of no value except as the hewers of wood and drawers of water. The Chinese conception of Tibetans are that they are as good as mechanical robots. Not to speak fundamental rights, a Tibetan is denied even the right to exist as a human being. Tibetans continue to be subjected in inhuman treatment and atrocities resulting in a heavy toll of lives. Yet, the one enduring fact is that as the measure of persecution grow in intensity, so has their determination to resist the aggressor. With an unshakable confidence and strength of mind they are all waiting for the day when their country can be free again. In the recent period, reports have reached us that the movement of resistance has even spread to the prisons and concentrations camps. Indifferent to the wrath and fury of the Chinese guards, Tibetans condemned to prison cells and labour camps keep up their morale by talking among themselves about the facts of Tibet being an independent nation and the armed violations of Tibetan sovereignty by the Chinese Communists. Those of the prisoners who have read about the history of Tibet are asked by other fellow mates to speak to them about the political history of free Tibet. Criticism and dislike of the alien rule are voiced by the prisoners and other enslaved people through songs which soon spread like a wildfire. The suffering people left in Tibet look upon us. To them we are a symbol of their hopes and aspirations in the fulfillment of the cherished goal of national freedom. It is for this reason that we have been making every effort to fulfill the hopes and trust that have been placed in us by our countrymen in Tibet.

The Tibetan question was raised several times in the United Nations. Constant efforts are being made to arouse the conscience of the world to the anguish and suffering to which the innocent people of Tibet are being subjected to, and to make known the true facts of Tibet. Likewise, we have adopted a multitude of other measures to draw support and sympathy for our cause. One should not be oblivious of the fact that the prime necessity of our waging a relentless struggle emerges from the gravity of the situation that has gripped our country, Tibet. It is because people in Tibet have fallen in the abyss of mental and physical miseries going beyond the limit of human endurance, and yet fired by the determined will to live as free people again that we have taken unto ourselves the great and sacred responsibility of unmitigated continuation of the national struggle. There is no point in our participation as a key figure in the national struggle for freedom if the masses of people left in Tibet were contented and at peace as the Chinese claim.

When the day comes for Tibet to be governed by its own people, it will be for the people to decide as to what form of government they will have. The system of governance by the line of the Dalai Lamas may or may not be there. It is the will of the people that will ultimately determine the future of Tibet. In particular, the opinion of the forward-looking younger generation will be an influential factor.

While mindful of the great responsibility that has fallen upon our shoulders, I can upon my countrymen to be wide awake to the developments that are taking place in this fast-changing world. There are many ways in which we can contribute our share to the enrichment of human knowledge. The scope, wealth and opulence of our own culture and learning are vast. Today, more and more people are giving their time and energy to the study and practice of the higher spiritual values. The philosophy of Buddhism, in particular, is attracting the attention of a growing number of people. People make great sacrifices, undergo travail and hardships, in their efforts to dig out and study the wisdom of Buddhist teachings. It is fortunate for us that our system of learning has diligent retained the complete Buddhist teachings including the profound and subtle subject of philosophy. And, we do not have to take the help of another language in understanding the subtle and deep meanings outlined in it. Our younger people should realize the value of these facilities. I hope more of our youth will make use of these rare facilities so as to contribute our mite to the world of learning and spiritual cultivation.

During the past ten years of our exile, much has been achieved in the education and rehabilitation of our people. The process of rehabilitation is fast nearing completion. When this is complete attempts should be made to achieve continued progress in the standard of living. We owe much to the government and the people of India for their sympathy and magnanimity which have made possible the favourable conditions we enjoy today. At the same time, it is essential for us who have been able to reach free countries to strive for the liberation of the majority of the Tibetan people still suffering under the yoke of Red Chinese oppression, and, towards the achievement of a free Tibet governed by Tibetans themselves. I call upon my countrymen to rededicate themselves to this sacred task. Whether Tibet will be free and independent in the near future depends on the efforts of the Tibetan people themselves.

The Chinese believe that all activities can be achieved only through violent means. That is why they are giving military training to the old as well as the young. They consider that the acquiring of arms, digging of trenches in strategic areas and the building of roads are the essential groundwork of military preparedness. Moreover, they believe in and strive towards the achievement of these goals purely through the application of Mao's teachings, assuming that these teachings contain the quintessence of wisdom. But as it is impossible for millions of people to think on the same line as one person, Red China is facing today, from what we learn from various sources, as enormous problem of ideological differences among the elder leaders who have for many years stood firmly and faithfully with Mao. The total outcome of these has been the creation of strife and dissension of a magnitude unknown in the past.

It is necessary for the Chinese to remember that oppression has never, anywhere, succeeded in suppressing the eternal desire of people to live as free man; free to think their own thoughts, free to act as they consider best for the common welfare and live as human beings and not as robots of slaves. Even if the Chinese leave nothing but ashes in our sacred land, Tibet will rise from these ashes as a free country even if it takes a long time to do so. No imperialist power has succeeded for all time to keep other people in colonial subjection for long.

38

Statement of His Holiness the Dalai Lama on the 11th Anniversary of the Tibetan People's National Uprising Day of 10th March, 1959

(MARCH 10, 1970)

MARCH 10TH has now become a symbol of our struggle for freedom, for justice and for the right to live as we wish. March 10th today stirs the hearts and minds of all Tibetans. Whether they are in the free countries or still under suppression in Tibet, March 10th 1959 marked a new era in the history of Tibet—it was on that day when the brave people of Tibet rose against the might of Communist China. It was on that day when unarmed men, women and children paraded through the streets of Lhasa calling for the restoration of Tibet's independence. It was on that day when the people of Tibet united as one force in a heroic attempt to free themselves from bondage. The world knows of the brutal and ruthless oppression that followed the national uprising. That was eleven years ago.

The situation in Tibet has ever since been gradually deteriorating, and conditions worsened with the advent of the so-called Cultural Revolution. Eleven years may not seem long to those of us who have been able to escape into free countries, but to those of our countrymen who are still in Tibet it has been a period of unending terror and suffering. Yet in the midst of such a desperate and difficult situation the flame of freedom, which was lit on March 10th, 1959, still burns persistently. The Communist Chinese regime in Tibet has experienced constant opposition from the Tibetan often in the form of violence. In 1969 alone, we learn of ambushes and raids by Tibetans on Chinese military camps and ammunition dumps in the areas of Chamdo, Poh, Lhoka, Tolung, Nyemo and Shang. There were also incidents were many Chinese officers were killed and many were held prisoners by the Tibetans during meetings organized by the Chinese. Above all, the Communists Chinese must have been shocked to find mounting opposition from the young Tibetans, many of whom have been educated and indoctrinated by the Chinese themselves in Tibet as well as in China. These are clear indications that all is not well in Tibet; that Tibetans are not contended and satisfied under the rule of alien power; that desperate resistance still continues; and that the spirit of liberty is still strong.

It is now nineteen long years since the armed forces of Communist China trampled Tibet under their feet. The Chinese have had all the time required to educate, indoctrinate and produce a new group of Tibetan leaders who would totally support their regime—but this has not happened. They have not been able to produce a single notable, young Tibetan leader. They are still using a few ex-members of the old Tibetan Government who are actually considered to be reactionaries according to the Chinese themselves. This is again a clear indication that the Tibetans, young and old, no matter how they are treated or brought up are not prepared to yield completely to the Communist Chinese rulers. Many of these Tibetans may be ideologically Communists, but they are definitely nationalist Communists. To these Tibetans their nations comes first, ideology second. We are fighting against colonialism and not against Communism.

When the hopes and aspirations of our countrymen, struggling to survive in a vast prison camp, is so strong and persistent; so unfailing and determined; it is not sufficient to dedicate this day only to the memory of those martyr who laid down their lives for the freedom of Tibet. We must, also, renew our pledge to hold high the torch of freedom and to continue the struggle so that the sacred cause for which six million Tibetans are still aspiring can be achieved. It is only fitting that we in the free countries shoulder this responsibility as our duty. We, therefore, solemnly rededicate this day and earnestly renew our pledge for the cause or Tibet's independence.

The world is ever changing. International changes are occuring almost every day of the year. A change in Tibet will definitely come about. The Chinese must realize that the spirit of freedom in the Tibetans is indomitable.

I take this opportunity to express on behalf of the people of Tibet and on my own behalf, our sincere and deep gratitude to the government and people of India for their generous and understanding assistance to the Tibetan refugees living in India. We also remember and remain deeply indebted to those countries, along with India, who have supported us in United Nations. Last but not least, we thank the various voluntary agencies that have come forth at a time when help was urgently and desperately needed. Much of what we have achieved in the fields of rehabilitation, education and cultural activities would not have been possible without their help.

Finally, while I call upon my people to strengthen their determination and toward conscientiously for the freedom of Tibet I also appeal to all those nations who cherish freedom to give us their firm and strong support in the just cause of Tibet's independence.

39

Statement of His Holiness the Dalai Lama on the 12th Anniversary of the Tibetan People's National Uprising Day of 10th March, 1959

(MARCH 10, 1971)

ON THE 10th of March 1959, the Tibetan people's uprising in Lhasa was crushed brutally by the Red Chinese Army. So why do we commemorate this day—a day of defeat when thousands of our people died and when Communist China proved her utter ruthlessness and her total disregard for human values? It may sound paradoxical of me to say that we not only dedicate this day to those who died for the cause of Tibet, but that we also celebrate this day as a day of victory. For it was on this day that the failure of the oppressive system of Red China in Tibet became apparent and that the Chinese in their frustration to cover up their deficiencies had to use violence to promulgate what is essentially the reverse to Communist ideals; colonialism. On the other hand, for us it was no defeat. Rather, it was a proof of the Tibetan courage and their determination never to live under alien rule.

A thousand more uprising may take place and a thousand times the Chinese may crush them, but they will never be able to break the spirit of liberty that resides in each one of us. My people will carry on the struggle till we see Tibet once again in its rightful place among the independent nations of this world. What more proof can I have of my words then the recent reports coming out of Tibet. Determined opposition against the Red Chinese resulted in the public shooting of 58 Tibetans around the months of February in 1970; while those executed behind closed doors and in prisons remain unknown. In July the same year, Radio Lhasa announced the successful suppression of an armed revolt. No other details were given. Later report said that revolt was wide-spread in South-Western Tibet inflicting more than 1,000 casualties of the Chinese army. 124 Tibetans were executed when the revolt was crushed. Three months later the Chinese unearthed a secret Tibetan resistance group in Lhasa called the 'Organization for the struggle of Tibet's Independence.' The Chinese executed nine of its members and sentenced the others to 20-30 years of imprisonment. All these has been happening despite the fact that the Chinese are now using tactics that would make their atrocities committed a few years back pale by comparison. I cannot describe in mere words the hunger, the misery and the death that my people face in our country today.

In spite of the fact that we Tibetans have to oppose Communist China I can never bring myself to hare her people. I believe that Tibet will be free only when its people become strong, and hatred is no strength. It is a weakness. The Lord Buddha was not being religious, in the popular sense of the term, when He said that hatred does not cease by hatred. Rather he was being practical. Any achievement attained through hatred can neither be lasting nor binding. It would only be inviting trouble sooner or later. And as for my people at this critical period, hatred would just be an extra mental burden. Moreover, how can we hate a race who do not know what they are doing? How can we hate the millions of Chinese whose very minds are regulated by their leaders? And how can we even hate those leaders who have themselves in the past been so persecuted and have suffered so much for their nation and for what they believe to be right. I do not believe in hatred, but I do believe, as I have always done, that one day truth and justice will triumph.

I believe in his even though I know that millions march in the Chinese army. She now even possessed mighty nuclear weapons that make her feared by the most powerful nations of this world. But history is unpredictable. Many great empires whose glory knew no bounds have crumbled and passes away. And although never in her history has China been so powerful as she is today, yet there is a weakness in the colossus. Her very foundations are based on fear. Like primitive beings, each person in China lives perpetually in fear of retribution for the slightest mistake from his new 'God'. Can such institution hope to remain? I say no. Nearly every totaliarian regime in history had this in similar—they never lasted long. Eventually China has to give why or break. And though tyrants and despots may continue to strut about in the world, truth and justice will ultimately triumph, and as ours is a just cause I say with confidence that the time will come when my people will fling away the yoke of Communist China's oppression and rise up to build a new Tibetan Nation.

In conclusion I take this opportunity again to thank all the countries and individuals who are continuing to give us moral and material support in our honour of need.

40

Statement of His Holiness the Dalai Lama on the 13th Anniversary of the Tibetan People's National Uprising Day of 10th March, 1959

(MARCH 10, 1972)

WE COMMEMORATE March 10 once more, for it records in history a significant nation-wide expression of the Tibetan people to free themselves of the shackles of foreign dominator. It is also a day when one remember of those who have lost their lives in this violent upheaval and of the thousands who have suffered, physically and otherwise, during these many years of cruel subjugation.

The past period of over a decade has been a time of great test for the people of Tibet, especially for those who are still the victims of this monstrous and alien on slaught on the very way of life that Tibetans cherish. Young Tibetans, both under Chinese control or in the lands where they have sought refuge, are becoming more conscious of their national identity—there is this new awareness in them of the Tibetan nation and the culture that once flourished there.

The truth about Tibet is spreading as each year passes by. And although this is happening much too slowly compared to the urgency of the actual situation, it is reaching nations and peoples of this world irrespective of the system of governments they follow or the continents to which they belong. This I believe is happening because more and more are beginning to recognize the justice and strength behind the people of Tibet's fight for freedom, and also because truth and justice can never be hidden. In fact, they must ultimately prevail and triumph if justice at all exists in this world—and I believe that justice does exist. One recent, encouraging example is the birth of a new nation in Asia—the emergence of Bangladesh. The indeed was a triumph of justice and a triumph of a people's determination. It is another historic landmark in man's never ending pursuit for the freedom to live as they wish.

Although the freedom of Tibet cannot be predicted, changes are bound to come. Even in the international scene great changes, unexpected a decade ago, have occurred. China too is changing and she is compelled to do so. She must break away from her isolation and outmoded ideas, for today, she is a responsible member of the United Nations and thus capable of doing much for the peace of mankind. We hope that is what she will do, and we also hope that she will one day recognize the true status of Tibet and the indomitable spirit of our people.

When we see the determination of the people; the national awareness of the youth; and the growing support for the cause; we can see that the future of Tibet is not dark. As long as there is this determination, this national awareness, and this growing support, there is hope for Tibet.

41

Statement of His Holiness the Dalai Lama on the 14th Anniversary of the Tibetan People's National Uprising Day of 10th March, 1959

(MARCH 10, 1973)

THIS YEAR marks the 2100th anniversary of the founding of the Tibetan Royal Dynasty by Nyatri Tsenpo. The year also marks the fourteenth anniversary of the Tibetan people's struggle against foreign domination. On this occasion when we remember and commemorate these two glorious anniversities, I send my greetings to all Tibetans both in and outside Tibet.

I would like to deal briefly with the history of these 2100 years. The earliest Tibetan Kings in dynastic succession were the seven Tris, the two Thengs, the six Legs, the eight Dhes and the five Tsens. During the reigns of these twenty-eight Kings Tibet made steady progress in handicrafts and education. In the reign of the twenty-eightieth King, Lha Thothori Nyentsen, Buddhism was first planted in Tibet. During the reigns of Songtsen Gampo, the thirty-third King, Trisong Detsen, the thirty-seventh King, and Tri Ralpachen, the fortieth, who are collectively known as the Three Great Religious Kings, Tibet emerged as the powerful state. In the field of religion, many Buddist scriptural texts were translated into Tibetan. Religious and civil codes were promulgated and Tibetan social behaviour was made decent and civilized. Politically, land was equally distributed to people and in summer and winter people's representatives held regular meetings. All this made the Tibetan social arrangement then prevailing democratic and modern. The fame of Tibet spread throughout Asia.

The forty-first King, Langdharma, suppressed the Buddhist faith and in his time Buddhism received a severe set-back. The two sons of Langdharma made rival claims to the throne of Tibet and Western Tibet was divided between them. Consequently the whole of Tibet was reduced to many petty principalities and the former strength of Tibet, both military and political, greatly decreased. The frontier provinces of Tibet seceded from Tibet and religion and politics suffered degeneration and decline.

Subsequently, since the time of Chogyal Phagpa of Skya, the successive dynastic reigns of Sakya, Pha-drupa, Rinpungpa and Tsangpa, made the strength of Tibetan politics firmer and the hold of religion deeper, unlike during the period of Tibetan disintegration. However, the standard they attained never reached that of the one which prevailed during the reigns of the Three Great Religious Kings of Tibet. Moreover Tibet was internally continually racked by disunity.

In the reign of the Fifty Dalai Lama, the political influence of the Tibetan Government grew and the Tibetan people enjoyed happiness and prosperity. However, in 1949 the Chinese communists invaded Tibet and since then we all know the extent of happiness which the Tibetan people enjoy.

As such, if we look back at Tibetan history, we will realise that during the time of the Three Great Religious Kings of Tibet the country did not only enjoy immense military strength but was culturally rich. Also, as we have seen, after Langdharma, Tibet disintegrated into many petty principalities and because of Tibetan weakness the country also suffered politically. Even in our times because of the fact that Tibet did not have a sustained strong central government it was easy for the Chinese communists to invade Tibet and the subsequent suffering which has been inflicted upon the Tibetan people is something which can be proved. Mere propaganda is unneccessary here. As such the Tibetans must at all time remember these and remain united. The determination to achieve their rights and freedom.

After the period of Tibetan disintegration and during the time of the Sakyapas and influence of the Mongol rulers of China was first felt in Tibet. After this during the time of the Manchu emperors, China began interfering in the affairs of Tibet. However at that time the Han Chinese themselves were under the domination of at first the Mongols and then the Manchus. The Yuan dynasty of the Mongols came to an end. The Manchus themselves were overthrown by the Chinese revolution of 1911, after which a republican government was established in China. At the same time, after the overthrow of the Manchus, Tibet declared its independence. However, some countries because of their territorial ambitions concluded several treaties which stated that Tibet was under the suzerainty of China. That these treaties contain neither truth nor they tell the objective reality can clearly be seen from that way earlier and later treaties were made. The violent aggression of the Chinese into Tibet and the way they forced the Tibetans to sign the 17-point Agreement was forcefully and clearly published by the Tibetans to the whole world. Besides, looking at any period of Tibetan history we know that Tibet existed as an independent nation.

Especially here I would like to touch on the real conditions in Tibet today. After being 'liberated' from the 'three big feudal lords' the Tibetans were made the "masters" of the country. Through such pleasing propaganda the Chinese are publicising that the progress achieved in Tibet under their rule is unprecedented and the Tibetan people are all happy.

The aim of the struggle of the Tibetans outside Tibet is the attainment of the happiness of the Tibetan people. If the Tibetans in Tibet are truly happy under Chinese rule then there is no reason for us here in exile to argue otherwise. Fourteen years have passed since the 10th March Uprising of 1959. It is needless for me to point to the Tibetans, since they have experienced all these, that out unique culture is being deliberately undermined, that the Tibetans in Tibet are denied the basic rights of religious worship, free expression and movement. The basic need of every human being is adequate food, clothing and shelter. But even here the Tibetans in Tibet face difficulties. Because of scarce food many of the Elder Tibetans fall sick and die. Every day most Tibetans live in fear, suffering and hardship and do not enjoy a moment of rest and relaxation. Even to the young Tibetans, whom the Chinese have reared and educated they, the Chinese, do not give jobs corresponding to the type of education which their youths have received. Envoking the ideal of "voluntary work", the Chinese drive the Tibetans like a herd of cattle to work in the fields, in road-building and construction. In short, the Tibetans in Tibet are not treated like human beings. Because the Tibetan people, like all other peoples in the world, are endowed with the capacity to differentiate good from bad, all of them, young, old and middle-age, despite their small individual differences, will never trust and put their faith in foreign aggressors. All of them will want their country to be ruled by their own people. This is the reason why we are continuing to struggle for the rights and freedom of the Tibetan people.

As such, considering the history of Tibet and the present aspirations of the Tibetan people, the present pitiable condition will never be continued to be borne by them for long. There are many changes which have occured and are occuring in the international political scene and I hope that the Chinese leaders will discard their present rigid and narrow-minded policy and listen to reason and see the reality that is lying all around them. There will be a satisfactory conclusion, and there will inevitably must be one, for the just cause of the rights and freedom of the Tibetan people. Without working hard at something there will never be a good, positive result. This is only natural. Consequently all Tibetans must continue to work towards their cause with one mind, and utmost dedication.

42

Statement of His Holiness the Dalai Lama on the 15th Anniversary of the Tibetan People's National Uprising Day of 10th March, 1959

(MARCH 10, 1974)

SIX MILLION Tibetans lost the right to determine their destiny, tens of thousands fled their homes and many more lost their lives in an era when scores of nations regained their freedom after a long period of colonial slavery. March 10 means all this and much more to us. Eighty-five thousand exiles are on this side of the mighty Himalayas and six millions on the other, but the spirit of March 10 binds us as one proud nation.

What is the spirit of March 10? We say it is the cause of Tibet. But what is the cause of Tibet? Is it a struggle against a race, a nation and an ideology? Or is it an unreasonable struggle waged by a minority in exile for their own interests? It is none of these.

The cause of Tibet is the cause of the Tibetan people; it is the cause of six million people. It is the struggle of a people to determine their own identity. Until they are satisfied the struggle for Tibet will continue.

I believe in justice and truth, without which there would be no basis for human hope. I also believe in the right of every nation to struggle for its freedom, including Tibet and its neighbouring states that have fallen victim to Chinese aggression.

Although there are signs liberalization in Lhasa itself and some border areas, this has in no ways alleviated the suffering of the vast majority of the people. Refugees still report that the overall situation in Tibet continues to be very grave. Under such circumstances, is it any wonder that the younger generation see a contradiction between the "socialist paradise" of factories, roads, airfields, and the simultaneous starvation of their countrymen? These imposing monuments of "progress" have no meaning to the common Tibetan; they only serve to high-light the dissatisfaction among the Marxist-educated younger generation of Tibetans.

So long as the people of Tibet are in such dire hardship and discontented with their lot, we have a duty to speak and act on their behalf. It is an onerous duty but one which we will push through with a determination equal to—if not more than—what our brethen are displaying in Tibet.

The future of Tibet is not a gloomy one. The international situation is extremely fluid; great changes are taking place all over the world. A change will definitely take place in Tibet also. Moreover, truth and justice are on our side. We have hope and we have the necessary determination—these are what ultimately count.

43

Statement of His Holiness the Dalai Lama on the 16th Anniversary of the Tibetan People's National Uprising Day of 10th March, 1959

(MARCH 10, 1975)

WHEREVER there is oppression there will always be opposition. Not wanting to be under the rule of another people, the Tibetans rose against the Chinese rule in Tibet and since then sixteen years have passed. Today when we commemorate the sixteenth anniversary of this struggle I send my warm greetings to the Tibetans in and outside Tibet.

During these last sixteen years we the Tibetans in exile have made commendable progress in material well-being, both individually and collectively. Especially in the education of our youths we have done remarkably. We enjoy full rights and live as complete human beings like others do in the rest of the world. However, the situation of our people in Tibet is just the opposite to our own in exile. It is common knowledge that the horrible conditions in Tibet are beyond words.

The Chinese aggressors have killed and jailed countless innocent Tibetans. Without caring for the starving people all around them the Chinese are channellising the productivity of the country into armaments. Through guilt the Chinese are digging trenches in the hillsides and to cover up their crimes and misdeeds, are churing out publications splashed with photographs of dance and drama performances and a few factories, which state that the Tibetans in Tibet are enjoying unprecedented happiness. This is done to fool the world public opinion. But a mere palm of the hand cannot hide the sun. Responsible and informed people everywhere in the world know that there can never be happiness in a society which is given the name of "new" but in which there is not even the fundamental material basis of adequate food, shelter and clothing. The elderly Tibetans through their own experience know, since they have gone through both societies, where there is greater happiness, in the old or the new society.

The Chinese are not only committing barbarous acts in Tibet far removed from normal international behaviour, but they are also trying to sabotage and stability of the Tibetan community in exile. There is a saying: you reap what you sow. One suffers the conseqeunces of one's own acts. No one will be able to change this. This is a natural law. Wherever there is oppression there will always be opposition and the Chinese actions mentioned above provide strength and inspiration to the Tibetan people's struggle.

The Tibetan people in Tibet, without caring the least for their personal welfare or safety, are courageously carrying on their struggle for the freedom of Tibet. Naturally this unremitting struggle of the Tibetans in Tibet is causing untold anxiety to be Chinese authorities. Consequently we the Tibetans in the free world, keeping our stand in conformity to the thinking of the masses of Tibet, will never stop our movement for the independence of Tibet. Apart from this we have no reason to interfere in the internal affairs of other people.

The Issue of Tibet is deeply linked with the charges in international politics and especially with the progress of the peace process in Asia. As such we must steer the ship of our struggle according to the shifting directions of the winds of international relations to reach the shore of Tibetan freedom and happiness. To attain this goal we must not only, be mere words, but through our acts and thoughts persevere and become ever more united.

44

Statement of His Holiness the Dalai Lama on the 17th Anniversary of the Tibetan People's National Uprising Day of 10th March, 1959

(MARCH 10, 1976)

SEVENTEEN years have passed since the Tibetans began their just struggle for their inherent rights of Tibetan national independence. On this Anniversary Day I remember with gratitude and reverence all those Tibetans who have sacrificed and who are continuing to sacrifice everything they hold dear for this supreme cause.

Realisation and promotion of the national interests and the national aspirations of the broad masses in Tibet is the cause and objective determining of our strivance and struggle for Tibetan freedom. Being subjected to coercion and restrictions under enemy's rule, the large masses of Tibetan people have no freedom of movement. Internally, they are afflicted with gnawing hunger and thirst, and the situation is such that when they meet and converse, they invariably first talk of food difficulties. However, the Tibetan people, not content with the sweet Chinese slogan of "equality and progress" and unmindful of the oppression and suppression, hunger and thirst unleashed by the enemy, are looked in waging an unceasing revolt against tyrannism and oppression. With courage that knows no frontier of defeat, and sacrifice of their very life-breath, our people are continuing to create a situation of desperate tension and crisis for the Chinese. They are doing for the fulfilment of the cherished goal of Tibetan freedom.

If our brethen in Tibet are waging such a glorious struggle, and that too against such odds and risks, surely it behoves those of us who are in exile to work with greater zeal and perseverance and without regret so that our brethen in Tibet are speedily emancipated from the anguished torments, and the common cause of the Tibetan freedom, which is cherished goals of all Tibetans, realized. Isn't it becomes all the more emphatic when we realise that those of us who are in the free countries of the world was free from the sufferings to which our people in Tibet are subjected to?

In this twentieth century, the world has witnessed the rise of the sun of equal freedom. People of many nations are enjoying the warmth of freedom which they did not have before. In ancient times, we Tibetans were known for our high degree of civilization and courage in all Asia. Should we always remain slaves of the barbarous, suffering under their dark domination?

The snow land of Tibet is blessed with a bountiful natural wealth, and rich natural beauty. Should this country of ours by converted into a warm-machinery manufacturing fortress, and the Tibetan people, its rightful owner, reduced to the status of a criminal perpetually subjected a oppression and humiliation?

By virtue of our secular Karma, we Tibetans have been endowed with priceless mineral resources of gold, copper, iron, oil, gas, coal and lead. Do you wish to allow the barbarous brigands who have no right whatsoever, to plunder and cart away these resources of ours as they are doing now?

My countrymen, beware of the yawning chasms. Forgetting the enemy who invaded and wrested the country, you indulge in squabbles and factionalism. Discarding the thoughts and motives to promote the interest of the larger masses of one's own people, you seek and work to promote your own interest only. Refusing to recognise the grave economic situation that the Tibetan people are in, you desire the emulate luxury life-style of other rich people. These are unhealthy trends and matters of serious concern. So, give a thought to these seriously.

Turning to the situation that the enemy is in, a time has now come when they are being reluctantly forced to admit the one and hundred acts of omissions and commissions they perpetrated in utter violation of their own documentary and oral commitments, their own principles and ideology.

All worldly phenomena are characterised by the inherent nature of arising, developing and passing away. Does it not behove us to wrestle with greater vigour and determination for the recovery of our rights, taking advantage of the ripe conditions and the timely opportunities?

Every year we commemorate the March Tenth Anniversary Day. This we do neither for gay pageantry and pleasure nor is this forced upon us by others. This solemn occasion is a time for uplifting one's spirit, for rethinking and summarising the present plight of the Tibetan people. Reminding ourselves of these, we should strive with renewed dedication and determination for freeing the Tibetan people from the present plight, and for realising the ultimate objective of Tibetan national freedom.

Banish the sense of timidity, lethargy and the effort to evade hardships. Cultivate and develop the spirit of complete self-reliance. Volunteer for challenges and hardships. Work with devotion and with pleasure in the sense that is in your own interest, and above all, in unity for achieving the goal of national freedom of the Tibetan people.

45

Statement of His Holiness the Dalai Lama on the 18th Anniversary of the Tibetan People's National Uprising Day of 10th March, 1959

(MARCH 10, 1977)

ON THIS commemoration of the March 10th anniversary, our thoughts turn inevitably to events taking place in Tibet. It is well-known that the invading Tibet, the Chinese Communists have stationed military personnel and civilian garrisons in extensive ares in the country. Parallel to this, Chinese settlements have even penetrated into the eastern and north-eastern frontiers of Tibet. In addition to this influx, Chinese migrants continue to arrive in Central Tibet. According to Radio Lhasa broadcast, between May 1975 and January 1977, 6,660 retired PLA veterans as well as graduate students from different parts of China were transported to Central Tibet to raise families and settle there. Forty-three separate batches were thus mobilised for this scheme on the pretext that they were volunteers who "had come to join the socialist revolution and socialist construction work in Tibet."

Those of our people left behind in Tibet continue to experience a life of poverty and relentless hard labour. To cite an instance of this, according to reports received on the construction of a new dam during the winter at Lhasa, at young and old, male and female inhabitants were summoned to the site of the construction and compelled to work round the clock without any break until the dam has been completed. Even those who developed open wounds on their backs had no alternative but to work without respite. Many became multilated as a consequence of severe frost-bite. From another report on construction work at Tak-tse, we learn that the inhabitants were forcibly put to labour on agricultural cultivation by day, and with the assistance of kerosene torches were compelled to work on an hydro-electric plant by night. These reports hae neither been fabricated nor exaggerated by us, but were broadcast by Radio Lhasa three or four weeks ago.

At a meeting convened to mourn the death of Mao a few months ago, 300 Tibetans were arrested and several were executed on the grounds that the accused portrayed a lack of genuine sorrow and grief at the meeting. A review of these facts will single-pointedly indicate the extent of forcible oppression and repression which the Chinese Communists have wrought on the Tibetan people.

At present, the campaign against hegemony and colonialism has taken precedence in international affairs and the call for the equality of all races has gained momentum. Yet the Communist Chinese persist in a policy of invasion and expansionism in Tibet, a renowned nation in the history of Asia, and have reduced it innocent and defenceless people to interminable oppression, suppression and torture. How is it justified to neglect and leave unattended such tragic happenings in Tibet?

Our struggle for the independent of Tibet is compatible with the hopes and aspirations of 6,000,000 Tibetans. It is fulfilment of our rights and duties, and is a just cause. Therefore, in order to realise this goal in its entirely, ever Tibetan must endeavour to work in unity, with resolve, courage and determination. It is the responsibility of every Tibetan, irrespective of age, to preserve, promote and personify the exemplary traditions inherited from our forefathers, to abide by truth and justice and to inculcate respect for our elders, tolerance of problems and difficulties in addition to benevolence to others, while at the same time remaining humble and modest. If deceitful and immoral means are adopted for insignificant and temporary gain and fame, not only will ridicule and abuse befall the subject of such indulgence, it will also be unbecoming of his status as an intelligent human being. It therefore becomes imperative for us all to cultivate the quintessence of a moral and prudent approach at all times.

46

Statement of His Holiness the Dalai Lama on the 19th Anniversary of the Tibetan People's National Uprising Day of 10th March, 1959

(MARCH 10, 1978)

Greetings to all Tibetans on this 19th anniversary of the Tenth March Uprising. On this occasion I also remember and pray for those who sacrificed their lives for the sake of our people and our country.

Recently the Chinese have intensified their propaganda about the "unprecedented happiness in Tibet today" through radio broadcasts and pictorial magazines. It is very difficult for the few selected foreign visitors, who are taken on guided tours for a few days and have to listen to explanations through interpreters carefully chosen by the Chinese, to know and tell us the actual, welfare and conditions of the Tibetan people. It is obvious to impartial observes that these reports which are artificial, biased, one-sided and unreliable, will not be accepted by people who are able to see both sides of the picture.

If the six million Tibetans in Tibet are really happy and prosperous as never before there is no reason for us to argue otherwise. If the Tibetans are really happy the Chinese should allow every interested foreigner to visit Tibet without restricting their movements or meetings with the Tibetan people. This would enable the visitors to really know that true conditions in Tibet. Further more, the Chinese should allow the Tibetans in Tibet to visit their parents and relatives now in exile. These Tibetans can then study the conditions of those of us in exile living in free countries. Similar opportunity should be given to the Tibetans in exile. Under such an arrangement we can be confident of knowing the true situation inside Tibet. This is morally right and practicable. Instead of doing this why are the Chinese indulging only in propaganda to woo the Tibetans in exile to return?

We must remember that nothing can be achieved if we lose courage. Every Tibetan should continue to be determined and dedicated to the goal that our nation, like other nations in this world, is governed by our own people.

47

Statement of His Holiness the Dalai Lama on the 20th Anniversary of the Tibetan People's National Uprising Day of 10th March, 1959

(MARCH 10, 1979)

TODAY, on the commemoration of the 20th Anniversary of the Tibetan National Uprising Day I express my warmest greetings to every Tibetan, inside and outside Tibet, united by one common language, race, traditions and customs while having a variety of ideology, behaviour and profession.

During the past 20 years 100,000 or so Tibetan refugees (mostly in India and 16 countries in the East and West) have been earning their livelihood by agriculture, small business, handicrafts, etc., and their living standard is improving and they are becoming self-sufficient. Of special importance is the over 20,000 Tibetan youths who provided with both the traditional and modern education, which are like the wings of a bird—are joining the mainstream of modern life. Our religion and culture—considered poison by the Chinese—are not only preserved and their centres firmly established in the Tibetan settlements in India but are also spreading among peoples of different social strata and races and gaining much interest and respect in the East and West Regarding our political situation, we follow the democratic system and tread the path of freedom, not only in word but in deed. And considering that we were forced to leave our land and wander in other people's lands, the fact that we have achieved a lot of success for the benefit of both the society and the individual is worth remembering.

We must not however, be content with what we have achieved so far, for we must still strive for greater progress. Especially since the main reason why we are in exile is the welfare of the 6 million Tibetans. Learning from our past experiences—without being discouraged by our tragedy—we must persevere and carry on the struggle until the day the 6 million Tibetans are fully satisfied and peace and freedom are fully restored in our land.

The Chinese, of course, say that we are against progress and revolution, against the Tibetan people and very oppressive, following the wrong path. It is not necessary for us to say repeatedly that these are lies, nor is there a need for us to lie. The free world knows that we have fought for change and reforms, what we have done to preserve our ancient culture and race and how we have tried to work, with justice and impartiality, for the welfare of our people; our actions are clear like a writing on a wall. If friends,enemies or observes investigate, it will be clear as to who is telling the truth, who is following the right path; and where it is that black is changed to white within only a year or two without a single basis for trust, and where earlier statement are contradicted by later ones and statements are like the words of a mad man.

We had no wish to challenge the Chinese military might, but the Tibetan masses in desperation, from 1955 onwards and in 1959, opposed, resisted and rose up in rebellion against the Chinese and cried; "Chinese Quit Tibet!" Tibet will be Governed by Tibetans!" This was a spontaneous feeling expressed by all Tibetans against the Chinese. But the Chinese declared that it was formented and led by external opponents who were the paper-tiger-American imperialists and the expansionist Indians, and the internal enemies who were a few reactionaries. They forcibly suppressed the Tibetan national uprising and misrepresented to the world that the Tibetan people actually supported the Chinese.

Similarly, in China, many campaigns were launched from the 1950s onwards, such as the Great Leap Forward, the Cultural Revolution, Learn from Tachai, which, as is known and accepted by all today, contained faults and mistakes and did not succeed but brought heavy losses. But, *at that time* the Chinese said these campaigns were great successes. Moreover, in China many old Chinese leaders who had worked for the Revolution for many years were purged under various pretexts and names; and when actual conditions necessitated their reinstatement they were appointed again on various excuses. In a short period it seems that in Chinese politics a person is purged many times and reinstated many times and thousands of reasons are given for the most unexpected changes. But, the Chinese are an intelligent people and can no longer believe the words of their leaders. Also, in the case of nations, the U.S.S.R., who was one a trusted and close friend of China, is now regarded as her chief enemy.

For a long time there were successive heavy losses and problems in the Chinese economy, education, and so forth. However, to hide these problems, propaganda about great success was drummed up; even workers and common cadres were made to publicise statistics learnt by rote. The amount of energy spent on these could have moved mountains and churned oceans but all these efforts achieved nothing and only exhausted the people.

So now, in order to catch up with the rest of the world, to cope with realities and to modernize China, great changes in Chinese politics have taken place recently. And, particularly, since their propaganda failed, the Vice-Premier Teng Hsiao-ping has been repeatedly making statement like; "seeking trust from facts", "if the masses feel some anger, we must let them express it", "if you have an ugly face, it is no use pretending to be handsome", "we must recognize our shortcomings and mistakes". Unlike the previous Chinese leadership, there now appears to be a desire for honesty, modernization and leniency.

The present Chinese leaders should give up the past dogmatic narrow-mindedness and fear of losing face and recognize the present world situation. They should accept their mistakes, the realities, and the right of all peoples of the human race to equality and happiness. Acceptance of this should not be merely on paper; it should be put in practice. If these are accepted and strictly followed, all problems can be solved with honesty and justice.

During the commemoration of the last 10th March Anniversary, I said that Tibetans inside Tibet who desire to travel abroad should be allowed to do so and those outside Tibet should be able to visit their country and meet with people. If this freedom existed, the truth about conditions on both sides would be clear to the Tibetans. This opportunity is the right of the Tibetans. Such a policy is also practicable and reasonable.

A beginning has now been made of granting

such an opportunity for the Tibetans in exile to meet their families and relatives. It is their right and so this is a welcome gesture. But, it is important that, besides the showcases, they must be permitted to see the actual conditions in Tibet, because so far the true conditions have been hidden from all foreigners who have visited Tibet. Such actions may serve the Chinese purpose a few times but will, in the end, bring only disgrace. This is clear from recent events in China. Therefore, I hope the Chinese will not resort to similar attempts when Tibetans visit Tibet in the future.

In short, to find the truth about conditions in Tibet from such visits we shall have to investigate whether all the conditions for a satisfactory meeting of the visitors and residents exist: I hope that any Tibetan who desires to travel outside Tibet will be able to do so without any restriction, and such an opportunity may not be denied on various excuses and pretexts as done in the past.

My statements, which have been based on our experiences of the past 20 years or so might not at first mean much to the present Chinese occupation forces and some Tibetan cadres, but if they discarded bias and chauvinism, and remembered past experiences, stopped being narrow-minded and egoistic and making statements like, "East Wind Will Prevail Over the West Wind," and instead considered the good and the bad aspects of the actual conditions and welfare of both the East and the West, I hope that believe that this statement becomes the basis for discovering the truth and thereby bringing improvement.

Finally, I would like to make special mention at the time of our 20 years in exile the assistance given by the Government of India to the Tibetan people in rehabilitating, education and in preserving and promoting our culture and religion. We also deeply appreciate India's humanitarian concern and the warm relationship that exists between the two countries from centuries ago and in particular our religious and cultural relationship, which may be described as that of one, between a teacher and student. The incalculable good-will and assistance that the Tibetan people have received from the people, the Central and state Government of India at a particularly tragic period in the history of Tibet, will never be forgotten and will be accorded an important chapter in the history of Tibet as well as the history of world Buddhism.

48

Statement of His Holiness the Dalai Lama on the 21st Anniversary of the Tibetan People's National Uprising Day of 10th March, 1959

(MARCH 10, 1980)

EVERY year on this day, the anniversary of the Tibet National Uprising I greet all my compatriots both in Tibet and in exile.

Twenty-one years have unfolded a shocking experience, which has never had any parallel in his history of Tibet. Never has there been so much systematic and extensive destruction of the religious, cultural, social and educational value of the Tibetan people. The frightening picture of abject poverty, wretched and helpless general conditions, persistent starvation and famine, has been experienced in Tibet for centuries.

In the past few years, the fluid international political scene has witnessed rapid new developments; the internal situation in China under the present leadership who are "seeking the truth from facts" is also undergoing changes. We hear of the repeated calls by the Chinese Government requesting us to return to our homeland. We also hear the so-called wave of moderation has begun to creep into China and, to some extent, into Tibet. However, it is still too early to predict the outcome of what may happen in the future. In response to these changes, as well as to the request by the Chinese government, I have despatched a fact-finding delegation to visit Tibet through China. It is for the first time in nearly twenty-one years that we have established contact with the Chinese Government, as well as our beloved countrymen.

In view of the present situation and development in Tibet we exiles have a tremendous obligation and responsibility to fulfil the hopes and aspirations of the 6,000,000 Tibetans in Tibet. We should make full use of the wonderful opportunity provided by the government and the people of India, for educating thousand of our young Tibetans as well as enabling us to preserve our religious and cultural identities.

It is for the future that we must prepare ourselves. Even though China, during the Manchu Dynasty had constantly tried to exploit and divide the Tibetans, the present adversity had unified all our people. Never in the history of Tibet have the people been so united as they are today.

It is upto us, the Tibetans in India and elsewhere, to work hard and take inspiration from our compatriots in Tibet. Any failure in our duties would be a mockery to the memory of those who have sacrificed their lives for the cause of Tibet, while undergoing tremendous hardship, but who have remained steadfast to the ideals for which we have left our country.

There is no question, despite the current leniency, that we in exile are much better off than our friends and relatives in Tibet. Here were have absolute freedom to go wherever we like, do what ever we like and practise every aspect of our religion and traditions without fear of censure from any quarter. Most important of all, our younger generation have at their disposal all the modern educational facilities of the free world. They can learn whatever they are interested in or whatever they feel will contribute something worthwhile to their community, whereas what passes for education in Tibet—still to this day—is what the authorities decide is good for them. This, I feel, is one of the worst aspects of the Chinese rule in Tibet—this lack of real education. Children of today are the makers of the future society. If the future of our society is in any way to be meaningful in terms of our being a member of the world community, then they must have a modern education, conducive to a cosmopolitan outlook of life, as well as being familiar enough with their own culture and tradition in order to retain their distinct identity.

The present policy of leniency favoured by the Chinese in Tibet, I think, has also room for our contribution towards overcoming this educational discrepancy of the youth in Tibet. There are some Tibetan refugees visiting Tibet now. Why don't some of our youth, who have received decent educational opportunities, offer their service to take up teaching posts in Tibet on a temporary basis, in schools there. And I see no reason, given the present situation, the Chinese authorities should put any objection to this. So on this 21st anniversary of our fight for truth and justice, I hope you youth will seriously consider this suggestion of mine.

In conclusion, once more I would like to remind everybody that the core of Tibetan issue is the welfare and ultimate happiness of six-million Tibetans in Tibet. The limited leniency that the Chinese have introduced is a welcome first step. But we are still nowhere near being satisfied that the Tibetans in Tibet are content. What the future holds in store only time will tell. The course I favour is to wait and watch to what extend the Chinese leaders are going to improve the conditions in Tibet.

49

Statement of His Holiness the Dalai Lama on the 22nd Anniversary of the Tibetan People's National Uprising Day of 10th March, 1959

(MARCH 10, 1981)

TODAY marks the twenty-second anniversary of the Tibetan people's struggle for their rights of national freedom, something to be commemorated not only by our own but also by future generations. Recognizing the nature and perspective of our struggle, we must on this occasion reinforce the strength of our courage and determination.

During the past twenty-odd years, the large masses of Tibetans left in Tibet have been subjected to sufferings of death, hunger and exploitation which defies description; while those who were able to flee were forced to become exiled from their homeland and to live in foreign countries. We Tibetans of the present generations have had to experience tremendous miseries and tribulations unparalleled in our entire past history. Nevertheless, there is no denying the fact that because of these very factors there will definitely be a realization of positive effects in the long-run. No matter how great negative trends such as hypocrisy, deception and arrogant aggression become in the world today, nevertheless as truth and justice always prevail, the true cause of our Tibet is becoming ever more clear to the world. Therefore, with conviction and never becoming discouraged, we should hold firm to our courage and dedication as in the past.

Although Tibet was not advanced in terms of scientific, technological or material progress, yet it is a nation rich in culture and having a history of more than two thousand years. By the power of this rich cultural heritage, the Tibetans are naturally a happy and well-adjusted people, thus forming a distinct society in the family of man. These are qualities praised and regarded as worthy of emulation by sensible people the world over.

Until the conditions ripen for all the people in this world to be come one great united fraternal family, each society should have the right to preserve and develop its unique traditional heritage and culture along with modern science and technology. Therefore, at present, one of our principal concerns in the struggle for the rights of six million people of Tibet should be the vigilant preservation and continuation of all those excellent aspects of our distinct cultural heritage that are of value to our society, without letting them decline. This is most important.

The Chinese policy towards Tibet in the past has been like the Tibetan proverb, "Before your eyes they show you brown sugar, but in your mouth they give you sealing wax." While outwardly spreading outrageous exaggerations which are clever, sweet-sounding, impressive and seemingly convincing, but which falsify the facts, they in actual practice have only been subjecting the Tibetans to torture and oppression. In the face of that, the Tibetans had justified cause to strive to free themselves from the bondage of their sufferings, because all people have the right to free themselves from their own suffering. If in actual fact the distinctly Tibetan way of life were being kept fully intact and the people were happier now than under the formal conditions, then there would be no point to argue.

In recent times the Chinese have realized that their past self-defeating policies of deception, exaggeration and empty propaganda have been of more harm then benefit and have now adopted a new policy of "seeking truth from facts" and are trying to implement what they preach. Their admission of their past mistakes, without trying to cover them up, is praiseworthy. However, since the thirty-odd years of actual experience the Tibetan people have had under the domination of the Chinese has not been a short time, it is definitely going to take sometime to develop confidence and conviction in a new lenient line. This is a natural way of thinking of sensible people.

Finally, anger cannot be vanquished by anger, and past history has disappeared into the past. What is more relevant is that in the future there actually be real and happiness through developing a friendly and meaningful relation between China and Tibet. For this to be realized, it is important for both sides to work hard to have tolerant understanding and be open-minded.

With prayers for the peace, happiness and welfare of all.

50

Statement of His Holiness the Dalai Lama on the 23rd Anniversary of the Tibetan People's National Uprising Day of 10th March, 1959

(MARCH 10, 1982)

TODAY on the 23rd anniversary of 10th March, and at a time when the truth of our cause is becoming ever clearer, I send, along with my appreciation, greetings to the Tibetan people in and outside Tibet.

In any society, the distinction, between truth and falsehood, benefit and harm, is ultimately revealed by time and history. Similarly, the actual history of these last twenty-three years had done a big summing-up of whatever was the truth and whatever the false in the Issue of Tibet. Without resorting to untruth and lies, without fabricating non-existing accomplishments or belittling past achievements and erasing their traces, it is important to apply the reasonable method of "seeking truth from facts" in analysing and learning lessons derived from a calm and objective study of the roots of right and wrong as they have been revealed and are being revealed by actual history.

At this moment, questions of the old and the new social systems, religion, differing ideologies and systems spring to the mind of many Tibetans in and outside Tibet. As I have mentioned many times before, on this question the Tibetans will have to keep pace with the progressive changes that are occuring in the twentieth-century world and move towards democratic revolution. The old social system will never be resurrected. The teachings of the Buddha, as contained in the Tripitikas (the three baskets) and three Higher Trainings, are beneficial to society since they are based on sound reason and actual experience. These we must preserve and promote. However, the livelihood of lamas and monks and the administration of the monastic establishment must be necessity change with the changing times. Like the fact that all the waters and rivers of different lands and climes have their ultimate meeting point in the ocean, so too the differing viewpoints on society, the variety of economic theories and the means to their attainment, must benefit, and they do certainly benefit, mankind itself. There is no point in indulging in dissension-creating discussions on differing ideologies. The fact that no positive result has accused from attempting to convert all man of different temperaments and likings into one common ideology and mode of behaviour can clearly be seen from the contemporary history of both the East and the West. If a few, without caring the least for the basic welfare of people and the larger interests of mankind, continue to give order, break and kill, and yet label this atrocious behaviour as 'revolutionary', they are only fooling themselves. This behaviour is both short-sighted and parrot-like. A recent time issue of Red Flag journal has criticised a few persons who, far from serving the people and looking after their welfare, literally sit on people's heads and do whatever comes to their mind. Persons who adopt such behaviour are not needed in any society and they certainly do not belong to the ranks of those thinking human beings who work for the benefit of themselves as well as that of others.

In the last two or three years the situation in Tibet has undergone some slight change. Because of this a number of people, comparing this to past suffering, feel content with the present liberalisation and hope that a good result will come about soon. On the other, a number of other people feel that the present liberalisation policy is a new attempt to fool the Tibetans and that in the end the Tibetan people will not be given rights to equal freedom. The Tibetans should neither suffer such inflated hopes nor ingrained suspicion. They should not be impatient and hold hasty views. The Issue of Tibet is the issue of people whose history goes back thousands of year and whose religious and cultural heritage is rich. It is also an issue which is deeply linked with the changes in the international political scene. Consequently the Issue of Tibet should inevitably undergo a proper, satisfactory and decisive change since the present situation will never remain as it is. As such all Tibetans must continue to struggle, broad mindedly, peaceably and truthfully, for both the short-and long-term happiness, interests and rights of our people. This struggle must continue right to the end.

51

Five Point Peace Plan for Tibet

By

THE DALAI LAMA

THE WORLD is increasingly interdependent, so that lasting peace—national, regional, and global—can only be achieved if we think in terms of broader interest rather than parochial needs. At this time, it is crucial that all of us, the strong and the weak, contribute in our own way. I speak to you today as the leader of the Tibetan people and as Buddhist monk devoted to the principles of a religion based on love and compassion. Above all, I am here as a human being who is destined to share this planet with you and all others as brothers and sisters. As the world grows smaller, we need each other more than in the past. This is true in all parts of the world, including the continent I come from.

At present in Asia, as elsewhere, tensions are high. There are open conflicts in the Middle East, Southeast Asia, and in my own country, Tibet. To a large extent, these problems are symptoms of the underlying tensions that exist among the area's great powers. In order to resolve regional conflicts, an approach is required that takes into account the interests of all relevant countries and peoples, large and small. Unless comprehensive solutions are formulated, that take into account the aspirations of the people most directly concerned, piecemeal or merely expedient measures will only create new problems.

The Tibetan people are eager to contribute to regional and world peace, and I believe they are in a unique position to do so. Traditionally, Tibetans are a peace loving and non-violent people. Since Buddhism was introduced to Tibet over one thousand years ago, Tibetans have practiced non-violence with respect to all forms of life. This attitude has also been extended to our country's international relations. Tibet's highly strategie position in the heart of Asia, separating the continent's great powers—India, China and the USSR—has throughout history endowed it with an essential role in the maintenance of peace and stability. This is precisely why, in the past, Asia's empires went to great lengths to keep one another out of Tibet. Tibet's value as an independent buffer state was integral to the region's stability.

When the newly formed People's Republic of China invaded Tibet in 1949/50, it created a new source of conflict. This was highlighted when, following the Tibetan national uprising against the Chinese and my flight to India in 1959, tensions between China and India escalated into the border war in 1962. Today large numbers of troops are again massed on both sides of the Himalayan border and tension is once more dangerously high.

The real issue, of course, is not the Indo-Tibetan border demarcation. It is China's illegal occupation of Tibet, which has given it direct access to the Indian sub-continent. The Chinese authorities have attempted to confuse the issue by claiming that Tibet has always been a part of China. This is untrue. Tibet was a fully independent state when the People's Liberation Army invaded the country in 1949/50.

It is my sincere desire, as well as that of the Tibetan people, to restore to Tibet her invaluable role, by converting the entire country—comprising the three provinces of U-Tsang, Kham and Amdo—one more into a place of stability, peace and harmony. In the best of Buddhist tradition, Tibet would extend its services and hospitality to all who further the cause of world peace and the well-being of mankind and the natural environment we share.

Despite the holocaust inflicted upon our people in the past decades of occupation, I have always strived to find a solution through direct and honest discussions with the Chinese. In 1982, following the change of leadership in China and the establishment of direct contacts with the government in Peking, I sent my representatives to Peking to open talks concerning the future of my country and people.

We entered the dialogue with a sincere and positive attitude and with a willingness to take into account the legitimate needs of the People's Republic of China. I hoped that this attitude would be reciprocated and that a solution could eventually be found which would satisfy and safeguard the aspirations and interests of both parties. Unfortunately, China has consistently responded to our efforts in a defensive manner, as though our detailing of Tibet's very real difficulties was criticism for its own sake.

To our even greater dismay, the Chinese government misused the opportunity for a genuine dialogue. Instead of addressing the real issues facing the six million Tibetan people, China has attempted to reduce the question of Tibet to a discussion of my own personal status.

It is against this background and in response to the tremendous support and encouragement I have been given by you and other persons I have met during this trip, that I wish today to clarify the principal issues and to propose, in a spirit of openness and conciliation, a first step towards a lasting solution. I hope this may contribute to a future of friendship and cooperation with all of our neighbours, including the Chinese people.

This peace plan contains five basic components:

1. Transformation of the whole of Tibet into a zone of peace;
2. Abandonment of China's population transfer policy which threatens the very existence of the Tibetans as a people;
3. Respect for the Tibetan people's fundamental human rights and democratic freedoms;
4. Restoration and protection of Tibet's natural environment and the abandonment of China's use of Tibet for the production of nuclear weapons and dumping of nuclear waste;
5. Commencement of earnest negotiations on the future status of Tibet and of relations between the Tibetan and Chinese peoples.

Let me explain these five components.

1. I propose that the whole of Tibet, including the eastern provinces of Kham and Amdo, be transformed into a zone of "Ahimsa", a Hindi term used to mean a state of peace and non-violence.

The establishment of such a peace zone would be in keeping with Tibet's historical role as a peaceful and neutral Buddhist nation and buffer state separating the continent's great powers. It would also be in keeping with Nepal's proposal to proclaim Nepal a peace zone and with China's declared support for such a proclamation. The peace zone proposed by Nepal would have a much greater impact if it were to include Tibet and neighbouring areas.

The establishment of peace zone in Tibet would require withdrawal of Chinese troops and military installations from the Country, which would enable India also to withdraw troops and military installations from the Himalayan regions bordering Tibet. This would be achieved under an international agreement which would satisfy China's legitimate security needs and build trust among the Tibetan, Indian, Chinese and other peoples of the region. This is in everyone's best interest, particularly that of China and India, as it would enhance their security, while reducing the economic burden of maintaining high troops concentrations on the disputed Himalayan border.

Historically, relations between China and India were never strained. It was only when Chinese armies marched into Tibet, creating for the first time a common border, that tensions arose between these two powers, ultimately leading to the 1962 war. Since then numerous dangerous incidents have continued to occur. A restoration of good relations between the world's two most populous countries would be greatly facilitated if they were separated—as they were throughout history—by a large and friendly buffer region.

To improve relations between the Tibetan people and the Chinese, the first requirement is the creation of trust. After the holocaust of the last decades in which over one million Tibetans—one sixth of the population—lost their lives and at least as many lingered in prison camps because of their religious beliefs and love of freedom, only a withdrawal of Chinese troops could start a genuine process of reconciliation. The vast occupation force in Tibet is a daily reminder to the Tibetans of the oppression and suffering they have all experienced. A troop withdrawal would be an essential signal that in future a meaningful relationship might be established with the Chinese, based on friendship and trust.

2. The population transfer of Chinese into Tibet, which the government in Peking pursues in order to force a "final solution" to the Tibetan problems by reducing the Tibetan population to an insignificant and disenfranchised minority in Tibet itself, must be stopped

The massive transfer of Chinese civilians into Tibet in violation of the Fourth Geneva Convention (1949), threatens the very existence of the Tibetans as a distinct people. In the eastern parts of our country, the Chinese now greatly outnumber Tibetans. In the Amdo province, for example, where I was born, there are, according to Chinese statistics, 2.5 million Chinese and only 750,000 Tibetans. Even in the so-called Tibet Autonomous Region (i.e., central and western Tibet), Chinese Government sources now confirm that Chinese outnumber Tibetans.

The Chinese population transfer policy is not new: It has been systematically applied to other areas before. Earlier in this century, the Manchus were a distinct race with their own culture and traditions. Today only two to three million Manchurians are left in Manchuria, where 75 million Chinese have settled. In Eastern Turkestan, which the Chinese now call Sinkiang, the Chinese population has grown from 200,000 in 1949 to 7 million, more-than half of the total population of 13 million. In the wake of the Chinese colonization of Inner Mongolia, Chinese number 8.5 million, Mongols 2.5 million.

Today, in the whole of Tibet 7.5 million Chinese settlers have already been sent, outnumbering the Tibetan population of 6 million. In central and western Tibet, now referred to by the Chinese as the "Tibet Autonomous Region", Chinese sources admit the 1.9 million Tibetans already constitute a minority of the region's population. These numbers do not take the estimated 300,000-500,000 troops in Tibet into account 250,000 of them in the so-called Tibet Autonomous Region.

For the Tibetans to survive as a people, it is imperative that the population transfer is stopped and Chinese settlers return to China. Others, Tibetans will soon be no more than a tourist attract and relic of a noble past.

3. Fundamental human rights and democratic freedoms must be respected in Tibet. The Tibetan people must once again be free to develop culturally, intellectually, economically and spiritually and to exercise basic democratic freedoms.

Human rights violations in Tibet are among the most serious in the world. Discrimination is practiced in Tibet under a policy of "apartheid" which the Chinese call "segregation and assimilation." Tibetans are, at best, second class citizens in their own country. Deprived of all basic democratic rights and freedoms, they exist under a colonial administration in which all real power is wielded by Chinese officials of the Communist Party and the army.

Although the Chinese Government allows Tibetans to rebuild some Buddhist monasteries and to worship in them, it still forbids serious study and teaching of religion. Only a small number of people, approved by the Communist Party, are permitted to join the monasteries.

While Tibetans in exile exercise their democratic rights under a constitution promulgated by me in 1963, thousands of our countrymen suffer in prisons and labour camps in Tibet for their religious or political convictions.

4. Serious efforts must be made to restore the natural environment in Tibet. Tibet should not be used for the production of nuclear weapons and the dumping of nuclear waste.

Tibetans have a great respect for all forms of life. This inherent feeling is enhanced by the Buddhist faith, which prohibits the harming of all sentient beings, whether human or animal. Prior to the Chinese invasion, Tibet was an unspoiled wilderness sanctuary in a unique natural environment. Sadly, in the past decades the wildlife and the forests of Tibet have been almost totally destroyed by the Chinese. The effects on Tibet's delicate environment have been devastating. What little is left in Tibet must be protected and efforts must be made to restore the environment to its balanced state.

China used Tibet for the production of nuclear weapons and may also have started dumping nuclear waste in Tibet. Not only does China plan to dispose of its own nuclear waste but also that of other countries, who have already agreed to pay Peking to dispose of their toxic materials.

The dangers this presents are obvious. Not only living generations, but future generations are threatened by China's lack of concern for Tibet's unique and delicate environment.

5. Negotiations on the future status of Tibet and the relationship between the Tibetan and Chinese peoples should be started in earnest.

We wish to approach this subject in a reasonable and realistic way, in a spirit of frankness and conciliation and with a view to finding a solution that is in the long term interest of all: the Tibetans, the Chinese, and all other peoples concerned. Tibetans and Chinese are distinct peoples, each with their own country, history, culture, language and way of life. Differences among peoples must be recognized and respected. They need not, however, form obstacles to genuine cooperation where this is in the mutual benefit of both peoples. It is my sincere belief that if the concerned parties were to meet and discuss their future with an open mind and a sincere desire to find a satisfactory and just solution, a breakthrough could be achieved. We must all exert ourselves to be reasonable and wise, and to meet in a spirit of frankness and understanding.

Let me end on a personal note. I wish to thank you for the concern and support which you and so many of your colleagues and fellow citizens have expressed for the plight of oppressed people everywhere. The fact that, you have publicly shown your sympathy for us Tibetans, has already had a positive impact on the lives of our people inside Tibet. I ask for your continued support in this critical time in our country's history.

Thank you.

FRAMEWORK FOR SINO-TIBETAN NEGOTIATIONS

We are living today in a very interdependent world. One nation's problems can no longer be solved by itself. Without a sense of universal responsibility our very survival is in danger. I have, therefore, always believed in the need for better understanding, closer co-operation and greater respect among the various nations of the world. The European Parliament is an inspiring example. Out of the chaos of war, those who were once enemies have, in a single generation, learned to co-exist and to co-operate. I am, therefore, particularly pleased and honoured to address this gathering at the European Parliament.

As you know, my own country - Tibet - is undergoing a very difficult period. The Tibetans—particularly those who live under Chinese occupation — yearn for freedom and justice and a self-determined future, so that they are able to fully preserve their unique identity and live in peace with their neighbours.

For over a thousand years we Tibetans have adhered to spiritual and environmental values in order to maintain the delicate balance of life across the high plateau on which we live. Inspired by the Buddha's message of non-violence and compassion and protected by our mountains, we sought to respect every form of life and to abandon war as an instrument of national policy.

I have thought for a long time on how to achieve a realistic solution to my nation's plight. My cabinet and I solicited the opinions of many friends and concerned persons. As a result, on September 21, 1987, at the Congressional Human Rights Caucus in Washington, D.C., I announced a Five Point peace Plan for Tibet. In it I called for the conversion of Tibet into a zone of peace, a sanctuary in which humanity and nature can live together in harmony. I also called for respect for human rights and democratic ideals, environmental protection, and a halt to the Chinese population transfer into Tibet.

The fifth point of the Peace Plan called for earnest negotiations between the Tibetans and the Chinese. We have, therefore, taken the initiative to formulate some thoughts which, we hope, may serve as a basis for resolving the issue of Tibet. I would live to take this opportunity to inform the distinguished gathering here of the main points of our thinking.

The whole of Tibet known as Cholka-Sum (U-Tsang, Kham and Amdo) should become a self-governing democratic political entity founded on law by agreement of the people for the common good and the protection of themselves and their environment, in association with the People's Republic of China.

The Government of the People's Republic of China could remain responsible for Tibet's foreign policy. The Government of Tibet should, however, develop and maintain relations, through its own Foreign Affairs Bureau, in the fields of commerce, education, culture, religion, tourism, science, sports and other non-political activities. Tibet should join international organizations concerned with such activities.

The Government of Tibet should be founded on a constitution or basic law. The basic law should provide for a democratic system of government entrusted with the task of ensuring economic equality, social justice and protection of the environment. This means that the Government of Tibet will have the right to decide on all affairs relating to Tibet and the Tibetans.

As individual freedom is the real source and potential of any society's development, the Government of Tibet would seek to ensure this freedom by full adherence to the Universal Declaration of Human Rights including the rights to speech, assembly and religion. Because religion constitutes the source of Tibet's national identity, and spiritual values lie at the very heart of Tibet's rich culture, it would be the special duty of the Government of Tibet to safeguard and develop its practice.

The government should be comprised of a popularly elected Chief Executive, a bi-cameral legislative branch, and an independent judicial system. Its seat should be in Lhasa.

The social and economic system of Tibet should be determined in accordance with the wishes of the Tibetan people, bearing in mind especially the need to raise the standard of living of the entire population.

The Government of Tibet would pass strict laws to protect wildlife and plant life. The exploitation of natural resources would be careful regulated. The manufacture, testing and stockpiling of nuclear weapons and other armaments must be prohibited, as well as the use of nuclear power and other technologies which produce hazardous waste. It would be the Government of Tibet's goal to transform Tibet into our planet's largest natural preserve.

A regional peace conference should be called to ensure that Tibet becomes a genuine sanctuary of peace through demilitarization. Until such a peace conference can be convened and demilitarization and neutralization achieved, China could have the right to maintain a restricted number of military installations in Tibet. These must be solely for defence purposes.

In order to create an atmosphere of trust conducive to fruitful negotiations, the Chinese Government should cease its human rights violations in Tibet and abandon its policy of transferring Chinese to Tibet.

These are the thoughts we have in mind. I am aware that many Tibetans will be disappointed by the moderate stand they represent. Undoubtedly, there will be much discussion in the coming months within our own community, both in Tibet and in exile. This, however, is an essential and invaluable part of any process of change. I believe these thoughts represent the most realistic means by which to re-establish Tibet's separate identity and restore the fundamental rights of the Tibetan people while accommodating China's own interests. I would like to emphasize, however, that whatever the outcome of the negotiations with the Chinese may be, the Tibetan people themselves must be the ultimate deciding authority. Therefore, any proposal will contain a comprehensive procedural plan to ascertain the wishes of the Tibetan people in a nationwide referendum.

I would like to take this opportunity to state that I do not wish to take any active part in the Government of Tibet. Nevertheless, I will continue to work as much as I can for the well-being and happiness of the Tibetan people as long as it is necessary.

We are ready to present a proposal to the Government of the People's Republic of China based on the thoughts I have presented. A negotiating team representing the Tibetan Government has been selected. We are prepared to meet with the Chinese to discuss details of such a proposal aimed at achieving an equitable solution.

We are encouraged by the keen interest being shown in our situation by a growing number of governments and political leaders, including former President Jimmy Carter of the United States. We are also encouraged by the recent changes in China which have brought about a new group of leadership, more pragmatic and liberal.

We urge the Chinese Government and leadership to give serious and substantive consideration to the ideas I have described. Only dialogue and a willingness to look with honesty and clarity at the reality of Tibet can lead to a viable solution. We wish to conduct discussions with the Chinese Government bearing in mind the larger interests of humanity. Our proposal will therefore be made in a spirit of conciliation and we hope that the Chinese will respond accordingly.

My country's unique history and profound spiritual heritage render it ideally suited for fulfilling the role of a sanctuary of peace at the heart of Asia. Its historic status as a neutral buffer state, contributing to the stability of the entire continent, can be restored. Peace and security for Asia as well as for the world at large can be enhanced. In the future, Tibet need no longer be an occupied land, oppressed by force, unproductive and scarred by suffering. It can become a free heaven where humanity and nature live in harmonious balance; a creative model for the resolution of tensions afflicting many areas throughout the world.

The Chinese leadership needs to realize that colonial rule over occupied territories is today anarchronistic. A genuine union or association can only come about voluntarily, when there is satisfactory benefit to all the parties concerned. The European Community is a clear example of this. On the other hand, even one country or community can break into two or more entities when there is a lack of trust or benefit, and when force is used as the principal means of rule.

I would like to end by making a special appeal to the honourable members of the European Parliament and through them to their respective constituencies to extend their support to our efforts. A resolution of the Tibetan problem within the framework that we propose will not only be for the mutual benefit of the Tibetan and Chinese people but will also contribute to regional and global peace and stability. I thank you for providing me the opportunity to share my thoughts with you.

[*Speech Delivered at the European Parliament, Strasbourg,* 15 June, 1988.]

52

His Holiness the Dalai Lama's Letter to Deng Xiaoping, 11 September 1992

DEAR MR. Deng Xiaoping,

I am pleased that direct contact has once again been established between us. I hope that this will lead to an improvement of relations and the development of mutual understanding and trust.

I have been informed of the discussions Mr. Ding Guangen had with Gyalo Thondup on June 22, 1992, and the position of the Government of China concerning negotiations for a solution to the Tibetan question. I am disappointed with the hard and inflexible position conveyed by Mr. Ding Guangen, particularly the emphasis on pre-conditions for negotiations.

However, I remain committed to the belief that our problems can be solved only through negotiations, held in an atmosphere of sincerity and openness, for the benefit of both the Tibetan and Chinese people. To make this possible, neither side should put up obstacles, and neither side should, therefore, state pre-conditions.

For meaningful negotiations to take place it is essential to have mutual trust. Therefore, in order to create trust, I believe it is important for the leaders and people of China to know of the endeavours I have made so far. My three representatives carry with them a letter from me, accompanied by a detailed note of my views and my efforts through the years to promote negotiations in the best interest of the Tibetan and Chinese people. They will answer and discuss my questions and points you wish to raise. It is my hope that through these renewed discussions we will find a way that will lead us to negotiations.

On my part, I have put forward many ideas to solve our problem. I believe that it is now time for the Chinese Government to make a genuinely meaningful proposal if you wish to see Tibet and China live together in peace. I, therefore, sincerely hope that you will respond in a spirit of openness and friendship.

Yours *sincerely*,
(H H the Dalai Lama)

53

Note Accompanying His Holiness the Dalai Lama's Letter to Deng Xiaoping, 11 September 1992

ON JUNE 22, 1992, Mr. Ding Guangen, head of the United Front works Department of CCP Central Committee, met with Mr. Gyalo Thondup in Beijing and restated the assurance given by Mr. Deng Xiaoping to Mr. Gyalo Thondup in 1979 that the Chinese Government was willing to discuss any issue with us except total independence.

Mr. Ding Guangen also said that, in the government's view, "the Dalai Lama is continuing with independence activities", but the Chinese Government was willing to immediately start negotiations as soon as I give up the independence of Tibet. This position, repeatedly stated in the past by the Chinese Government, shows that the Chinese leadership still does not understand my ideas regarding the Tibetan-Chinese relationship. Therefore, I take this opportunity to clarify my position through this note.

1. It is an established fact that Tibet and China existed as separate countries in the past. However, as a result of misrepresentations of Tibet's unique relations with the Mongol and the Manchu Emperors, disputes arose between Tibet and the Kuomintang and the present Chinese Government. The fact that the Chinese Government found it necessary to conclude a "17-Point Agreement" with the Chinese Government in 1951 clearly shows the Chinese Government's acknowledgment of Tibet's unique position.

2. When I visited Beijing in 1954, I had the impression that most of the Communist Party leaders I met there were honest, straightforward and openminded. Chairman Mao Zedong, in particular, told me on several occasions that the Chinese were in Tibet only to help Tibet harness its natural resources and use them for the development of the country, General Zhang Jingwu and General Fan Ming, were in Tibet to help me and the people of Tibet, and not to rule the Tibetan Government and people, and that all Chinese officials in Tibet were there to help us and to be withdrawn when Tibet had progressed. Any Chinese official who did not act accordingly would be sent back to China. Chairman Map went on to say that it had now been decided to establish "Preparatory Committee for the Establishment of the Tibet Autonomous Region" instead of the earlier plan to put Tibet under the direct control of the Chinese Government through a "Military-Political Commission."

At my last meeting with Chairman Mao, before I left China, he gave me a long explanation about democracy. He said that I must provide leadership and advised me on how to keep in touch with the views of the people. He spoke in a gentle and compassionate manner which was moving and inspiring.

While in Beijing, I told Premier Zhou Enlai that we Tibetans were fully aware of our need to develop politically, socially and economically and that in fact I had already taken steps towards this.

On my way back to Tibet. I told General Zhang Guohua that I had gone to China with doubts and anxiety about the future of my people and country, but had now returned with great hope and optimism and a very positive impression of the Chinese leader. My innate desire to serve my people, especially the poor and the weak, and the prospect of mutual cooperation and friendship between Tibet and China made me feel hopeful and optimistic about the Tibet's future development. This was how I felt at that time about the Tibetan-Chinese relationship.

3. When the "Tibet Autonomous Region Preparatory Committee" was set up in Lhasa in 1956, there was no alternative but to work sincerely with it for the interest and benefit of both parties. However, by then the Chinese authorities had already started to use unthinkable brutal force to impose Communism on the Tibetan people of the Kham and Amdo areas, particular in Lithang. This increased the resentment of the Tibetans against Chinese policies, leading to open resistance.

I could not believe that Chairman Mao would have approved of such repressive policy because of the promises he had made to me when I was in China. I, therefore, wrote three letters to him explaining the situation and seeking an end to the repression. Regrettably, there was no reply to my letters.

In late 1956, I visited India to attend Buddha Jayanti, the anniversary of the birth of Buddha. At that time, many Tibetans advised me not to return to Tibet, and to continue talks with China from India. I also felt that I should stay in India for the time being. While in India, I met Premier Zhou Enlai and told him how deeply saddened I was by the military repression inflicted upon Tibetans in Kham and Amdo in the name of "reforms." Premier Zhou Enlai said that he regarded these matters as mistakes committed by Chinese officials and that "reforms" in Tibet would be carried out only in accordance with the wishes of the Tibetan people, and that in fact the Chinese Government had already decided to postpone the "reforms" in Tibet by six years. He then urged me to return to Tibet as soon as possible in order to prevent further outbreaks of unrest.

According to the Indian Prime Minister, Jawaharlal Nehru, Premier Zhou Enlai told him that the Chinese Government "did not consider Tibet as a province of China. The people were different from the people of China proper. Therefore, they [the Chinese] considered Tibet as an autonomy." Prime Minister Nehru told me that the had assurance from Premier Zhou Enlai that Tibet's autonomy would be respected and, therefore, advised me to make efforts to safeguard it and cooperate with China in bringing about reforms.

By then, the situation in Tibet had become extremely dangerous and desperate. Nevertheless, I decided to return to Tibet to give the Chinese Government another opportunity to be able to implement their promises. On my return to Lhasa through Dromo, Gyangtse and Shigatse I had many meetings with Tibetan and Chinese officials; I told them that the Chinese were not in Tibet to rule the Tibetans, that the Tibetans were not subjects of China, and that since the Chinese leader had promised to establish Tibet as an autonomous region with full internal freedoms, we all had to work to make it succeed. I emphasised the point that the leaders of China had assured me that all Chinese personnel in Tibet were there to help us, and that if they behaved otherwise, they could be going against the order of their own government. I believe, I was once again doing my best to promote cooperation between Tibet and China.

4. However, because of the harsh military repression in the Kham and Amdo parts of

eastern Tibet, thousands of young and old Tibetans, unable to live under such circumstances, began to arrive in Lhasa as refugees. As a result of these Chinese actions the Tibetan people felt great anxiety and began to lose faith in the promises made by China. This led to greater resentment and worsening of the situation. Nevertheless, I continued to counsel my people to seek a peaceful solution and to show restraint. At the risk of losing the trust of the Tibetan people I did my best to present a breakdown of the communications with the Chinese officials in Lhasa.

But the situation continued to deteriorate and finally exploded in the tragic events of 1959 which forced me to leave Tibet.

Faced with such a desperate situation, I had no alternative but to appeal to the United Nations. The United Nations, in turn, passed three resolutions on Tibet in 1959, 1961 and 1965, wherein it called for the cessation of practices which deprive the Tibetan people of their fundamental human rights and freedoms including their right to self-determination and asked member States to make all possible efforts towards achieving that purpose.

The Chinese Government did not respect the United Nations resolutions. in the meantime, the Cultural Revolution started and there was absolutely no opportunity for solving the Tibetan-Chinese problems. It was, in fact, not even possible to identify a leader with whom we could talk.

5. Inspite of my unfulfilled hopes and disappointments in dealing with the Chinese Government, and since Tibet and China will always remain as neighbours, I am convinced that we must strive to find a way to co-exist in peace and help each other. This, I believe, is possible and worthy of our efforts. With this conviction I said in my statement to the Tibetan people on March 10, 1971: "Inspite of the fact that we Tibetans have to oppose Communist China, I can never bring myself to hate her people. Hatred is not a sign of strength, but of weakness. When Lord Buddha said that hatred cannot be overcome by hatred, he was not only being spiritual. But his words reflect the practical reality of life. Whatever one achieves through hatred will not last long. On the other hand, hatred will only generate more problems. And for the Tibetan people who are faced with such a tragic situation, hatred will only bring additional depression. Moreover, how can we hate a people who do not know what they are doing. We cannot even hate the Chinese leaders for they have suffered tremendously for their nation and the cause which they believe to be right. I do not believe in hatred, but I do believe, as I have always done, that one day truth and justice will triumph."

In my March 10 statement of 1973, referring to the Chinese claim of Tibetans being made the "masters of the country" after being "liberated from the three big feudal lords" and enjoying "unprecedented progress and happiness", I stated: "The aim of the struggle of the Tibetans outside Tibet is the attainment of the happiness of the Tibetan people. If the Tibetans in Tibet are truly happy under the Chinese rule then there is no reason for us here in exile to argue otherwise."

Again, in my March 10, 1979 statement, I welcomed Mr. Deng Xiaoping's statement "to seek truth from facts", to give the Chinese people their long cherished rights, and of the need to acknowledge one's own mistakes and shortcomings. While commending these signs of honesty, progress and openness, I said: "The present Chinese leaders should give up the past dogmatic narrow-mindedness and fear of losing face and recognise the present world situation. They should accept their mistakes, the realities, and the right of all people of the human race to equality and happiness. Acceptance of this should not be merely on paper, it should be put into practice. If there are accepted and strictly followed, all problems can be solved with honesty and justice." With this conviction I renewed my efforts to promote reconciliation and friendship between China and Tibet.

6. In 1979, Mr. Deng Xiaoping invited Mr. Gyalo Thondup to Beijing and told him that apart from the question of total independence all other issues could be discussed and all problems can be resolved. Mr. Deng further told Mr. Thondup that we must keep in contact with each other and that we could send fact-finding delegations to Tibet. This naturally gave us great hopes of resolving our problems peacefully and we started sending delegations to Tibet.

On March 13, 1981, I sent a letter to Mr. Deng Xiaoping in which I said, "The three fact-finding delegations have been able to find out both the positive and negative aspects of the situation in Tibet. If the Tibetan people's identity is preserved and if they are genuinely happy, there is no reason to complain. However, in reality over 90% of the Tibetan are suffering both mentally and physically, and are living in deep sorrow. These said conditions has not been brought about by natural disasters, but by human actions. Therefore, genuine efforts must be made to sole the problem in accordance with the existing realities in a reasonable way.

In order to do this, we must improve the relationship between China and Tibet as well as between Tibetans in and outside Tibet. With truth and equality as our foundation we must try to develop friendship between Tibetans and Chinese in future through better understanding. Time has come to apply our common wisdom in a spirit of tolerance and broadmindedness to achieve genuine happiness for the Tibetan people with a sense of urgency. In my part, I remain committed to contribute to the welfare of all human beings and in particular the poor and the weak to the best of my ability without making any distinction based on national boundaries.

I hope you will let me know your views on the foregoing points."

There are no reply to my letter. Instead, on July 28, 1981, General Secretary Hu Yaobang gave Mr. Gyalo Thondup a document, entitled "Five Point Policy towards the Dalai Lama."

This was a surprise and a great disappointment. The reason for our consistent efforts to deal with the Chinese Government is to achieve lasting and genuine happiness for six million Tibetans who must live as neighbours of China from generation to generation. However, the Chinese leadership chose to ignore this and, instead, attempted to reduce the whole issue to that of my personal status and the conditions for my return without any willingness to address the real underlying issues.

Nevertheless, I continued to place hope in Mr. Den Xiaoping's statement "seeking truth from facts" and his policy of liberalisation. Therefore, I sent several delegations to Tibet and China and wherever there was an opportunity we explained our views to promote understanding through discussion and dialogue. As initially suggested by Mr. Den Xiaoping I agreed to send Tibetan teachers from India to improve the education of Tibetans in Tibet. But for one reason or the other the Chinese Government did not accept this.

These contacts resulted in four fact-finding delegations to Tibet, two delegations to Beijing, and the start of family visitations between the Tibetans in Tibet and in exile. However, these steps did not lead to any substantial progress in resolving the problems between us owing to the rigidity of the Chinese leaders' positions which, I believe, failed to reflect Mr. Den Xiaoping's policies.

7. Once again, I did not give up hope. This was reflected in my annual March 10 statements to the Tibetan people in 1981, 1983, 1984 and 1985, wherein I said the following:

"....Past history has disappeared in the past. What is more relevant is that in the future there actually must be real peace and happiness through developing friendly and meaningful relations between China and Tibet. For this to be realised, it is important for both sides to work hard to have tolerant understanding and be open-minded." (1981)

"The right to express one's ideas and to make every effort to implement them enables people everywhere to become creative and progressive. This engenders human society to make rapid progress and experience genuine harmony....The deprivation of freedom to express one's views, either by force or by other means, is absolutely anachronistic and a brutal form to oppression...The people of the world will not only appose it, but will condemn it. Hence, the six million Tibetan people must have the right to preserve, and enhance their cultural identity and religious freedom, and find fulfillment of their free self-expression, without interference from any quarters. This is reasonable and just." (1983)

"Irrespective of varying degrees of development and economic disparities, continents, nations, communities, families, in fact, all individuals are dependent on one another for their existence and well-beings. Every human being wishes for happiness and does not want suffering. By clearly realizing this, we must develop mutual compassion, love, and a fundamental sense of justice. In such an atmosphere there is hope that problems between nations and problems within families can be gradually overcome and that people can live in peace and harmony. Instead, if people adopt an attitude of selfishness, domination and jealously, the world at large, as well as individuals, will never enjoy peace and harmony. Therefore, I believe that human relations based on mutual happiness." ((184)

". . . in order to achieve genuine happiness in any human society, freedom of thought is extremely important. This freedom of thought can only be achieved from mutual trust, mutual understanding and the absence of fear. . . In the case of Tibet and China too, unless we can remove the state of mutual fear and mistrust, unless we can develop a genuine sense of friendship and goodwill the problems that we face today will continue to exist.

It is important for both of us to learn about one another... It is now for the Chinese to act according to the enlightened ideals and principles of the modern times; to come forward with an open mind and make a serious attempt to know and understand the Tibetan people's viewpoint and their true feelings and as irritations... It is wrong to react with suspicion or offence to the opinions that are contrary to one's own way of thinking. It is essential that differences of opinion be examined and discussed openly. When differing view-points are frankly stated and sensibly discussed on an equal footing, the decisions or agreements reached as a result will be genuine and beneficial to all concerned. But so long as there is a contradiction between thought and action, there can never be genuine and meaningful agreements.

So, at this time, I feel most important thing for us is to keep in close contact, to express our views frankly and to make sincere efforts to understanding each other. And, through eventual improvement inhuman relationship, I am confident that our problems can be solved to our mutual satisfaction. (1985)

In these and other ways I expressed my views clearly. But, there was no reciprocity to my conciliatory approaches.

8. Since all the exchanges between Tibetans and Chinese yielded no results I felt compelled to make public my view on the steps necessary for an agreeable solution to the fundamental issues. On September 21, 1987, I announced a Five Point Peace Plan in the United States of America. In its introduction, I said that in the hope of real reconciliation and lasting solution to the problem, it was my desire to take the first step with this initiative. This plan, I hoped, would in the future contribute to the friendship and cooperation among all the neighbouring countries including the Chinese people for their good and benefit. The basic elements were :

1. Transformation of the whole of Tibet into a zone of ahimsa (peace and non-violence);
2. Abandonment of China's population transfer policy which threatens the very existence of the Tibetans as a people;
3. Respect for the Tibetan people's fundamental human rights and democratic freedoms;
4. Restoration and protection of Tibet natural environment and the abandonment of China's use of Tibet for the production of nuclear weapons and dumping of nuclear waste;
5. Commencement of earnest negotiations on the future status of Tibet and of relations between the Tibetan and the Chinese peoples.

As a response to this initiative, Mr. Yang Mingfu met Mr. Gyalo Thondup on October 17, 1987 and delivered a message containing five points criticising me for my above peace initiative and accusing me of having instigated demonstrations in Lhasa of September 27, 1987 and of having worked against the interest of Tibetan people.

This response, far from giving serious thought to my sincere proposal for reconciliation, was disappointing and demeaning.

Despite this, I tried once again to clarify our views in a detailed 14 Point response on December 17, 1987.

9. One June 15, 1988, at the European Parliament in Strasbourg, I once again elaborated on the Five-Point Peace Plan. I proposed as a framework for negotiations to secure the basic rights of the Tibetan people, China could remain responsible for Tibet's foreign policy and maintain a restricted number of military installations in Tibet for defence until a regional peace conference is convened and Tibet is transformed into a neutral peace sanctuary. I was criticised by many Tibetans for this proposal. My idea was, to make it possible for China and Tibet to stay together in lasting friendship and to secure the right for Tibetans to govern their own country. I sincerely believe that in the future a demilitarised Tibet as a zone of Ahimsa will contribute to harmony and peace not only between Tibetan and Chinese, but to all the neighbouring countries and the entire region.

10. On September 23, 1988, the Chinese Government issued a statement that China was willing to begin negotiations with us. The announcement stated that the date and venue for the negotiations would be left to the Dalai Lama. We welcomed this announcement form Beijing and responded on October 25, 1988, proposing January1989 as the time and Geneva, an internationally recognized neutral venue, as our choices. We accounced that we had a negotiation team ready and named the members of the team.

The Chinese Government responded on November 18, 1988, rejecting Geneva and expressing preference for Beijing or else Hong Kong, as the venue. They further stated that my negotiation team could not include "a foreigner" and consist only of "younger people", and that it should have older people, including Mr. Gyalo Thondup. We explained that the foreigner was only a legal advisor and not an actual member of the negotiating team and that Mr. Gyalo Thondup would also be included as an advisor to the team.

With a flexible and open attitude we accommodated the Chinese Government's requests and agreed to send representatives to Hong Kong to hold preliminary meetings with representatives of the Chinese Government. Unfortunately, when both sides had finally agreed on Hong Kong as the site for preliminary discussions the Chinese Government refused to communicate any further and failed to live up to their own suggestion.

11. Although I championed this proposal for over two years there was no evidence of consideration or even an acknowledgment from Chinese Government.

Therefore, in my March 10th statement in 1991 I was compelled to state that unless the Chinese Government responded in the near future I would consider myself free from any obligation to abide by the proposal I made in France.

Since there appeared to be no benefit from the many solutions I had advocated concerning Tibet and China, I had to find a new way. Therefore, in a speech at Yale University on October 9, 1991, I said :

. . . I am considering the possibility of visit to Tibet myself on the spot and communicate directly with my people. By doing so, I also hope to help the Chinese leadership to understand the true feelings of Tibetans. It would be important, therefore, for senior Chinese leaders to accompany me on such a visit, and that out-side observers, including the press be present to see and report their findings.

Second, I wish to advise and persuade my people not to abandon non-violence as the appropriate form of struggle. My ability to talk to my own people can be a key factor in bringing about a peaceful solution. My visit could be a new opportunity to promote understand and create a basis for a negotiated solution.

Unfortunately this overture was immediately opposed by the Chinese Government. At that time, I was asked on many occasions by the press whether I was renewing the call for Tibetan independence since I had declared that the Strasbourg proposal was no longer valid. To these questions, I stated that I did not want to comment.

12. The Chinese Government has, with great doubt and suspicion, described our struggle as a movement to restore the "old society" and that it was not in the interest of the Tibetan people but for the personal status and interest of the Dalai Lama. Since my youth, I was aware of the many faults of the existing system in Tibet and wanted to improve it. At that time I started the process of reform in Tibet. Soon after our flight to India we introduced democracy in our exile community, step by step. I repeatedly urged my people to follow this path. As a result, our exiled community now implements a system in full accordance with universal democratic principles. It is impossible for Tibet to ever revert to the old system of government. Whether my efforts for the Tibetan cause are as charged by the Chinese for my personal position and benefit or not is clear from any repeated statements that in a future Tibet, I will not assume any governmental responsibility or hold any political positions Furthermore, this is reflected clearly in the Charter which governs the Tibetan Administration in Exile and in the "Guidelines for Future Tibet's Policy and the Basic Features of Its constitution," which I announced on February 26, 1992.

In the conclusion of these guidelines relationship with its neighbours on equal terms and for mutual benefits. It shall be devoid of hostility and enmity."

Similarly, in my statement of March 10th 1992, I stated, "When a genuinely cordial relationship is established between the Tibetans and the Chinese, it will enable us not only to resolve the disputes between our two nations in this century, but will also enable the Tibetans to make a significant contribution through our rich cultural tradition for mental peace among the millions of young Chinese."

My endeavours to establish a personal relationship with Chinese leaders include my offer, presented through your Embassy in New Delhi in the latter part of 1980, for a meeting with General Secretary Hu Yaobang during one of his visits abroad at any convenient place. Again in December 1991, when Premier Li Peng visited New Delhi, I proposed to meet him there. These overtures were to no avail.

13. An impartial review of the above points will clearly show that my ideas and successive efforts have consistently sought solutions that will allow Tibet and China to live together in peace. In the light of these facts it is difficult to understand the purpose to the Chinese Government's position that Mr. Den Xiaoping's statement on Tibet of 1979 still stands and that as soon as "the Dalai Lama gives up his splittist activities", negotiations could start. This position has been repeated over and over again with no specific responses to my many initiatives.

If China wants Tibet to stay with China, then China must create the necessary conditions for this. The time has come now for the Chinese to show the way for Tibet and China to live together in friendship. A detailed step-by-step outline regarding Tibet's basic status should be spelt out. If such a clear outline is given, regardless of the possibility or an agreement or not, we Tibetans can then make a decision whether to live with China or not. If we Tibetan obtain our basic right to our satisfaction then we are not incapable of seeing the possible advantages of living with the Chinese.

I trust in the far sightedness and wisdom of China's leaders and hope that they will take into consideration the current global political changes and the need to resolve the Tibetan problem peacefully, promoting genuine lasting friendship between our two neighbouring peoples.

[*Translated from the original Tibetan*.]

54

Statement of H.H. the Dalai Lama on the 35th Anniversary of Tibetan National Uprising Day, 10 March 1994

TODAY, as we observe the 35th anniversary of our National Uprising Day, I wish to take stock of our 14 years' effort to find a peaceful and realistic solution to the Tibetan issue through honest negotiations with the Chinese Government. In my endeavour to restore freedom, peace and dignity to our country and people, I have always sought to be guided by realism, patience and vision.

For the past 14 years, I have not only declared my willingness to enter into negotiations, but have also made maximum concessions in a series of initiatives and proposals which clearly lie within the framework for negotiations as stated by Den Xiaoping in 1979, that "except for the independence of Tibet, all other questions can be negotiated." The ideas put forward in my Five Point Peace Plan for Tibet in 1987 and the Strasbourg Proposal in 1988 envisage a solution which does not ask for the complete independence of Tibet. However, the Chinese Government has even refused to enter into negotiations of any kind. It has also avoided discussing any question of substance, insisting that the only issues to be resolved are those pertaining to my personal return to Tibet. The issue is not about my return to Tibet. I have stated this time and again. The issue is the survival of the six million Tibetan people along with the protection of our distinct culture, identity and civilization.

I have made it clear that the negotiations must centre around ways to end China's population transfer policy, which threatens the very survival of the Tibetan people, respect for Tibetans' fundamental human rights and entitlement to democratic freedom, the demilitarization and de-nuclearization of Tibet, the restoration of the Tibetan people's control over all matters affecting their own affairs, and the protection of Tibet's natural environment. Moreover, I have always emphasized that any negotiation must comprise the whole of Tibet, not just the areas which China calls the "Tibet Autonomous Region."

I have maintained this approach for the last 14 years in spite of the disappointment and criticism expressed by many Tibetan to my moderate stand. I have not forgotten that 1.2 million Tibetans have died and that Tibet has suffered immeasurably since the occupation of our country by Communist China. I also know that every Tibetan hopes and prays for the full restoration of our nation's independence.

Nevertheless, I had hoped that my middle way approach would eventually create an atmosphere of mutual trust conducive to fruitful negotiations and exert a restraining influence on the repressive Chinese policies in Tibet. Here, I appreciate the many Tibetans who have supported my initiatives and felt they were a practical necessity.

The Chinese Government has rejected my overtures one after another and has consistently attempted to confuse the real issue. Meanwhile, the magnitude and gravity of the situation inside Tibet has dramatically escalated. Developments in Tibet have been marked by an intensification of the Chinese policy of suppression, the marginalization of the Tibetan people in our own country, the gradual extermination of our unique culture and religion, and the destruction and exploitation of Tibet's environment.

I must now recognize that my approach has failed to produce any progress either for substantive negotiations or in contributing to the overall improvement of the situation in Tibet. Moreover, I am conscious of the fact that a growing number of Tibetans, both inside as well as outside Tibet, have been disheartened by my conciliatory stand not to demand complete independence for Tibet. Because of my statements, some Tibetans have come to believe that there is no hope at all the Tibetan people regaining their basic rights and freedoms. This, and the lack of any concrete results from my conciliatory approach towards and Chinese Government over the past 14 years have caused disillusionment and undermined the resolve of some Tibetans.

Internationally, my initiatives and proposals have been endorsed as realistic and reasonable by many governments, parliaments, and non-governmental organizations. But, despite the growing support of the international community, the Chinese Government has not responded constructively.

I have left no stone unturned in my attempts to reach an understanding with the Chinese. We have had to place our hopes on international support and help in bringing about meaningful negotiations, to which I still remain committed. If this fails, then I will no longer be able to pursue this policy with a clear conscience. I feel strongly that it would then be my responsibility, as I have stated many times in the past, to consult my people on the future course of our freedom struggle. Just as the late Indian Prime Minister, Jawaharlal Nehru, stated in the Indian Parliament on December 7, 1950, I too have always maintained that the final voice with regard to Tibet should be the voice of the Tibetan people. Whatever, the outcome of such a consultation, it will serve as a guideline for our future dealings with China and the reorientation of the course of our freedom struggle.

I continue to remain committed to finding a peaceful and negotiated resolution to the issue of Tibet with the Chinese Government directly. But the Chinese are merely paying lip service to this approach. It is evident that only increased international political and economic pressure can bring a sense of urgency to bear on the Chinese leadership not merely to pay lip service but to resolve the problem of Tibet peacefully and amicably. The tragedy of Tibet can be relieved through the determined and concerted efforts of various governments and NGOs championing human rights, liberty and democracy the world over.

If the Tibetan issue can be resolved peacefully, through mutual openness and understanding, I am convinced that it will help alleviate the anxiety felt in the minds of the six million residents of Hong Kong. It will also have a positive effect to China's relationship with Taiwan and enhance its international image.

Today, we remember those brave Tibetans who fought and died for the cause of our nation and those who are languishing in Chinese prisons. We also pay our respects to our courageous brothers and sisters in Tibet who are continuing the struggle for the freedom of our people under extremely adverse conditions. The course of history and the present world atmosphere are favourable to the aspirations of our nation. Our cause is gathering momentum. Fearful of these developments,

China has now formulated policies to undermine our administration in exile as well as to create discord and division in our community. Therefore, every one of us must be alert and renew our commitment to the just cause of our country. I firmly believe that the day is close when our beloved Land of Snows will not longer be politically subjugated, culturally ravaged, and economically and environmentally exploited and devastated. Our dedication, sacrifice and hard work will eventually lead our captive nation to freedom and peace in dignity. However, it is important that our struggle must be based on non-violence.

On behalf of all the Tibetan people, I want to take this opportunity to express our deep appreciation and gratitude to our many friends throughout the world for their support of our cause. I must also think the many parliaments and governments that have started to take a serious look at the Tibetan problem. Another positive development of recent years is support for our cause even amongst the Chinese people. For example, a long letter written on October 5, 1992, by the well-known Chinese dissident, Wei Jingsheng, to deng Xiaoping, speaking out against his government's unjust claims over Tibetan and their misguided, policies there, has just become public. These expressions are the manifestations of genuine human respect for truth and justice. I take this opportunity especially to thank our Chinese brothers and sisters the world over their support and encouragement. Finally, I wish to reiterate our immense gratitude and appreciation to all the countries where Tibetan exiles have been given asylum, particularly to the people and government of this country, which has become a second home for the majority of the Tibetans in exile.

My prayers for the peace and welfare of all sentiment beings.

55

Statement of His Holiness the Dalai Lama, 10 March 1995

THE WORLD is today undergoing major changes. While there is a spirit of reconciliation and peace emerging in many troubled parts of the world, unfortunately new conflicts are also breaking out. We have endeavoured to find a peaceful resolution to the Tibetan issue and hoped that positive changes would also come to Tibet. But, as we commemorate the 36th anniversary of our people's uprising, I must state with sadness that little has changed in our homeland and our people continue to suffer. In fact, the Chinese Government has intensified its repression in Tibet. Recent Chinese policies demonstrate more clearly than ever their intention to resolve the question of Tibet through force, intimidation and population transfer.

The Chinese authorities have lately adopted a series of new measures to tighten political control in Tibet. Under a programme of investigation and scrutiny" tighter security measures were imposed and a new crackdown on advocates of human rights and independence has been launched. Victims of this new political persecution include Tibetans who work for the preservation include Tibetans who work for the preservation of Tibetan culture, which includes teaching the Tibetan language and opening private schools. Tibetan cadres and members of the Chinese Communist Party are made to undergo political reeducation, reminiscent of the days of the Cultural revolution. Those suspected of harbouring religious and national feelings are being purged. Monasteries have been raided by the People's Armed Police and the chain of political arrests has now been extended to rural areas. The rebuilding and construction of new monasteries has been prohibited and the admission of new monks and nuns stopped. Tibetan travel agents and tourist guides have been dismissed in order to control the flow of information and Tibetan children are no longer permitted to study abroad. Those who are presently studying abroad have been ordered to return.

At a high-level meeting in Beijing last July these policies were sanctioned and 62 new "economic development projects" in Tibet were announced. As in the past, these projects are designed primarily "to increase the immigration of Chinese into Tibet and ultimately drown the Tibetans in a sea of Chinese. Similarly, China's proclaimed intention to build a railway to Central Tibet is particularly alarming. Under the present circumstances this will enable a dramatic acceleration of China's population transfer policy. We only need to look at the large influx of Chinese who are arriving by train every week in different parts of Eastern Turkestan to understand the impact such a railway will have on the survival of the Tibetan people with its unique cultural heritage.

Over the past 15 years, I have tried to resolve the Tibet-China problem in a spirit of genuine friendship and cooperation, discarding any feelings of enmity towards the Chinese. I have consistently and sincerely made attempts to engage the Chinese Government in earnest negotiations over the future of Tibet. Regrettably China has rejected my proposals for a negotiated resolution of our problem. Instead she has set the pre-condition that I formally recognise Tibet to be "an inseparable part of China" before any negotiations can start. The true nature of the historical relationship of Tibet and China is best left for Tibetan and Chinese historians to study objectively.. I also encourage other scholars, as well as international jurists and their institutions, to study the history of Tibet and draw their unbiased conclusions.

In the past I have deliberately restrained myself from emphasising the historical and legal status of Tibet. It is my belief that it is more important to look forward to the future than dwell in the past. Theoretically speaking it is not impossible that the six million Tibetans could benefit from joining the one billion Chinese of their own free will, if a relationship based on equality, mutual benefit and mutual respect could be established. If China wants Tibet to stay with China, then she must create the necessary conditions. However, the reality today is that Tibet is an occupied country under colonial rule. This is the essential issue which must be addressed and resolved through negotiations.

In the past few years our cause has gained increasing international importance and support. This is reflected in the United Nations' debates on the situation in Tibet: in the General Assembly's Third Committee, in the Commission for Human Rights, and in the reports of the United Nations' Rapporteurs. Last year I appealed to the international community for help in facilitating negotiations between my representatives and the Chinese Government. A number of Asian and Western Governments have supported my call for negotiations publicly and through diplomatic channels and have offered their good offices to bring them about. I take this opportunity to think these governments for their support. It is important that the international community, and especially democratic countries, continue to send a clear message to China that their behaviour in Tibet is deplorable and that the question of Tibet must be resolved through peaceful negotiations without pre-conditions. The need to make real progress in resolving the problem of Tibet is urgent. The present lack of progress increases the danger of violent conflicts breaking out in Tibet.

Many Tibetans have; voiced unprecedented criticism of my suggestion that we should compromise on the issue of total independence. Moreover, the failure of the Chinese Government to respond positively to my conciliatory proposals has deepened the sense of impatience and frustration among my people. Therefore, I proposed last year that this issue be submitted to a referendum. However, as long as I lead our freedom struggle, there will be no deviation from the path of non-violence.

The referendum should seek to clarify the political course of our struggle. A thorough and honest discussion of the various options open to us must take place among the Tibetan people. I hope that this historic exercise will be carried out carefully and thoroughly. I realise that under the present conditions it would be impossible to hold a fair referendum inside Tibet. Nevertheless, we will be able to find ways to collect representative opinions from different parts of Tibet and to conduct the plebiscite properly among our exiled community.

While we prepare ourselves for this referendum, I also wish to state that I remain open to any Chinese overtures for negotiations. I am still committed to the spirit of my "middle way" approach, and I am hopeful that continued international efforts to persuade the Chinese Government to enter into negotiations with us may eventually yield tangible results. Our negotiating team remains ready to resume talks any time at a mutually agreeable venue. Sooner or later, a flexible and open-minded Chinese leadership must realise the wisdom of resolving the issue of Tibet through negotiations in a spirit of reconciliation and compromise. This is the only proper way to ensure stability, which the Chinese leadership assert, is their primary concern. However, true stability must be based on the mutual trust, consent and benefit of all concerned, not on the use of force.

Tibet's geographic position in the heart of Asia gives it enormous strategic importance. For centuries Tibet acted as a buffer ensuring peace in the region. The implications of China's presence in Tibet go well beyond Tibet's borders. Over the last more than forty years Tibet has undergone an unprecedented militarisation. Coupled with the increased transfer of Chinese population into Tibet, this has changed the peaceful character of the Tibetan plateau. If this alarming trend continues, it will not only threaten the survival of the Tibetan people and their culture, but will have serious repercussions for the region as a whole.

Tibet's spiritual and cultural traditions have contributed to peace in Asia. Buddhism not only turned Tibetans into a peace loving nation following a period of great military might, but also spread from the Himalayas to Mongolia and other places in Central Asia and provided millions of people with a spiritual foundation of peace and tolerance. Buddhism is not alien to China, and I strongly believe that Buddhism can be of great service in providing spiritual values, peace of mind, contentment and self-discipline to millions of Chinese in the future.

With the occupation of Tibet, Tibetan Buddhism has been robbed of its cradle and homeland, not only violating the Tibetan people's right to freedom of religion but also endangering the very survival of this rich spiritual and cultural tradition in Tibet and Central Asia. This is particularly true of China's policy of cutting Tibet up into many separate administrative units, most of which have been incorporated into neighbouring Chinese provinces. Historically, the contribution of Tibetans from these areas to Tibet's cultural and spiritual heritage has been immense. But as tiny minorities in Chinese provinces it will be very difficult for these Tibetans to preserve their Buddhist culture and distinct identity in the long term. The Tibetan entities outside the so-called Tibet Autonomous Region (TAR) comprise a larger portion of the Tibetan area and roughly four of the six million Tibetans. A solution to the question of Tibet cannot be found without all these parts of Tibet being incorporated into one Tibetan entity. This is essential to the survival of Tibetan culture.

Finally, I wish to pay homage to the brave men and women of Tibet, who have died for the cause of our freedom. I pray also for our compatriots who are enduring mental and physical suffering in Chinese prisons at this moment. Not one day passes without my fervent prayers for an early end to the suffering of our people. I believe that today the question is not whether Tibet will ever be free, but rather how soon.

56

Statements of H.H. the Dalai Lama

Current Situation in Tibet

Alexander Solzhenitsyn described the Chinese rule in Tibet "more brutal and inhuman than any other communist regime in the world." In 1960s, the International Commission of Jurists found, after extensive investigations, that China had committed acts of genocide in Tibet. The UN passed three resolutions in 1959, 1961 and 1965 expressing their "grave concern" over the violation of fundamental human rights of the Tibetans and stated that Tibetan people were deprived of their inalienable rights to self-determination. Notwithstanding all these universal condemnations China continued its dubious rule in Tibet.

Since the Chinese invasion of Tibet in 1949, China has been working for the extermination of Tibetan identity to secure its full control, legitimise its rule over Tibet and to put an end to the Tibetan resistance. She has committed glaring acts of genocide against the Tibetans. Over 1.2 million Tibetans have been killed; more than 6,000 monasteries, and the institutes of learning have been destroyed and precious artifacts have been vandalised and sold. Tibetans are denied of the basic rights of expression, speech, movement, religion, etc. Tibetan women are subjected to forced abortion and sterilisation. Tibetan children are denied of their childhood and basic education. 70% of the Tibetans are still illiterate. Arbitrary arrests, repression, torture, intimidation, imprisonment have been the regular feature for the last 45 years. Thousands of Tibetans still languish in various Chinese prisons. Most of them are young people, who are below 25 years of age. Majority of Tibetans still live in their old homes while Chinese reside in new colonies with modern amenities. Tibetans are forced to live in the high hills while Chinese occupy all the low and fertile lands. 7.5 million Chinese have outnumbered 6 million Tibetans in Tibet. Tibet has been amputed to six parts and what the Chinese refer to Tibet now is a part of Tibet (the so-called Tibet Autonomous region). The other five divisions are incorporated neighbouring Chinese provinces. China has turned Tibet into a military arsenal. Tibet's fragile environment has been devastated. Majority of Tibet's forest have been cleared and mineral resources exploited. Today, Tibet looks more barren than ever.

Chinese Population Transfer and the Future of Tibet

The most critical threat confronting the Tibetan people is the massive influx of Chinese civilians into Tibet. The influx, which has its roots in early Communist directives, is assimilating Tibet and Tibetans into China. It has now reached a point where the distinct identity of the Tibetan people and their ancient civilisation is being overwhelmed, and its continued separate existence in jeopardy. Today, the six million Tibetan people have been outnumbered by the 7.5 million Chinese population in Tibet. In 1949, when the Chinese invasion of Tibet began, there were only a handful of Chinese in what is today the "Tibet Autonomous Region." In eastern Tibet, now under the jurisdiction of Sixhuan Province, there was a small population consisting mainly of traders. Only in north-eastern Tibet, which is now under the jurisdiction of Qinghai Province, was there any sizable Chinese populations and that was confined to the northwest corner of the province.

The first indication that China would establish policies to settle the Tibetan Plateau with Chinese came in 1952, in the "Directives of Work in Tibet" issued by Mao Tse-tung himself. He said: "Tibet covers a large area but is thinly populated. Its population should be increased from the present 2 or 3 million to 5 or 6 million, and then to over ten million."

A massive and largely hidden wave of Chinese in the 1960s and 1970s were prisoners, shipped off to China's gulag in Hainan, Habibei and Haixi Tibetan Autonomous Prefectures in Qinghai Province. Over one million prisoners were shipped to these Tibetan prefectures.

Up until 1981, the flow of Chinese into the "TAR" was very low. However, it is still estimated that over 2 million Chinese are settled in "TAR." In the Tibetan province of Amdo which is now turned into a Chinese province called Qinghai, to quote China's own statistics, out of the total population of 4.45 million in 1990 only 20% are Tibetans and rest are Chinese. The situation is even worse in Kham province where all the major towns like Dartsedo, Derge, Kanze and Markham are reported to be inhibited by 95-100% Chinese. Today the Chinese population in Kham alone is reported to be well over 3.6 million.

The inevitable effects of population transfer are clearly illustrated in areas that have been successfully overwhelmed by ethnic Chinese settlers. In a *New York Times* opinion piece, His Holiness the Dalai Lama noted: "Today, only two to three million Manchurians are left in Manchuria, where 75 million Chinese have settled. In eastern Turkistan, which the Chinese now call Sinkiang (Xinjiang), the Chinese population has grown from 200,000 in 1949 to seven million, more than half of the total population of Inner Mongolia, Chinese now outnumber the Mongols by 8.5 million to 2.5 million."

To encourage ethnic Chinese settlement in Tibet, the Chinese Government offers an array of benefits for this "hardship" post. These benefits include enticements for Chinese settlers to extend long-term assignments and/or retire in Tibet. Annual wages for Chinese personnel are 87% higher in Tibet than in Chinese provinces, according to one government figure for every 18 months of work in Tibet. Chinese personnel typically receive a 3-month vacation back to China, all expenses paid. Housing, health care, cultural and educational facilities are all part of an enormously expensive undertaking to provide for Chinese in Tibet. The cost of keeping one Chinese in Tibet is equal to that of four in China.

As a result of population transfer, Tibetans are generally marginalised in economic, political and social spheres. However, the most serious impact is on the long-term identity of the Tibetan people as a distinct people and culture. Besides, China's policy of coercive birth control in Tibet also threatens the Tibetan identity. Till date, thousands of Tibetan women in Tibet have undergone forced abortion and sterilisation.

There is new evidence that China is redoubling its efforts to put an end to the Tibetan resistance, and ultimately, to the distinct Tibetan identity. At a high-level secret meeting of Chinese officials held on May 12, 1993, it was decided that the further flooding of Tibet with Chinese nationals would offer the final solution to the Tibetan problem. This "solution" is aimed at making it demographically "impossible for the Tibetans to rise as is in the case of Inner Mongolia and Xinjiang (East

Turkistan)." This evidence disproves China's official denial of population transfer into Tibet.

Systemic Destruction of Tibetan Culture and Religion

From the very beginning of the invasion of Tibet, Chinese started undermining the Tibetan culture an religion. Soon this escalated into the dreaded 'struggle sessions' in which religious figures and local leaders were tortured and murdered, often by members of their own families who were threatened with similar treatment if refused.

By 1959, there were more than a total of 6,259 monasteries with about 592,558 resident monks and nuns. These religious centres also housed tens and thousands of statues, religious artifacts made of gold, silver and other metals. Tibetan national identity became indistinguishable from its religion. Buddhism has become the essence of Tibetan life, culture and civilisation. However, Chinese occupation of Tibet has resulted in destruction of all but 13 monasteries. All religious statues and artifacts were either destroyed or stolen. In a recent meeting, Chinese banned the possession of photos of HH the Dalai Lama. His Holiness is the source of spiritual refuge to all believers in Tibetan Buddhism. Denying the right of Tibetans to possess his photo is a contravention of their religious freedom. Today, China is using Tibetan culture as a tool in achieving its political and economic ends. Chinese policy is aimed at bringing about a gradual and natural death of Tibetan culture and religion.

Environmental Destruction of Tibet

Under the Chinese rule, the systematic destruction of environment of Tibet is unprecedented. The rich wildlife, forests, plants, minerals and water resources have all suffered irreplaceable degradation and Tibet's ecological balance is being seriously disturbed.

Research indicates that the Chinese authorities denuded some 54 billion dollars worth of timber at the end of 1985 from the rich forest reserves of Tibet. In Amdo province alone, nearly 50 million trees have been felled since 1955 and millions of acres of forest area amounting to at least 70% cleared. A similar condition prevails in other parts of Tibet, particularly in eastern and southern Tibet. The massive and unchecked deforestation in Tibet is causing irreversible soil erosion and also increases the deposits of silt in the rivers, which in turn causes landslides and reduces potential farming land. Since Tibet is the source of the major rivers in Asia, there is a serious threat to environmental conditions in South and South-Eastern Asis — as seen in the tragic floods in Bangladesh. The deforestation in Tibet also increases the risk of imbalancing the monsoon which then may herald disaster to Indian agriculture.

The systematic and large scale mining in Tibet began in the early 1960s and has been continuing since then. Today, the Chinese authorities are extracting over 126 different types of minerals in Tibet which includes uranium and oil. The unrestrained exploitation of mineral resources poses serious threat to the survival of the remaining rain forest in Tibet.

Militarisation and Nuclearisation of Tibet

China has turned the once peaceful and buffer state between India and China into a vast military zone. China's occupation forces serve to keep its control over Tibet and to further China's strategic aims in the region. The militarisation of the Tibetan platueau profoundly affects the geopolitical balance of the region and causes serious international tension.

With the Chinese occupation of Tibet, Indian and Chinese troops today face each other on the Himalayan border for the first time in history. The first ever bloody war between the two countries was fought in 1962. China's on-going assistance to Pakistan in building up nuclear power, large concentration of military personnel and nuclear build-up in Tibet, military infiltration in India an persistent assistance to the military regime in Burma and particularly to build up a naval base in the Bay of Bengal further destabilise the Indian subcontinent.

Today, Chinese military presence in Tibet includes an estimated 300,000 to 500,000 troops, of which 200,000 are permanently stationed in Central Tibet near the Indian border; 17 secret radar stations; 14 military airfields; 5 missile bases in Kongpo Nvitri, Powo Tramo, Rudok, Golmu and Nagchu; at least 18 ICBMs, 70 medium range missiles and 20 intermediate range missiles.

Besides, China also utilises Tibet for chemical warfare exercises and dumping nuclear waste from other countries. The recent report published by the International Campaign for Tibet, an organisation based in Washington, USA, confirms the existence of a Chinese nuclear station in Tibet known as "Ninth Academy" near Lake Kokonor in Amdo province.

[*Issued by the Eighth Tibetan Non-Governmental Organisations in Exile*, 1995.]

Part C

INTERVIEWS / DIALOGUES

57

We Tried to Resist All Change

FOR THIRTEEN years, Tenzin Gyatso, the fourteenth Dalai Lama and the spiritual and temporal leader of Tibet, has lived in exile in northern India while the Chinese have occupied and ruled his country. In this rare interview, with *Newsweek's* Tony Clifton, the Dalai Lama takes a realistic and dispassionate view of his own and Tibet's future.

Clifton: What do you hear about conditions in Tibet today?

Dalai Lama: Conditions are very grave, although there has been some relaxation since the end of the cultural revolution. For example, it is easier for Tibetans to move from one district to another. But there is still no freedom of religion for ordinary people and there is a very serious food shortage. A constant fear is present. If a person sighs heavily he can be questioned about his motives at a self-criticism session, and people who even look in the direction of several places can be accused of being "reactionaries." Opponents of Chinese have just disappeared or been executed.

Q. Is the opposition widespread?

A. I think it is. These groups print illegal pamphlets and put up anti-Chinese posters, and they also commit sabotage. The members are not older men who want to restore the traditional Tibet they remember. The resistance has many young men who were actually educated in China and are even Communists. What makes them resist and binds them together is that they are nationalists who want Tibet to be free again.

Q. Do you think that in your position you should encourage this movement?

A. I do what the people want me to do. I am carrying out their wishes now by telling you what they are doing.

Q. Does that mean that if the people in Tibet eventually decided to accept Chinese rule, you would accept their decision?

A. I would accept their wish. After all, there are 6 million people in Tibet and only 80,000 of us outside, so that if the people in Tibet willingly accepted Chinese rule we would have to respect what the majority said. I would not like to live like an exiled European king surrounded by his court and holding views which were not the views of his people. I realize that this means that one day I might lose Tibet. Well, I am a simple monk, and the Lord Buddha himself gave up a kingdom. So this might be a good opportunity for me.

Q. Could you accept Tibet as part of China?

A. My answer, speaking entirly for myself as a religious person, is that nationality itself is not important.

Q. You speak of yourself as a religious person but in Tibet you were the political leader as well. Would you be prepared to give up your political role in the future?

A. I could accept being purely a religious

leader although now I am involved in many fields, including politics.

Q. Do you think the traditionalist Tibet which you knew must disappear?

A. I think it is inevitable there must be great changes, but this is not necessarily a bad thing. The future Tibet will be entirely different. How can a nation stand still? We suffered because we were very conservative and tried to resist all change. I think that if at the start of the century we had tried to develop with the rest of the world and took a part in world affairs we might have avoided what has happened to us now.

Q. Are these new views of yours?

A. No I was thinking like this in Tibet, although you must remember that I was 16 when the Chinese invaded just a student in the Potala Palace. But later I wanted to bring about reforms, reforms that would suit Tibetan Society. The Chinese did not want to do it that way; they wanted to do things their way. But it doesn't matter what I thought then. All that is past now.

Q. Do you think the Chinese took advantage of your youth?

A. I think they probably did. It might have helped if I had been older. But I did not think that I would have been able to stop them regardless of how old I might have been. And perhaps if they hadn't come I would have become a very conservative old man, which might have been a very bad thing. So I have one thing to thank them for.

Q. Do you really hope you might get-back to Tibet again one day?

A. Of course I hope I will return, if there is no hope there is no reason to struggle. Our hope lies with the determination of the Tibetan people. As long as the Chinese continue to oppress us, then that determination will be there. I hope that the Chinese will understand that if they want real harmony they will have to treat the Tibetans as brothers.

Q. Why don't they do that now?

A. They want to make us conform, although there is a great difference between the Tibetans and the Chinese, in culture, in race, in geography, even in food. Their officials did not seem to understand the feelings of the people and they don't want to discuss anything. They say they are non-believers, but they believe completely in one man, Mao. But Mao is being misunderstood by them. He was a peasant and he suffered and fought. He had a good brain and he thought for himself. He did great things for the Chinese, helped free them. But these men oppress our people in his name.

Q. Has exile changed your view of your own role?

A. Some people think that the Dalai Lama and Tibet are inseparable, but Tibet was a powerful nation before the accession of the first Dalai Lama. For the past few centuries the Dalai Lama has helped the Tibetan nation by being a leader and be the last a unifying force, but perhaps he is not so useful now. I might be the last Dalai Lama. It is not important. What is important is that Tibet should benefit, whatever happens to the Dalai Lama.

58

Tibet Remains a Vast Prison

Pringle: Your Holiness, since last November there has been a period of general liberalization in China. Have these events had any effect on the situation in Tibet?

Dalai Lama: Only slightly. Something is moving but it is difficult to know where it is going. There are fewer restrictions for our people now, but basically Tibet still remains a vast prison.

Q. Do you believe Deng Xiaoping, China's Deputy Prime Minister, is a man with whom you would find it easier to deal?

A. Certainly, I remember tell a quotation of his that I like very much: "seeking truth from facts." Absolutely good. Deng has the courage to admit mistakes. In the past it was rare for the top Chinese leadership to speak with such realism about political matters. If China's leaders are now sincere about change, and hold to it for a generation, that will be very good. But I really doubt they will.

Q. Recently, the Panchen Lama (another influential Tibetan lama) appealed to you from Peking to return. Would you consider doing so in view of the changes that have taken place?

A. At the moment there is no question of returning. I must remain here for our people. The Chinese leaders have said for twenty years that I am "anti-people", and that Tibetan refugees live under the Dalai Lama's suppression. Now they say they are very much concerned for their "friends" in exile and hope they will return soon. Overnight, they have decided we are their brothers. So, you see, there is no logic in their thinking.

Q. I understand that wall posters, similar to those in Peking, have been put up in Lhasa.

A. That is true. At least one poster I heard of outlined Tibetan history, stating that the country has been separate from China. Other posters complained that Tibetans working in the civil administration received lower pay than the Chinese doing the same jobs.

Q. It looks as though the Chinese want to open Tibet to tourists from the United States and Europe. What is your attitude toward that?

A. Good, very good. Isolation was part of the suppression, and to keep Tibet isolated would be an advantage to them (the Chinese). Of course, tourists will be controlled and it will be very difficult to mix with the Tibetans. But our country is very beautiful. There is no pollution. Water is very clear. So is the sky. You can have a few days of enjoyment, and the Tibetans can see a few foreigners.

Q. What will you be doing in Mongolia and the Soviet Union?

A. Tibet's relationship with Mongolia is an old one that goes back many centuries. We pray in the same language. But my motive in going to each country is purely religious. I hope to visit Mongolian monasteries and see rare artifacts in Leningrad museums.

Q. The Chinese have indicated that you are "playing with fire" by taking this trip. Does this worry you?

A. Those people who fight fires are also playing with fire sometimes.

Q. Concerning relations with China, do you think your demands for Tibetan autonomy might not be construed as being rather inflexible now that there is same relaxation in China? Don't you feel you could position somewhat and create conditions for a dialogue?

A. The Chinese explanation of the Tibet picture is that it is very simple. Our explanation is that it is very complex. The Chinese should do as Deng Xiaoping says and seek truth from facts. They must change their attitude. The Chinese occupied Tibet in the name of liberation. If they would really help us and respect the Tibetan culture and way of thinking, then our thinking may change. I will follow the will of the majority of our people.

Q. Do you still hope one day, if circumstances are favourable, to live in Tibet again yourself?

A. Of course. If the Chinese change and show respect to Tibet, I think we will find a solution.

Q. Your goal, then, is to return to a free and independent Tibet, separate from China?

A. During the past 30 years, we have gained nothing from China; therefore it should be obvious why we want to remain separate country. Now, if the Chinese attitude changes and they respect the Tibetan people's wishes and come to Tibet as liberator and helper, we may think of some mutually beneficial terms. Before, they followed an attitude that compelled us to make an effort to separate from the Chinese. If the Chinese have something to offer us, the picture might be different—especially if we get some benefit from a union with them. After all, we are only 6 million people. We have no sea route. We are inaccessible because we live at such a high altitude. We are rich only in minerals, and you can't eat minerals.

Q. Can you foresee a situation in which you would be prepared to think in terms of a close relationship with China?

A. Yes, but not China as such. China represents the Han people. Throughout history the Chinese have emphasized the differences between China and the "Middle Kingdom." They said we Tibetans and the Chinese were equal as brothers, each as part of the "Middle Kingdom." These days they say we Tibetans are also Chinese. This is nonsense.

Q. If the Chinese said that "you Tibetans are Tibetans but if we all work together in a great `Middle Kingdom,' it would be for the benefit of everyone," would you be more prepared to negotiate?

A. I think the 6 million Tibetan people must be prepared first. Then, after that, I would be prepared.

[From *Newsweek*, 18 June, 1979.]

59

Statement of His Holiness the Dalai Lama on the 37th Anniversary of Tibetan National Uprising Day, 10 March 1996

As WE commemorate today the thirty seventh Anniversary of the Tibetan people's uprising, we are witnessing a general hardening of Chinese government policy. This is reflected in an increasingly aggressive posture towards the peoples of Taiwan and Hong Kong and in intensified repression in Tibet. We also see rising fear and suspicion throughout the Asia-Pacific region and a worsening of relations between China and much of the rest of the world.

Within the context of this tense political atmosphere, Beijing has once again sought to impose its will on the Tibetan people by appointing a rival Panchen Lama. In doing so, it has chosen a course of total disregard both for the sentiments of the Tibetans in general and the Tibetan spiritual tradition in particular, despite my every effort to reach for some form of understanding the cooperation with the Chinese government. Significantly, the official Chinese media compares the present political climate in Tibet with that in Poland during the Solidarity years of the 1980's. This demonstrates a growing sense of insecurity on the part of the Chinese leadership as a result of which, through a continuing compaign of coercion and intimidation, Bejing has greatly reinforced its repression throughout Tibet. I am therefore saddened to have to report that the situation of our people in Tibet continues to deteriorate.

Nevertheless, it remains my strong conviction that change for the better is coming. China is at a critical junction: its society is undergoing profound changes and the country's leadership is facing the transition to a new generation. It is obvious too that the Tiananmen massacre has failed to silence the call for freedom, democracy and human rights in China. Moreover, the impressive democratization in process across the Taiwan Strait must further invigorate the democratic aspirations of the Chinese people. Indeed, Taiwan's historic first direct presidential elections later this month are certain to have an immense political and psychological impact on their minds. A transformation from the current totalitarian regime in Beijing into one which is more open, free and democratic is thus inevitable. The only outstanding question is how and when and whether the transition will be a smooth one.

As a human being, it is my sincere desire that our Chinese brothers and sisters enjoy freedom, democracy, prosperity and stability. As a Buddhist monk, I am of course concerned that a country which is home to almost a quarter of the world's entire population and which is on the brink of an epic change, should undergo that change peacefully. In view of China's huge population, chaos and instability could lead to large-scale bloodshed and tremendous suffering for millions of people. Such a situation would also have serious ramifications for peace and stability throughout the world. As a Tibetan, I recognize that the future of our country and our people depends to a great extent on what happens in China during the years ahead.

Whether the coming change in China brings new life and new hope for Tibet and whether China herself emerges as a reliable, peaceful and constructive member of the international community depends to a large degree on the extent to which the international community itself adopts responsible policies towards China. I have always drawn attention to the need to bring Beijing into the mainstream of world democracy and have spoken against any idea of isolating and containing China. To attempt to do so would be morally incorrect and politically impractical. Instead, I have always counselled a policy of responsible and principled engagement with the Chinese leadership.

It became obvious during the Tiananmen movement that the Chinese people yearn for freedom, democracy, equality and human rights no less than any other people. Moreover, I was personally very moved to see that those young people, despite being taught that, "political powers comes out of the barrel of a gun" pursued their aims without resorting to violence. I, too, am convinced that non-violence is the appropriate way to bring about constructive political change.

Based on my belief in non-violence and in dialogue, I have consistently tried to engage the Chinese government in serious negotiations concerning the future of the Tibetan people. In order to find a mutually acceptable solution. I have adopted a middle-way' approach. This is also in response to, and within the frame work of, Mr. Deng Xiaoping's stated assurance that "anything except independence can be discussed and resolved."

Unfortunately, the Chinese government's response to my many overtures has been consistently negative. But, I remain confident that his successors will realize the wisdom of resolving the problem of Tibet through dialogue.

The Tibet issue will neither go away of its own accord, nor can it be wished away. As the past has clearly shown, neither intimidation nor coercion of the Tibetan people can force a solution. Sooner or later, the leadership in Beijing will have to fact this fact. Actually, the Tibet problem represents an opportunity for China. If it were solved properly through negotiation, not only would it be helpful in creating a political atmosphere conducive to the smooth transition of China into a new era but also China's image throughout the world would be greatly enhanced. A properly negotiated settlement would furthermore have a strong, positive impact on the peoples of both Hong Kong and Taiwan and will do much to improve Sino-Indian relations by inspiring genuine trust and confidence.

For our part, we seek to resolve the issue of Tibet in a spirit of reconciliation, compromise and understanding. I am fully committed to the spirit of the 'middle-way approach.' We wish to establish a sustainable relationship with China based on mutual respect, mutual benefit and friendship. In doing so, we will thing not only about the fundamental interests of the Tibetan people, but also take seriously the consideration of China's security concerns and her economic interests. Moreover, if our Buddhist culture can flourish once again in Tibet, we are confident of being able to make a significant contribution to millions of our Chinese brothers and sisters by sharing with them those spiritual and moral values which are so clearly lacking in China today.

Despite the absence of positive and conciliatory gestures from the Chinese government to my initiatives, I have always encouraged Tibetans to develop personal relationships with Chinese. I make it a point to ask the Tibetan to distinguish between the Chinese people and the policies of the totalitarian government in Beijing. I am thus happy to observe that there has been significant progress in our efforts to foster closer interaction amongst the people of our two communities, mainly between exile Tibetans and Chinese living abroad. Moreover, human rights activists and democrats within China, people like the brave Wei Jingsheng, are urging their leaders to respect the basic human rights of the Tibetan people and pledging their support of our right to self-rule. Chinese scholars outside China are discussing a constitution for a federated China which envisages a confederal status for Tibet. These are most encouraging and inspiring developments. I am, therefore, very pleased that the people-to-people dialogue between the Tibetans and chinese is fostering a better understanding of our mutual concerns and interests.

In recent years we have also witnessed the growth of a world-wide grass-roots movement in support of our non-violent struggle for freedom. Reflecting this, many governments and parliaments have come forward with strong expressions of concern and support for our efforts. Notwithstanding the immediate negative reactions of the Chinese regime, I strongly believe that such expressions of international support are essential. They are vital in communicating a sense of urgency to the minds of leadership in Beijing and in helping persuade them to negotiate.

I would like to take this opportunity to thank the numerous individuals, also the members of governments, of parliaments, of non-governmental organizations and of religious orders who have supported my appeal for the safety and freedom of the young Panchen Lama, Gedhun Choekyi Nyima. I am grateful for their continued intervention and efforts on behalf of this child who must be the world's youngest political prisoner. I also wish to thank our supporters all over the world who are commemorating today's anniversary of the Tibetan people's uprising with peaceful activities in every part of the globe. I urge the Chinese government not to construe such support for Tibet as anti-Chinese. The purpose and aim of these activities is to appeal to the Chinese leadership and people to recognize the legitimate rights of the Tibetan people.

In conclusion, I am happy to state today that our exile community's experiment in democracy is progressing well without any major setbacks or difficulties. Last autumn, the Tibetans in exile participated in preliminary polls to nominate candidates for the Twelfth Assembly of the Tibetan People's Deputies, the parliament in exile. Next month, they return to the polls to elect the members themselves. Thus accords with my conviction that democracy is the best guarantee for the survival and future of the Tibetan people. Democracy entails responsibilities as well as rights. The success of our struggle for freedom will therefore depend directly on our ability to shoulder these collectively. It is thus my hope that the Twelfth Assembly will emerge as a united, mature and dedicated representative of our people. This will ultimately depend on every franchised member of our community. Each one is called upon to cast his or her vote with an informed and unbiased mind, with a clear awareness of the need of the hour and with a strong sense of individual responsibility.

With my homage to the brave men and women of Tibet, who have died for the cause of our freedom, I pray for an early end to the suffering of our people.

60

Dialogue between the Dalai Lama and Indian Policy Experts, New Delhi, 10 August 1993

SUDHINDRA BHADORIA (*Secretary General, South Asian Forum for People's Initiative*):

I consider it a matter of honour and privilege to welcome His Holiness the Dalai Lama and Indian policy experts for a dialogue about the Tibetan issue. The South Asian Forum for Peoples' Initiative believes that all the countries of the South Asian region have common dreams and challenges in the context of freedom, democracy and development. We all need peace and security. We consider that the struggle of Tibetan people is a matter of common concern for all Asian countries and people. It is a movement for a world order of Gandhi's vision based upon justice, dignity, democracy and non-violence. It is a movement which must receive our full support at various levels. We hope that this gathering of distinguished Indian parliamentarians, ex-army generals, foreign policy experts, diplomats, academicians, human rights activists, women leaders, environmentalists, and social action groups will be enlightened by today's dialogue on "Implications of Recent Developments in Tibet for Security, Prosperity and Peace in Asia." I request our former Ambassador to China and one of the most distinguished foreign secretaries Shri A.P. Venkateshwaran for his introductory remarks.

A.P. Venkateshwaran (*Ex-Foreign Secretary and former Ambassador to China; Centre for Policy Research*):

It is a matter of privilege and pleasure for me to initiate the discussion before such a distinguished audience. We have made great advances in the material and mental realm but we have not kept moral values at the same level. This meeting has a special significance for us as the foremost spiritual leader in the world of today, His Holiness the Dalai Lama, is present here and will address the seminar. I hope that he will give us a direction through which we can try and restore some of the values which we are in danger of losing forever.

Firstly, let me say that when His Holiness with a large number of his followers crossed over to India in 1959, he had like a good guest taken on the responsibility of looking after his people and looking after our interests in the sense that he refrained from political activities. Therefore, it is upon us, the Indians, to focus upon the issue of Tibet and to realize what the presence of His Holiness and the Tibetan people in India means to us in this country. First and foremost India has no border with China. India has a border with Tibet. Secondly, Tibet has been an independent country for large periods of time. It has never been an integral part of China as is being made out. In any case from 1911 onwards up to the invasion of Tibet in 1950 by People's Liberation Army. Tibet was certainly fully independent and sovereign as a state. Many of the member nations of the United Nations today have less number of years as independent states than

Tibet had, when China forcibly took over by military operation.

Let me now make a few other points which are very relevant. Even as early as 820 A.D., there was a treaty between Tibet and China which was inscribed in both the Chinese and Tibetan languages on three stone pillars in Gorbumeru, Lhasa, and Changan. It is said in the treaty, and I quote, that "Tibet and China agree that they will abide by their searches whereby all to the east constitutes China and all that is to the west constitutes Tibet and neither side will wage a war or seize the other's territory." However that may be, we all know what happened in 1950-51 when Mao Tse-tung announced that Tibet will be liberated. Now when such a statement is made which was in contradiction with what Mao himself had said and it has been quoted by Edgar Snow in *Red Star Over China,* when he passed through some regions of Tibet during the Long March and was helped by the Tibetan people with food and shelter for his forces Mao had said: "This is our only foreign debt and one day we must pay the Manchus and the Tibetans for it." Instead China decided to take over Tibet itself.

What is extremely important here is to remember that the concept of suzerainty was invented by the British. And Napoleon once described the British as perfidious Albion for very good reasons. Suzerainty was a concept by which Britain was trying to keep out the Russians. She preferred Chinese presence in Tibet to the Russian presence. Because there was this fear that Russia was trying to reach the warm water ports of the Indian Ocean. Russia was more frightening in the minds of West European nations than China. Because China at that time was not particularly powerful in military terms. Later this concept of suzerainty obscured the vision of our leadership when the invasion of Tibet took place. Our Prime Minister Jawaharlal Nehru had been inspired by the vision of two of the biggest countries of Asia and world, China and India cooperating for development and peace, he felt that this will be a force which will affect the process of development and peace in the whole world. Unfortunately the Chinese never shared this vision of Nehru. As we all know about what happened in 1962. But it was this vision which obscured Nehru's perception when China forcefully occupied Tibet. At that time we had a Consulate General in Tibet who had sent one of the most stirring telegrams which I can ever recall in reading the diplomatic annals. The telegram was: "The Chinese have entered Tibet. The Himalaya has ceased to exist." What he meant to convey was that now you cannot consider the Himalayas as a secure frontier on which you may rely for your own security. Because till then we had friendly Tibetans who had the closest relationship with us, whose spirituality and whose sense of friendliness could not be surpassed. I can further say that this is visible from the Tibetan population now in India which for last 35 years have not given a single cause for complain to the Indian authorities for any misbehaviour of any kind. If there has been any misbehaviour, it has been on our part in unnecessarily beating up the Tibetans a year ago when Premier Li Peng had come to Delhi and in an overreaction our security forces had used unwarranted force on these innocent and peaceful people.

Now, what is the real consequence of the Chinese occupation of Tibet? When they occupied it, they stayed there and they had got a 17 Point Agreement signed, under compulsion and duress by the Tibetan side. His Holiness the Dalai Lama did not renege because he felt that perhaps the Chinese could be persuaded to see reason and a better understanding may be reached. One interesting aspect of the 17 Point Agreement was that in this agreement, which had been drafted by the Chinese themselves, Tibet was granted full administrative and political autonomy. It also gave assurance that no interference will be made in the established status, powers and functions of the

Dalai Lama and the Panchen Lama. But the events proved otherwise. That is why in 1956, when His Holiness had come to India for the 2500 Birth Anniversay of Lord Buddha he told Pandit Nehru that he will not like to return to Tibet due to obvious reasons. He talked of the pressures being exerted upon him and his government by the Chinese. Nehru persuaded His Holiness to return, counselling him that perhaps the problem could be solved out slowly. In any case, if the problem had to be sorted out with the Chinese the presence of His Holiness back in Tibet was necessary. But in 1959, with the kind of insensitivity and the kind of pressures and the forces used by the Chinese, His Holiness had to leave his country. The rest is history.

A final point must be made before I conclude. We have the border problem with China which is yet to be sorted out. But we keep on saying that things have improved. It is further stated that we have agreed that peace and tranquillity will prevail on border. The Chinese have not told us till today about where this so-called line of actual control exists. So along which line are we making this peace and tranquillity? We are puzzled about it. When I ask my friends in the Ministry of External Affairs, I am told that we are puzzled about it. When I ask my friends in the Ministry of External Affairs, I am told that we are still deciding where this line runs. I am willing to say that the Chinese are never going to tell you where this line runs. Because it is always a shifting line for them, a line by which they can push their interest to the maximum extent possible depending upon their strength and weakness of their opponent.

India's border in the eastern sector is the most important and we base it on the so-called McMahon Line, which runs across the highest watershed ridge of the Himalayas. It was negotiated under the Simla discussion in 1914 Chinese refused to sign the agreement. It was a tripartite meet. The Chinese refused to sign it not because they disagreed in separating the inner and outer Tibet. Anyhow any legal basis for claiming that the McMahon Line was agreed as the border depends upon the recognition of the Tibetan signature. If we say that Tibet was not independent at that time, then obviously there is no McMahon Line Agreement. On the other hand, if Tibet was independent then we can have our claim and continue negotiations with whoever is the authority at present in Tibet.

His Holiness the Dalai Lama:

I am extremely happy to have this opportunity and I would like to thank the organizers for this seminar [*in Tibetan*].

Now I will try to speak my own broken English. But let me also make it clear that my English is so poor that there is always danger of wrong understanding or misunderstanding. So be careful when you listen Dalai Lama's English.

Recently, I have noticed that the Indian public, specially the intellectuals and media, are showing deeper interest about the Tibet issue. I think there is developing a deeper understanding of what Tibet means to this country. Of course, this is very encouraging. Actually, we have always been looking at this country during last 42 or 43 years. When we got trouble from our eastern neighbour then naturally we have to look to our southern neighbour. Today, there is worldwide recognition that the Tibetan civilization, its spirituality, and culture are unique. It is quiet relevant in the context of crating a peaceful world, peace with fellow human beings, peace with animals, peace with environment. People expect contribution from the Tibetan culture about it. That unique cultural heritage has developed actually on the basis of Indian culture, Indian thought, and Indian philosophy. Let us know that.

For human beings, economy and day-to-day life are important. But in deeper human mind, at the emotional and intellectual levels, the culture and spirituality are very important. In our case, we have had close relations with China. But because of the spiritual relationship with India, it is not only a unique but also very deep connection. This is why, even before the Chinese occupation, Tibet always looked to this country. For last 34 years, we as refugees, consider this country as saviour of our nation. Therefore, I am really encouraged about the increasing interesting in this country about the Tibetan issue.

Of course, I know that from the President of India to ordinary Indians — they all have very strong feelings for Tibet. There is no doubt about that. But this nation is like an elephant which takes time to move, as was reminded by Nehru in 1962 when the Chinese military hostilities had started. Once it moves it becomes a force. For last thirty years, I have sometimes expressed a little complaint. It is that the policy of the Government of India towards China and particularly about Tibet is a little over cautious. I am hopeful that if you really make commitment on the moral as well as the practical basis, it is going to be a tremendous benefit for us.

I do want to express my appreciation of this programme. I am particularly impressed by the speech by my old friend [Shri A.P. Venkateshwaran]. Your speech is most forceful. But you also have been a bit diplomatic on this issue in the past. Today, you have given the true picture of Tibet issue. Therefore I am not going to repeat what has been already stated in the opening remarks by me dear friend. I congratulate you on this statement.

In my view the issues of land and boundary are important but the concern for human-community is much more basic and most important. If there was real benefit to the Tibetan people because of the Chinese occupation then the situation may have been completely different. The majority of Tibetans would have welcomed. But what has really happened. The liberators, they call themselves as liberators, brought upon us more misery than happiness. Of course, nobody can deny that some development has taken place in the fields of education, health, and some aspect of economy. But the destruction side is immense. Even late Panchen Lama, just two days before his sudden death, publicly expressed his views about it and said that the amount of destruction cannot match by the progress. Therefore, even those Tibetans who wanted to believe or trust the Chinese due to ideology or some other reason now realize that their trust is an illusion. The Chinese occupation has caused loss of freedom and a lot of destruction and human suffering. These historical and human realities give us the legal and moral right to overcome this problem. This is the real basis for my struggle.

In my view, it is significant that more and more Indians are realizing that Tibet is important for this country. Tibet is important for India at two levels - geographical situation and the mental affinity. Before the Chinese invasion, the long northern border was a peaceful border. With the changes due to Chinese occupation, this country is compelled to spend a lot of money to protect that border. The large sum of money which was spent on this border since 1962 could have been utilized for education, health, and several other development activities. I am sure that substantial progress would have been achieved.

Tibet acted as the buffer state in the past. Since Chinese occupation of Tibet that situation got changed. In recent times the Sino-Indian relations are apparently improving. Even though there is no sign of reduction of the Chinese forces in Tibet, it is in fact increasing. Any sign of reduction of missiles in Tibet is also not available. In this connection, it is my firm belief that if the northern border of India is safe, then it will have great impact up to in the western and eastern borders of India. Because of the large presence of the Chinese forces on the northern borders, the other neighbours also find more courage.

In the context of mental affinity, it is clear that the Chinese have only occupied the Chinese territory and not the Tibetan mind. We Tibetans do not consider ourselves as Chinese. At that level we are much closer to India. The majority of Tibetans are Buddhist. Even the followers of ancient pre-Buddhist religion, who are a few hundred thousand, feel much loser to India due to the Buddhist influence. It is a centuries old relationship. Thus the entire Tibetan nation mentally looks to India. I am sure that as long as the Tibetan nation is there, this mental attitude will also be there. Furthermore, in spite of the Chinese army control Tibet is a hostile land to them. Although the Chinese soldiers have reached the Indian borders but the real China is at least 2000 kms. away from it. They will have to bring their soldiers only after going through a large area which is essentially hostile.

Of course, the population of Chinese is always increasing in Tibet. There is failure of Chinese control of Tibet in spite of 40 years occupation and the protest activities are increasing. Therefore, the Chinese Government is pursuing another policy. I have definite information that Chinese authorities have decided to increase and encourage Chinese migration into Tibet to increase their influence. So that the Tibetans become a minority in their own land forever. They always say that it is not their policy but according to my information they are deliberately doing it. In fact, the Chinese Government is providing incentive for it. Now all the bigger towns of Tibet have a larger number of Chinese than the Tibetans. I consider this as a very serious issue.

It automatically creates tension between the Tibetans and the Chinese. There is a clear demarcation between them in the schools, offices, jobs and even in prisons. It is affecting the social climate and there is a serious threat to Tibetan people and their identity due to the Chinese policy of population transfer. It is also creating new pressures upon Nature and a number of wild species are endangered. The mining activities by the Chinese are creating havoc for our environment. It is being carried out without appropriate arrangements. A large scale deforestation without necessary replantation has depleted the Tibetan forest cover. The overall damage to the environment is getting worse because of the Chinese indifference about it.

I me a Tibetan recently who has visited Tibet recently. He was nobody in Tibetan clothes neither he could hear anyone speaking in Tibetan. When he asked some of the younger Tibetans about it, he was told that we are being forced to dress like the Chinese, speak and read Chinese the follow the Chinese way of life. It is true about the conditions in the so-called Inner Mongolia. There are a number of reports about the overwhelming presence of Chinese in various parts of Mongolia.

I feel that the time is running out for this unique culture of Tibet. We have to save the Tibetan nation. There is no other way except to communicate directly with the Chinese Government about it. This is my thinking. When we are appealing directly to the Chinese Government there is no point in talking about independence. One thing I have made clear to the Chinese government that eventually Tibet should be made a zone of peace. Irrespective of its political status my life is dedicated to that goal. In the global context my rest of life is dedicated to demilitarization of this whole planet.

I am still in favour of persuasion policy, but my efforts of last 34 years have proved that it also needs more and more international pressure. The support of this country is very important for us. I take this opportunity to express my appreciation of the continuity of support from the Indian people to our cause: Besides the moral issue, the practical considerations are also in favour of an increased interest and understanding among the Indians particularly the media and the policy experts about what Tibet means to this country.

Lot of damage is already done. If the situation is allowed to worsen for another ten years, then it will be beyond any kind of solution of us. Therefore, you have to appreciate the need of immediate efforts for saving the unique culture of Tibet.

Brajesh Mishra (*former representative of India at the United Nations and former Ambassador of India to China*):

This has been an inspiring address with very valuable information for India about the current situation of Tibet. Sino-Tibetan relations require that the international community is made aware of the realities and it is equally necessary that the Tibetans and the Chinese negotiate. If we keep these two aspects in mind we may come to a via media which should not be difficult for the Government of India to follow. I do remember that in December 1991 the Chinese Premier told a group of us that China is willing to negotiate other issues except independence. He later said it publicly also in Delhi. And we hear today from His Holiness, not for the first time that it is important for the Tibetans to negotiate that independence is not being insisted upon in this situation. This is a situation which is much more amenable for discussions and negotiations that the demand for independence of Tibet. Otherwise we will be putting up hostile forces, hostile to the Tibetan people, in the forefront. In the view, we should keep in mind that the international situation is in a flux today.

The old alignments have not yet changed. We do not know what is going to be the shape of Sino American. Sino-Japanese, or Sino-Russian relations. We hear that the Western world is putting pressure on China about human rights. It includes the question of Tibet. At the same time, we see their decision to treat China as most favoured nation. We have to be extremely careful about it.

We should not become pawns in the hands of the others. We realise the importance of Tibet to us — spiritually, culturally, strategically. We know that if Tibet were a free nation it would have been far more favourable for India. But we must not follow a policy in our desire to help Tibet which may invite hostility of China. It will not help and we have proof about it from our past experiences. Therefore, the new situation should be recognised as hopeful. We should in India fight for this cause. But we should be aware of the international situation and various support sources for this cause.

S. Shahabuddin (*former Ambassador of India and Editor*, 'Muslim India'):

I admire the dignity with which the Tibetan people and His Holiness the Dalai Lama have been facing the adversities before them. Your laugh and smiles are proof of your confidence in the destiny and future of the Tibetan people's culture and their nation. I will only like to assure your that the Indian elephant is slow to move but it stood up and is ready to be counted. I do not regard Tibet as a lost cause. We do not have to wait for the next turn of the wheel. I also do not regard the Tibetan question in the perspective of international law only. Sometimes it guides our nations and their conduct. But sometimes human conduct influences the laws. Tibet is not a territorial question, it is a moral question. It is a cultural question. How the international community should save the life and soul of a people? We cannot afford to wait. Therefore, the question of Tibet today is primarily a question of human right and then a question of ethnicity. Today in the age of ethnicity when the submerged ethnic groups are resurfacing and asserting themselves all over the globe, the Tibetan people deserve our recognition on the basis of a distinct history, culture, language, geography and in any other basis. They have a right to self-determination and they must have right to their ethnicity. And to their homeland. The political arrangement for it is to be decided by His Holiness and his people. We cannot advise about it. It is obvious that we will have to follow a two track approach for it keeping the Tibetan issue alive in the international community and never fear to negotiate. I am concerned about what the Chinese are doing in Tibet. I am concerned about it not only as an Indian. It is an Asian question and a human question. You have told about their demographic policies which is adversely affecting the Tibetan ecology. Their military presence up to our borders has become possible only because of occupation of Tibet. But what concerns me most is their nuclear programme. They are mining uranium in Tibet and are engaged in nuclear programmes without the international safeguards. The nuclear waste is being dumped at the river sources in Tibet. It is a factor for environmental pollution and is a matter of concern for the future of the whole region which is irrigated by these rivers. Asian security has been affected by the enslaving of Tibet by Chinese army and it is not allowing the construction of a zone of peace, which you history and culture. In the long-term perspective the Chinese empire is the last empire which is on the line of disintegration. But how long it may take is not clear.

Environmentally there is desertification in Tibet and greater silting in rivers like Brahmaputra. This is a long-term crisis. Therefore, I support the Tibetan movement for restoration of cultural and ethnic autonomy. I also support your efforts for negotiation without any preconditions in the true Buddhist spirit..

General J.S. Arora *(Convenor, Sikh Forum):*

This is a fight between spiritualism and materialism. It is also a fight between a national state and people of diverse cultures and ethnic identities. Whether they will be allowed to survive or not? There is no doubt that the nation-state at the moment is dominant. But with the disappearance of Soviet Russia. I do feel that in the long run the world will be a happier place to live in if the various people were permitted to live with a certain amount of autonomy than a national state trying to dominate and repress people. How long it will take is not known to me? With the bi-polar world having disappeared you find that the unipolar world has not come into its own. We see that the might is still right as evident in Yugoslavia. On the other hand eventually the moral values have to succeed. I feel that the humanity has continued to survive in spite of domination for centuries. Poland is one example of it. I am sure that with the moral and spiritual values that Tibet has it will survive and eventually come on the top. What help can we give them from India. The Indian Government is not feeling so strong within and therefore cannot be strong in world affairs. But we Indians as a nation must stand and show that we are with Tibet and its moral struggle.

H.H. The Dalai Lama

The Chinese Government has been approached by my personal emissaries in late 1970s. It was told to them by Deng Xiaoping that besides independence anything can be negotiated. Since then for last 14 years I have sent about six delegations to China. From my side I have made ample efforts to start a meaningful negotiation. But whenever I have brought any concrete idea the Chinese have always avoided to come forward about it. Fortunately, there is some change in their attitude due to international pressure. This shows that we need more pressure.

The second issue is about independence. I am full committed to the middle way — not complete separation from China and at the same time not allowing the continuity of the present arrangement. I am concentrating on the present crisis — the Tibetan nation must be saved. The ultimate Tibetan future will be decided by the Tibetan people. But in the meantime it is extremely important to make it clear that Tibet is not part of China. It becomes extremely difficult to negotiate with the Chinese. Even if the Chinese themselves say about it then it is to be asked what was the reason to make the 17 point agreement. Though it was drafted by the Chinese and the seal was made in Beijing. What was the compulsion for the Chinese to have this agreement? In 1956, and on many other occasions the Chinese Prime Minister Chou Enlai had made it clear that China does not consider Tibet as another province of China. It is given a special treatment. It also has implications for the concept of suzerainty. It involves the condition of autonomy for any kind of Sino-Tibet relation. The present case of Tibet is becoming worse than British rule over India. In the Indian case, there was no danger of the extinction of the people of this country. In our case, we are only 6.5 million and the invaders are 1000 millions.

Aravind Deo (*Editor, P.O.T. and India's last Consul General in Tibet*):

Today, I recall my life's precious 13 months spent in Tibet between 1961 and 1962 and I am aware of the great cultural invasion of Tibet. One cannot but be moved by the fact that this torrent of history has attempted to wash away much of the cultural heritage which cannot be recovered. Because some of it was physical and much of it was spiritual. I think we in India must be grateful to His Holiness for having graced our land in spite of great adversities and given us his guidance. His Holiness has mentioned that he is aware of the realistic possibilities and I have no doubt that the solution when it comes would be satisfying the people of Tibet. I do believe that the emergence of an area of peace in Tibet is a natural corollary because Tibet has no record of having expanded its boundaries in other parts of world.

Muchkund Dube (*Professor, Jawaharlal Nehru University and former Foreign Secretary of India*):

The leaders of all major countries have recognised the compassion and spirituality of H.H. the Dalai Lama and he is the representative of Tibetan people in the eyes of the world. It seems to me that the major countries are dealing with the great challenge of Tibet issue at two levels. On one level, they are showing great concern for the violation of human rights. They also express appreciation and admiration for the indomitable courage of the Tibetan people. They openly show their respect for the Dalai Lama and his vision. But at the official level, they still fall short to recognizing the autonomy and independence of Tibet. They are not actively working for it. I do see a link between the levels and hope that the one would lead to the other level very soon. The recent changes in Tibet are very negative and they carry a warning to the whole world and above all to India. I think the elephant has now not only to get up but also to move.

If we look at the problem from a strategic perspective for South Asia and Southeast Asia, we find that China is going to be a major factor in the overall situation of our region. Economically China is progressing by leaps and bounds. By the end of this century it is likely to attain a per capita income which may well be equal to that of UK and France. On the military side, its policies are highly militaristic. It is not taking any initiative for peace and stability in the region. It is indulging in series of activities which have just the opposite effect for us in South and Southeast Asia. I have in mind the determination of the Chinese Government to acquire all the weapons of modern nuclear war. They have enough of missiles. Now they are building up nuclear submarines so that they have sea base capacity.

They are also going for heavy bombers. There is preparation for emerging as the superpower of this region with military strength at land, in sea and from air. In the changed context of the post-Cold War era, there are some efforts to establish a new paradigm of mutual consultation and increasing involvement of United Nations for security purposes but China is one of the countries which is giving a clear rebuff to these initiatives, particularly to the efforts of the Australian Foreign Minister and the Canadian Prime Minister. It is obvious that the Chinese see their interests in maintaining the status quo which may promote continuity of the Cold War imperatives, alliances and fears.

In such a scenario, Tibet has a very important role to play. Tibet symbolises spirituality of the East and has a leader of the stature of His Holiness who has carried the message of peace and compassion all over the world. Tibet has a remained a de facto zone of peace in the region. Now it should be de jure declared as a zone of peace because its importance depends upon the stature of Tibet in the comity of nations. I think the new paradigm of security is very relevant for this region and the forces working for it are not insignificant. But I am not sure whether India is still a force in this context. Of late India has put on many chains around its feet and is not able to move in the manner which we could do until a few years ago. We are only becoming a silent witness to the unfolding of the situation which is determined by other major powers in the world. I assume that most of these powers want to perpetuate [the] status quo with some minor changes in the arrangements and institutions of Cold War days. Here we can look forward to His Holiness the Dalai Lama and his leadership. He has been influencing the world leadership in his own unique way for a right direction and we should all be grateful for it. But it may become so much more effective if we have voice of a genuinely independent Tibet under the leadership of His Holiness at the global platform with all the strength of spirituality and peace that has been there in Tibet throughout the millennium.

B. Vivekanandan (*President, Jayaprakash Foundation, New Delhi*):

The first three decades after the second World War had witnessed freedom of almost all imperial possessions of European colonial powers in Asia, Africa and Latin America. This was achieved through a combination of concerted pressures mounted on the Western imperial powers through freedom movements inside the colonies complemented by pressures exerted by the international community and partly due to the realisation on the part of the imperial powers that, in the long run, holding on to the colonies any longer in the face of uprisings and revolts would prove costly for them. Therefore, they decided that it was better to gracefully quit the colonies.

It took another one-and-a-half decade for the Soviet Union to understand this lesson of history and let off the territorial acquisitions it made, using the opportunities provided by the Second World War, in the Baltic — Estonia, Lithuania and Latvia — and in the Eastern Europe, besides Afghanistan which it occupied in 1979. The Soviet military power, its superpower status backed by a regimented dictatorial system, could not help the Soviet Union to retain those new imperial possessions for long. Although repeatedly, movements in these countries for freedom and democracy were suppressed with the help of tanks and machine guns—in Hungary in 1956 and in Czechoslovakia in 1968 for example — those perceived advantages the Soviet Union enjoyed in the world proved no match for people's urge for restoration of their freedom in all these countries.

One should have thought that there is a good lesson for China to learn from the experience of the Soviet Union vis-a-vis its own imperial possession of Tibet and gracefully quit Tibet and restore the freedom that country enjoyed before its occupation by China in 1950. Instead, China holds on to its occupation of Tibet, despite repeated revolts of the Tibetans. It tries to establish its grip over Tibet by effecting demographic change in the country by inducting more and more Chinese in Tibet for settlements. That way, China has indeed put into motion a policy of cultural genocide in Tibet and denied basic human rights to the Tibetan people and has reduced certain areas of Tibet as dumping grounds of nuclear waste and other toxic materials, and thus further endangering the health of the Tibetans.

Tibet is clearly an independent state, presently under the Chinese occupation. The Chinese arguments against that fact hold no water. There are clear evidences that from 1911 onwards up to the Chinese occupation, on 7 October 1950, Tibet remained an independent country, exercised its powers and dealt with other nations accordingly. Tibet participated along with China and British India at the Simla Convention in 1914 as an equal partner. During the Second World War other powers also dealt with Tibet independently. Tibet refused its consent to China for example in 1941 when China wanted to develop a road communication, through Tibet to Assam to facilitate supplies during the War. In 1947, Tibet participated at the Asian Relations Conference, convened in New Delhi as an independent country. Moreover, a document like the so-called 17-Point agreement which the Chinese produce as a justification to perpetuate their occupation of Tibet, was cooked up by the Chinese after they occupied Tibet and has no moral or legal validity as it was "negotiated" and concluded by a "delegation" headed by Ngabo Ngawang Jigme who himself was a prisoner in Peking and the Chinese Government through intimidation and deceit and without any proper consultation with the Dalai Lama. He was kept all along in the dark about the terms of negotiation at Peking or its outcome. The fact that the Dalai Lama refused to put his seal on this so-called 17-Point Agreement of 23 May 1951 which for the first time said that Tibet, was a part of China deprives it of all moral and legal authority.

The other relevant document which needs the scrutiny of jurists is the Trade Agreement concluded between India and China in 1954 by which India agreed to the "sovereignty" of China over Tibet. It is not clear who gave India this right to barter sovereignty of Tibet to China without the consent of the people of Tibet. The Simla Convention of 1914, in which India, China and Tibet participated as equals, did not confer any such right to India to do so. Therefore, the 1954 Trade Agreement between India and China is null and void. However, it needs the scrutiny of jurists to examine whether India had any right to confer upon China sovereignty over Tibet as it referred to in the 1954 Sino-India Trade Agreement. If so, India should review its position and rectify this mistake publicly.

M. L. Sondhi (*Convener, Tibet Swaraj Committee*):

I think at this stage one should offer some practical suggestions for our future steps in the context of the present state of our government and the Indian political system. I remember that there have been high points in our Tibet policy and I refer to the regime of Shri Lal Bahadur Shastri. He brought a certain dignity to India through his policies in the national and international context. Today it is essential to remember that Lal Bahadur Shastri came very near to recognising the Government of Tibet in exile. As a matter of fact the policy papers indicate that he was in the process of announcing recognition to the Government of Tibet in exile under the leadership of His Holiness. I do not think that Shastriji was not connected with our national interests. Or the Foreign Office at the time was made of people who had not evaluated its implications for

Indian interests. So a proper point of departure for us has to be the recognition of Tibetan Government-in-exile. I do not think that the present Indian Government is at all weak in the sense it is made out to be except that it refuses to take advantage of certain peace dividends which are there after the end of the Cold War. Secondly, we must explore the possibilities of using radio waves for spreading the message of Swaraj for the Tibetans. "Swaraj" is a very good word which cuts across independence, association, sovereignty, suzerainty, self-wareness, etc. It is a Gandhian word with association of our own national movement against the British imperialism. On these issues our bureaucrats are unnecessarily apprehensive. If our radio and TV carry the message of the Dalai Lama across the Himalayas it is not going to lead the PLA to march to India. In any case, we have evidence now that Indian army is quite adequately equipped to defend the frontiers of India against any adventurism of any of our neighbours.

There is a need of new policy framework which is essential based upon peace dividends. Peace dividend means the money saved from the reduction of defence expenditures. Our country is not in a position to spend five crores a day on defence due to the occupation of Tibet by China. This money through new policy initiatives may become available for our national development provided the Tibetan Government-in-exile is recognised and made to participate in the unfolding resolution of the Tibet issue. It will certainly have begin effect upon the Kashmir scene, too.

The nuclear challenge of China also has to be settled. It should be resolved on the basis of either adequate security, mutual security, or cooperative security. But we cannot allow the present situation to continue which is absolutely contrary to the post-Cold War world order. It can be solved through establishment of Tibet Swaraj, because a free Tibet is the best guarantee against Chinese military threat and nuclearization of the region.

India cannot keep quiet on the question of cultural genocide and suppression of human rights in Tibet. It needs very important changes in the minds of Indian decision-makers and that can be achieved if we channelize our nationalism along the middle path of Lord Buddha. It will bring peace in the region along with dawn of Swaraj for the Tibetan brothers and sisters through strengthening of the role of UN in the emerging world order.

Kamal Mitra Chenoy (*President, JNU Teachers Associations*):

It is important to underline that in spite of our various positions about China and Tibet, there is absolute agreement that no government and no state has the right to oppress any people including its own. And just as we believe that there was no right to kill the students at Tiananman Square, we also believe that there is no right to oppress people in Sinkiang, in Mongolia or in Tibet. We have to oppose the so-called process of cultural assimilation in Tibet which is in fact very oppressive cultural imperialism and an attempt to destroy the cultural identity of the Tibetan people. I was extremely pleased and struck by the plea of His Holiness for human rights, peace and communal amity even in India. If we really want to strengthen our case, we must say that autonomy and human rights are not divisible and it must be applicable for Tibet, Kashmir and other similar situation in the region and the world. The call of Dalai Lama for demilitarization and denuclearization and conversion of Tibet into a zone of peace is really in the interest of this region and all of us must support it in all possible ways.

A.P. Venkateshwaran: At this point, there is a need to recapitulate two points which His Holiness made and which would activate all of us, particularly those who are Indian citizens. The first point is about the relationship between making Tibet as an area of peace and reduction of pressure our northern border. It will also contribute towards improving the situation in the eastern and western sectors. His Holiness uses the term of peace with non-violence as they cannot exist without each other. Thus Tibet as a zone of peace will create a regional environment for peace and non-violence in South Asia. The second point for our attention has not been made by His Holiness. He only hinted about it. It is to be remembered that the negotiating strength of Tibet freedom movement is reduced by statements about Tibet as an integral part of China. In last four years this statement has been gratuitiously made during the visits of top leaders from one side to the other. It was first stated when Prime Minister Rajiv Gandhi went to China in 1989. And I understand that the Chinese held that you cannot have a joint communique unless you include this paragraph that Tibet is an integral part of China. Our side caved in. Although I do not see any reason why we should have. Then when Premier Li came in December 1990, the same statement was repeated, the explanation given is amusing as they said that we included it because it was included in 1989. But it is really humiliating for me as an Indian citizen that the Chinese do not think of returning the courtesy by referring to Kashmir as an integral part of India. Nor for that matter they are willing to accept Sikkim as a part of India. This calls for writing letters and articles to activate movements in favour of stopping our government from making such statements in future on the Tibet issue. This will not cause any backing away from our position on Tibet in the U.N. and elsewhere.

Anand Kumar (*Convenor, Committee for Solidarity with Tibet Liberation Movement:*

It is a pleasant duty for me to convey our gratitude to all the participants of this unique dialogue between Indian policy experts and His Holiness the Dalai Lama. His Holiness talked to us as a teacher about our present crisis in the context of Tibet.

We as a nation are prisoners of our past mistakes and we need him as a Guru and guide of the whole human family, and not only as the leader of the Tibetan people in exile. We are extremely satisfied that he talked to us like one of us and not as guest or someone in exile. It helped us in elevating ourselves by getting out of the inferiority syndrome which has imprisoned our thinking since the Chinese aggression and our humiliation in 1962.

It was rare opportunity for all of us to participate in this extraordinary seminar where the speakers included His Holiness, three of the most distinguished Indian foreign secretaries, our representatives to U.N. China and Tibet, of ex-army generals, parliamentarians, representatives of human rights and environment movement and students and youth movements. Our audience included some of the most distinguished scholars from various research institutes, universities, and non-governmental organisations, as well as representatives of various women organisations, human rights group, and socio-cultural associations. We are grateful to all of you for joining in this dialogue for freedom of Tibet and peace and development in Asian countries.

This meeting gives us a new confidence as we have realised that we are not alone in fighting our shame regarding China and Tibet. His Holiness is also there is guide us in this hour of darkness in our foreign policy and defence policy. He is there to help us in restoring the moral basis for our policies which must be in harmony with heritage of Buddha and Gandhi. Our nation has lost its stature in the comity of nations due to repeated mistakes regarding China and Tibet in last forty years. We have to regain our self-respect and dignity by joining the global campaign for free Tibet and for a peace initiative against the focus of militarization, nuclearization and colonization.

